Chicken Soup
for the Soul.

A Book of
Christmas
Miracles

Chicken Soup for the Soul: A Book of Christmas Miracles
101 Stories of Holiday Hope and Happiness
Amy Newmark

Published by Chicken Soup for the Soul, LLC www.chickensoup.com
Copyright ©2017 by Chicken Soup for the Soul, LLC. All Rights Reserved.

Front cover illustration of angel courtesy of iStockphoto.com/vitamasi (©vitamasi)
Front cover artwork of star background courtesy of iStockphoto.com/DavidMSchrader
(©DavidMSchrader)
Back cover and interior artwork courtesy of iStockphoto.com/STILLFX (©STILLFX)
Photo of Amy Newmark courtesy of Susan Morrow at SwickPix

Cover and Interior by Daniel Zaccari

LCCN 2017947985

Distributed to the booktrade by Simon & Schuster. SAN: 200-2442

Publisher's Cataloging-In-Publication Data
(Prepared by The Donohue Group, Inc.)

Names: Newmark, Amy, compiler.
Title: Chicken soup for the soul : a book of Christmas miracles : 101
    stories of holiday hope and happiness / [compiled by] Amy Newmark.
Other Titles: Book of Christmas miracles : 101 stories of holiday hope and
    happiness
Description: [Cos Cob, Connecticut] : Chicken Soup for the Soul, LLC,
    [2017] | Summary: "Compilation of 101 stories about holiday miracles
    and joy from Chicken Soup for the Soul's library of past books."--
    Provided by publisher.
Identifiers: ISBN 978-1-61159-972-5 (print) | ISBN 978-1-61159-272-6
    (ebook)
Subjects: LCSH: Christmas--Literary collections. | Christmas--Anecdotes. |
    Miracles--Literary collections. | Miracles--Anecdotes. | Joy--Literary
    collections. | Joy--Anecdotes. | LCGFT: Anecdotes.
Classification: LCC GT4985 .C453 2017 (print) | LCC GT498 (ebook) | DDC
    394.2663/02--dc23

PRINTED IN THE UNITED STATES OF AMERICA
on acid∞free paper

25 24 23 22 21 20 19 18 17   01 02 03 04 05 06 07 08 09 10 11

A Book of
Christmas
Miracles

101 Stories of
Holiday Hope
and Happiness

Amy Newmark

Chicken Soup for the Soul, LLC
Cos Cob, CT

Changing lives one story at a time®
www.chickensoup.com

Table of Contents

❸

~Christmas Spirit~

❹

~Holiday Angels~

5

~The Joy of Giving~

6

~Family Matters~

7

~The Gift of Gratitude~

⑧
~Answered Prayers~

⑨
~The Best of All Gifts~

⑩

~Through the Eyes of a Child~

Introduction

I t's been Christmas in July at the Chicken Soup for the Soul offices as we've put together this special collection of stories for you. We've loved the process — reading through hundreds of our past books to find the most intriguing stories about holiday miracles in our vast library. What we've gathered in one place for you will surely be a treat, as you read about divine intervention, the joy of giving, answered prayers, holiday angels, family reunions, and many other stories that will make you say "wow."

At the end of each story, you'll see the *Chicken Soup for the Soul* book in which the story previously appeared. It's a wonderful review of our twenty-four years of publishing — our favorite stories about holiday miracles, from Thanksgiving to New Year's.

We're excited that this book is serving as a fundraiser for the U.S. Marine Corps Reserve Toys for Tots program as well. Toys for Tots has created miracles for millions of families with their gift-giving program. I'm sure you've seen the collection bins in your own communities, and maybe you've even donated a toy.

There's nothing better than giving during the holiday season — I think it's what we all love the most. But it's hard to choose what's best about the holidays, right? There are also family reunions, the wonder on the face of a child, and the chance to gather with our communities at church, at school, and even at the mall to share the special spirit of the season, brightening those long winter nights.

However you celebrate, we want to wish you and yours a very

happy holiday season. We hope you'll have a little time off to curl up in front of the fire and have a good read.

And rest assured that this collection, like all our Christmas books, is appropriate for young readers. We work closely with Santa to keep the magic alive for all ages.

~Amy Newmark
Publisher and Editor-in-Chief, Chicken Soup for the Soul

Chapter
1

A Book of
Christmas
Miracles

Divine Intervention

Medically Impossible

Miracles come in moments. Be ready and willing.
~Wayne Dyer

I remember it was almost Christmas because carols softly played on the radio in the nurses' station. I walked into Jimmy's room. A small seven-year-old, he seemed dwarfed by the big, indifferent, mechanical hospital bed with its starchy white sheets.

He looked up at me through suspicious eyes, hidden in a face puffed up from the use of steroids to control his kidney condition. "What are you gonna do to me now?" they seemed to ask. "What blood tests are you gonna order? Don't you know they hurt, Doc?"

Jimmy had a disease called nephrotic syndrome, and it was not responding to any therapy we had tried. This was his sixth month with the illness, his second week in the hospital. I was feeling guilty — I had failed him. As I smiled at him, my heart felt even heavier.

The shadow of defeat had dulled his eyes.

Oh no, I thought, *he's given up.* When a patient gives up, your chances of helping that patient lower dramatically.

"Jimmy, I want to try something."

He burrowed into the sheets. "It gonna hurt?"

"No, we'll use the intravenous line that's already in your arm. No new needles." What I planned I had tried a few weeks earlier without success. I gave him intravenous Lasix, a drug that is supposed to "open up" the kidneys.

This time I planned a new twist, which the nephrologist said probably would not work but was worth a try. A half hour before I injected the Lasix I would inject albumin, a simple protein that would draw water from the bloated cells into the bloodstream. Then, when I gave the Lasix, the water flooding the bloodstream might flow into and open up the kidneys. The problem was, if it didn't, the "flooded" blood vessels could give Jimmy lung congestion until his body readjusted. I had discussed this with his parents. Desperate, they agreed to try.

So I gave albumin into his intravenous line. A half hour later I came back to give the Lasix. He was breathing harder and looked scared. I had an idea. I never believed in divine intervention, but Jimmy came from a very religious family.

"You pray a lot?" I asked.

"Yes, "he answered. "I pray every night. But I guess God don't hear me."

"He hears you," I replied, not knowing in all honesty if God did or didn't, but Jimmy needed reassurance. And belief. "Try praying as I give this medicine to you. Oh, and I want you to pretend you see your kidneys—remember all those pictures of them I showed you awhile back?"

"Yes."

"Well, I want you to picture them spilling all the extra water in your body into your bladder. You remember the picture of your bladder I showed you?" I figured I might as well try visualization. This was in the early 1970s. Some articles had been written about visualization and some evidence existed that it worked—in some cases, anyway.

"Yeah."

"Good. Start now. Concentrate on your kidneys." I placed my hands there and shut my eyes, concentrating—just to show him how, you understand. Then injected the Lasix.

Jimmy closed his eyes and concentrated, and mouthed a prayer.

What the heck. I also prayed, even though I knew it wouldn't work. I did not believe in divine intervention. When I died I would have a few choice questions for God about why he allowed certain terrible things to happen to certain children. One of my friends suggested that when I did die, God would probably send me the other way just to avoid me. But in for a penny, in for a pound.

"How long will it take to work?" the nurse asked as she adjusted the dripping intravenous line. I motioned for her to step from the room.

"In a person with normal kidneys, maybe twenty minutes — fifteen minutes tops," I replied. "With Jimmy, I'm hoping a half hour. But I have to tell you, it's a real long shot. Stay with him. If he has trouble and needs oxygen, call me. I'll be at the nurses' station writing all this down."

I sat down and opened Jimmy's cold, metal-jacketed chart, almost cursing the irony of the Christmas carol on the radio: "Oh Holy Night." Before I had scribbled one sentence, the nurse stuck out her head from Jimmy's room. "A half hour to work?" she asked.

"For normal kidneys."

"Otherwise fifteen minutes 'tops,' right, Doc?"

"That's what I said."

"Well, the floodgates have opened: He's urinating like crazy. Within just two minutes he asked for the urinal. I've got to go get another."

Two minutes? Impossible. I went to the room as fast as my cane would allow me to walk. Jimmy had already filled the plastic yellow urinal. The nurse rushed in with another two. He grabbed one and started filling that one, too. He grinned at me, the light back in his blue eyes.

I left the room, a numbness coursing through my mind and body. It couldn't be. If he diuresed — if his kidneys opened up — he was on the way to a cure. No, it just could not happen that fast. Impossible. Medically impossible. And yet...

Was it sheer pharmacology and physiology breaking the rules? Was it the visualization?

I could clearly hear a fragment of a carol on the radio. I felt goosebumps: "Fall on your knees, oh hear the angel voices..."

A paraphrase of the last line from *Miracle on 34th Street* came to me: "And then again, maybe I didn't do such a wonderful thing, after all."

~John M. Briley Jr., M.D.

A 5th Portion of Chicken Soup for the Soul

The Miracle of a Precious Stone

I miss thee, my Mother! Thy image is still
the deepest impressed on my heart.
~Eliza Cook

I should have been happier. It was two days before Christmas and I was driving alone on a country road in our small mountain community delivering homemade cookies to shut-ins. A light dusting of snow covered the barren cornfields, giving hope to every child who prayed for a white Christmas.

I had spent the last couple of days with church friends, mixing dough, shaping date balls, melting chocolate, baking dozens and dozens of different Christmas cookies. We had covered every surface in my kitchen with cookies, laughing uproariously at our own jokes, singing off-key one familiar Christmas carol after another.

Driving along the familiar roads that late afternoon, I was having a conversation with my Lord about the death of my mother four months earlier. We had had this conversation before, and each time God had provided a measure of peace.

And yet, the same questions surfaced again and again. Why did my mother have to endure so many years of mind-numbing pain before her death? Why didn't I have peace about where she was?

I delivered all of my cookies, warmly greeting the shut-ins. Their homes were decorated with small white pines or blue spruce cut from the deep forests surrounding the community.

At my final stop, Miss Ruby, a beloved eighty-three-year-old known for her quiet benevolence, was slow to respond to my persistent knock on her front door. I started to get concerned because she had fallen on Thanksgiving Eve while preparing dinner for several neighbors who would be alone that holiday.

Finally, I heard the steady rhythm of her wooden cane as she slowly made her way to the door.

"I guessed you'd be coming by, my dear, so I've made some hot chocolate to entice you to stay a little longer. It gets lonely here on Long Bottom Road in the winter, and even more so now that I can't get outside in this cold weather while my hip is healing."

We chatted while I balanced my cup on my knee and found myself wishing her grown children lived nearer to provide companionship and care for her. As I was leaving, she put her arms around me, kissed me on the check and whispered, "You're an angel, do you know that?" I was hardly an angel, but I thanked her and promised to visit again after Christmas when the holiday rush was over.

Back in the car, I drove a short distance down the dirt road before easing to a stop next to a weathered split-rail fence. No farmhouses were in view.

I laid my head down on the steering wheel and wept.

"I miss you, Mother," I cried out, looking heavenward to the overcast skies, hoping she heard me.

This was my first Christmas season without her. I knew well the verse, "to be absent from the body is to be present with the Lord." Still, I wept alone on that country road, unable to accept the peace that God was so willing to give me.

Finally, in desperation, and with no thought of Biblical precedent, I asked the Lord for a sign, a sign that He cared, a sign that He heard me, a sign that He loved me, a sign that my mother was safe in heaven with Him.

Wiping my eyes, I returned to our country home where I quietly prepared dinner for my husband. We were alone; our sons were married and living in another part of the state. This was their year to spend Christmas with their wives' families.

The next morning, while dressing for church, my husband turned to me in surprise and asked, "Where on earth did you find this?"

"Find what?" I asked, straightening my skirt before the mirror.

"The ruby!" he replied. "Isn't that your ruby there on the bedspread?"

I rushed to the bed, picked up the ruby, held it close to my breast and began to weep.

It had become a custom for my parents' seven children to pool our resources each time one of us celebrated a fortieth anniversary and to present the happy couple each with a ruby, the stone traditionally associated with that anniversary. On our anniversary the previous year, I was given a lovely ruby set in a pendant on a simple gold chain.

The first week I wore it, the stone had come loose from its setting and was never found, leaving me distraught.

I had searched for nearly a year, combing the carpets, checking our closets, looking in the most unlikely places for this ruby which had lovingly tied me to my siblings.

And now, on this Sunday morning, the ruby appeared from nowhere in the center of our bedspread. More curiously, I had made the bed less than a half hour before.

My husband, sensing my suspicion, placed his hands firmly on my shoulders. "I know you must think I found the ruby and laid it on the bedspread where you'd quickly see it. But I can assure you before God that this is the first I've seen it since you lost it last year. I promise you!"

It was my sign. There could be no other explanation. And I sought none.

~Mariane Holbrook

Chicken Soup for the Soul: Miraculous Messages from Heaven

Bell of Truth

*And everyone who has left houses or brothers or sisters
or father or mother or children or fields for my sake
will receive a hundred times as much and
will inherit eternal life.*
~Matthew 19:29

I was nineteen years old, alone in a studio apartment in Kansas City. It was the Christmas season and self-pity had gotten the best of me. With no job and the rent barely paid, all I had was a box of cereal, a carton of milk, five dollars in my bank account, and a single one-dollar bill in my purse.

Earlier that year, I'd made a fateful decision. I was forced to quit college due to lack of money. So, I packed up two suitcases and got on a bus with only fifty dollars in my pocket. My parents were getting a divorce, and I had no financial support. My temporary minimum wage job had ended. I was new to town, alone and friendless.

So here I was in Kansas City, sitting on my Murphy bed, staring out the window. I began to think, "No one really cares if I live or die. I could be lying in the gutter somewhere and it wouldn't make a difference."

I thought, "I've got to get out of here, get out of this room, before I do something I'll regret."

I buttoned up my old lime green coat. It had once been part of my new college wardrobe. Now it had holes in the elbow and was torn at the shoulder where white stuffing poked out.

I walked down the five flights of stairs with the dollar in my pocket. I opened the door to bitter cold. The icy wind smacked me in the face, making my eyes tear. I began to walk. And walk. I had no destination. I just knew I had to get out of the apartment. Eventually, I came to a park with benches and a fountain, where I could sit, cry and pray.

With my eyes closed, begging God for help, His wisdom, a sign, anything, I heard a voice. A man was speaking to me. Was it a sign? I opened my eyes to find a homeless drunk sitting next to me and asking me for a date!

I headed back toward the apartment. By now the sky had opened up, delivering a combination of rain, sleet and snow. Without a hat or umbrella, my tattered coat soaked up the freezing rain like a sponge and wet hair covered my face.

Walking past fancy stores that were beautifully decorated for the Christmas season, I felt embarrassed by my "little match girl" appearance. A few steps later I stood outside a small coffee shop, gazing in the window. Here, even in this coffee shop, women were wearing furs and beautiful clothes. What would it feel like to be sitting and chatting with friends over a nice warm cup of tea, looking good, watching the dreary weather outside? I wondered if my one dollar could buy me a cup of tea. Then it occurred to me that with tax and tip, I couldn't afford the tea and I continued homeward.

Cold and wet, I asked myself, "Could life get any more miserable?"

It was then that I came upon a Salvation Army woman ringing the bell in front of a red bucket.

"Well," I thought to myself, "you've got your arms and legs, your eyesight and your health, so you're a lot luckier than a lot of these folks The Salvation Army people are trying to help." So I reached in my pocket and gave my last dollar to The Salvation Army.

Back at my apartment, I opened my mailbox to find one envelope, my bank statement. I already knew what it said. But when I opened it to file it away, I noticed something wrong on the statement. It did not show the expected $5 balance, but now reflected a $105 balance.

I always knew exactly what I had in my account, balanced to the penny. Something was wrong. I wasn't about to spend money that was not mine. I called the bank. I wasn't taking any chances. The bank employee said it was indeed my money, but I knew better.

Donning the tattered, wet green coat, I marched back out into the cold. My bank happened to be directly across the street from the fountain I had sat at crying just a couple of hours earlier.

I walked in. "May I see the bank manager, please?"

I'm sure I looked an awful sight; well-dressed people were staring at this cold ragamuffin demanding that the bank officer remove the mistaken overage.

While he went into back offices to check out the error, I waited patiently in a leather chair that squeaked when I shifted in the seat, water dripping from my hair. Upon his return, he looked puzzled and sat down, scratching his head. "I can't make any sense of it," he said, "but it is indeed your money."

"That's impossible. I know what I had to the penny, and this appeared out of nowhere."

He said he understood my concern because it had not appeared on previous statements. "Our records indicate that a deposit was made into your account last July and we just now caught it. That's why it appears on your bank statement for the first time in December. But it is definitely your money and you need not worry that we'll be asking for it back."

When money is tight, a person keeps track of each and every cent. I knew without question that I'd never made such a deposit back in July, but I couldn't convince him.

I walked home, thanking God for the extra money, which I used for a discount plane ticket to visit family for Christmas. My spirits healed as I shared that holy holiday with them.

A few months later, I told someone about the mysterious appearance of the $100.

"Hadn't you just given your last dollar to charity?" she asked.

"Well, yes."

"So, don't you see?" she replied. "You were rewarded hundredfold!"

The tiny hairs went up on my arms and a chill moved up my back.

I call this the bell of truth ringing my spine. I had just experienced a blessing, a Christmas miracle.

~Morgan Hill

Chicken Soup for the Soul: A Book of Miracles

Reflections of Hope in the Snowstorm

It only takes a thought and your angels will be there…
for although you may not see them, you're
always in their care.
~Author Unknown

I was homesick. My husband, Keith, was attending Utah State University in Logan, Utah. We lived eight hundred miles away from my parents and family back home in Northern California. We couldn't afford to go home for Christmas. We would just stay home in Hyrum, and have a simple Christmas with our baby, Ann.

Then a most unexpected gift arrived in a Christmas card: enough money for gas for the eight-hundred-mile drive home. We were so excited. Keith took time off from his part-time job and we packed the car. We had family prayer, asking humbly for safety and good traveling conditions.

We drove all day through Nevada, over the Sierras, to the west coast of California. Everything went well and we finally drove up the familiar driveway, honking the horn to signal our arrival. My family rushed out to greet us, welcoming us with love and Christmas cheer.

We celebrated Christmas in my childhood home, all of us together again for the first time in three years. My family rejoiced when we announced that we were expecting our second child in the spring.

All too soon, the time came for us to return to Utah. My parents gave us some money for gas. With tears and hugs, we started on our way. Hoping to make good time, we drove steadily through the day.

Toward evening, we arrived in Wendover, on the border between Nevada and Utah. Snow flurries swirled around the car. We stopped just long enough to fuel up the car. With no credit card and very little cash, we did not even consider staying overnight in a motel.

If the road and weather conditions were good, we had about two hours of driving to get to Salt Lake City. We thought if we could just make it to Keith's parents' home in nearby Bountiful that night, we could rest. Then we could go on to Hyrum in the morning, and he would make it to work on time.

We drove into the darkening night. Frantic flurries of snow swirled wildly about the car. Keith was having trouble seeing the road, as the headlights seemed dim. He pulled over, and got out to brush the snow away from them.

Then he climbed back into the driver's seat and told me the bad news. "We have only one headlight." A simple statement, but loaded with dread.

With another heartfelt prayer for safety and protection, we felt we had no choice but to head slowly out onto the nearly deserted freeway. Our car bravely slogged through the snowy darkness. We desperately tried to keep our eyes on the white line in the road, but it was vanishing quickly in the accumulating snow. We seemed to be all alone on that dark stretch of freeway. There was no traffic in either direction, and the visibility was near zero.

We knew that our parents were praying us safely through the night. We prayed too, for traction and safety.

Suddenly, out of nowhere, a semi-truck appeared, gaining quickly upon us. It splattered a spray of snow onto our windshield as it passed. Then it pulled into our lane, directly in front of our car. Our meager headlight reflected off the shiny silver doors on the back of the truck.

The driver could have sped ahead. Instead, he stayed right with us, lighting our way. The steady flurry of relentless snowflakes dashed against our windshield. The wipers could barely keep them brushed away. The white line of the road was no longer visible. We cautiously crept along, following the truck.

In those anxiety-filled moments, I felt our unborn baby kick for the first time! The miracle of new life growing within me filled us with wonder. We felt that there were angels protecting us that night, and there was a curious peace in our hearts.

Hours later, we reached the welcome streetlights and plowed roads of Salt Lake City. To signal our gratitude, Keith blinked our one headlight at the semi-truck driver in front of us. This man had stayed with us for more than 120 miles on that drive between Wendover and Salt Lake City. Our one headlight had reflected off the back of his truck as he had lighted our way in the dark night.

It turned out that this storm deposited eighteen inches of snow in twenty-four hours, closing the Salt Lake City airport for twenty hours. But we had traveled safely through the massive storm. We offered a heartfelt prayer of thanksgiving for this miracle.

As I gratefully closed my eyes at last that night, the images of the steadily blowing snow drifted before them. More importantly, though, my mind's eye fixed upon the reflection of the unseen angels and the semi-truck driver who had stayed with us, giving us hope through the darkest hours of that snow-filled night.

~Valaree Terribilini Brough

Chicken Soup for the Soul: Hope & Miracles

A Gift to Each Other

Where thou art — that — is Home.
~Emily Dickinson

I was born with a wandering spirit. After college, I joined a theatre company and traveled all over North America and Europe. I was far away and broke most of the time, but no matter where I wandered, I made it home to Colorado for Christmas. This was a fairly significant feat, and yet I had managed to do it every year without fail. It sometimes involved days and nights of driving through blizzards, gallons of espresso, twelve-hour plane rides, lost baggage, and customs officials who always seemed to pick me for scrutiny.

Our holiday traditions were pretty average — tree, presents, way too much food, Christmas Eve service at church, watching the movie *White Christmas* with my sister. Nothing extraordinary happened, but living so far away made it essential to be there. I needed to stay current in my siblings' lives. I wanted to know my nieces and nephews and have them know me. If I wasn't there for Christmas I feared I would just fade out of the family.

My fiancé Calvin and I traveled back to Colorado for our wedding, which was the "opening ceremony" of a huge Fourth of July family reunion. I wasn't a girl who imagined my wedding as the pivotal point of human history anyway, so a simple affair was just my style. But even small and simple broke the bank for us. We headed back to work in Europe knowing there would be a slim chance of another trip home anytime soon. Christmas would likely be a cozy twosome.

"This is okay," I told myself. "We're our own family now. It will be romantic." Plus, our tour ended in Switzerland, so that's where we'd be stuck for Christmas. Definitely worse places to be!

But as the tour drew to a close, my morale crumbled. Watching our teammates excitedly depart, talking about cherubic nieces and nephews, trees, stockings, and family traditions, left me feeling less than lucky about my own situation. Yes, I was a newlywed and the world was supposed to be rosy, but in truth, spending our first six months of marriage in a van with a team of kooky performers and sleeping on pull-out couches in people's dens had placed a strain on the marital bonding process. Our harmony was a little off-key, to put it mildly. Three solid weeks of undiluted togetherness was looking about as awkward as the sixth grade dance and even less appealing. A little padding of friends and family would have been so much less stressful.

The lack of company wasn't the only check in my negative column, either. We had no home. Like I said, we traveled in a van and were housed as part of our performance contracts. Being on break meant that we'd have to find a place to stay. Someplace free. And who wants a couple of bickering vagabonds hanging around at Christmas? Even if someone did take pity and invite us into their "stable," I was really stretching to dig up any gratitude for someone's pull-out couch.

Then there was the shortage of trappings and trimmings. Our performing-artist-lifestyle left us without discretionary funds, so gifts were pretty much out. And to top it all off, Calvin got sick with an infected wisdom tooth. He was delirious with pain. So much for romance.

First things first. Although Calvin and I were alternately ticked off and bewildered by one another, I did still have regular moments of fondness toward him. I didn't enjoy seeing him in pain. Especially because it made him all whiny and meant I had to do all the driving. We needed to get that tooth taken care of. We prayed.

"Lord, we haven't been very nice to each other lately and we know that bothers You. We're going to try and improve, but in the meantime Calvin's in a lot of pain and it's Christmas and all, and we were hoping that maybe You could toss us a miracle or something. A little sprinkle of healing power. Please."

It was something like that. Not a very spiritual sounding prayer, just desperate. We stopped on our way out of town at the home of our area representative, Jean-François, to drop off a calendar for our next tour.

He took one look at Calvin and declared with widened eyes "zut alors!" This can mean many things, but in this case it was an expression of alarm.

He made a phone call. He spoke way too fast for me to follow his French, but it sounded very emphatic and convincing and twenty minutes later the source of distress was being extracted from Calvin's jaw by Jean-François' friend, who also happened to be a dental surgeon and who also decided he didn't want to be paid since it was two days before Christmas. God is so cool, and His people can be really cool sometimes too. On this day He was also really speedy, which was such a nice bonus.

While Calvin was being repaired, I wandered the streets of Lausanne soaking up Christmas Spirit from all the colors and lights and using my tiny store of Swiss francs to buy a few chocolate coins, a nice writing pen, a recording of Calvin's favorite artist, and a few other tidbits. I could wrap each one separately and tie little bows and we could have a miniature Christmas. It would be a peace offering — my promise of a fresh start. Our harmony had already improved with the pressure of touring off our shoulders. A little privacy might be tolerable after all.

With that thought came the reminder that we needed a place to stay. We actually had an offer but I had put off phoning them. Timothy and Pierette were the elderly uncle and aunt of a colleague. They lived in a remote mountain village a couple of hours from Geneva, and we had met them earlier that tour. Timothy was an egg farmer and Pierette ran the general store in the village. They mentioned that they had a little apartment in their basement and that we were welcome to stay anytime, including the holidays.

Why hadn't I called them? I had a picture in my mind of a

spider-infested stairway leading to a dank room with a bare flashlight hanging down, a chamber pot in one corner and a hot plate with questionable wiring in the other. I was thinking WWII, French Resistance. This would be the space between two walls where they hid Jewish neighbors and secret radios. Of course this was neutral Switzerland, so none of that actually happened here, but my imagination always tended toward the dramatic. There would be an old wooden door with a broken latch. Chickens would be pecking outside the door and snow would blow in through the cracks. We'd sleep on separate army cots under threadbare blankets and we'd have scrambled eggs for Christmas dinner. Truthfully, I was kind of reveling in the whole sad and wretched picture and imagining the screenplay.

I was brought back to reality when Calvin arrived, all swollen-cheeked. "Tho, dith joo make dath phwone cawwl?"

Darn. We really had no alternatives, but I was sure the experience itself wouldn't be as fun or glamorous as the eventual movie version. I prayed again. "God, I miss my family. So far, marriage is not really what I expected, and I feel like Heidi going to stay on some mountainside in a scary basement with some old people I don't really know. I want to make the best of this. I know it's really not all about me. I know I should ask You to help me grow up and be selfless like You, but I also want to pray that we have a really nice, fun holiday together."

I made the call, got directions, and turned the van up the winding mountain road. As we pulled into the little town we had to wait for a herd of cows making its way down the main street. With Calvin mumbling the directions through wads of cotton we arrived at Pierette's general store.

I knocked hesitantly. The door flew open and Timothy and Pierette greeted us like their own grandchildren back from a war, or a refugee camp, or from just having received a Nobel Prize. We were ushered directly into the parlor where a fire was crackling and a tree was twinkling. There were cookies right out of the oven, and hot chocolate with lots of whipped cream.

Over steaming cups they asked us all about our tour, all about our wedding, all about our families. We learned all about egg farming and life in a tiny Swiss village. We laughed, and smiled and ate cookies. God had answered our prayer. He knew what our marriage needed, and He prepared this place for us long in advance. This was the most calm, nurturing place in the world to spend Christmas, or any other day for that matter. Of course I hadn't seen the little apartment in the basement yet, but Pierette said we were welcome to join them upstairs as much as we liked, so maybe we wouldn't have to hang out with the spiders.

The phone rang, disrupting our relaxed conversation. We heard a "zut alors!" in the conversation. Timothy returned to us with a frown.

The village was in an uproar. The pastor was sick. He had a fever and had lost his voice. There would be no Christmas Eve program. This was a considerable crisis, tantamount to the plague or a foreign army marching over the Alps. Timothy and Pierette exchanged distressed glances and Pierette immediately began clearing away the dishes. Whenever a solution is unclear, it's always helpful to tidy up in Switzerland.

Calvin raised an eyebrow at me, and I answered with a grin and a nod. This was a no-brainer! We jumped up and offered to save the day.

We'd been doing nothing but Christmas programs for weeks. We had a vast repertoire to choose from. Relief spread over our hosts' faces.

We began gathering props, running lines, and planning all the music we could do with only the two of us. With a quick change of clothes we set off. We chose a play about two lonely people who meet in an airport on Christmas Eve. As the characters hesitantly begin to converse, they share their stories, their loneliness, and a reminder of God's gift to us in the birth of Jesus. My character, a believer, realizes that they were put there for that reason — put there to answer one another's need. They read the Christmas story from the book of Matthew, and share an impromptu celebration.

Calvin's character, with spiritual eyes opening for the first time, declares, "You'll have to lead me. I've never had a real Christmas before."

We were in the zone. We were a perfect team that night, and I remembered why I had chosen to spend the rest of my life with this man. Performing this play on Christmas Eve, for these people, was perfect. As I spoke my lines, the truth of them penetrated my own heart—we answered each other's need. We were put here for that reason. The paradox of God's sovereignty struck me. Somehow, in the complexity of God's love and provision, He cares about my smallest details and desires. And yet, at the same time, it's all about Calvin, and it's all about the man in the front row with tears streaming down his cheeks, and it's about Pierette and her general store, and the dental surgeon, and all of my teammates at home with their families. We are God's gift to each other. Like a master composer, He brings all the instruments together, each with a different tone, each playing a different part, and He makes it turn out so beautifully.

After the program we were invited to the evening meal, full of cheese and chocolate and all the yummiest Swiss things. Not a single scrambled egg. Later, we grabbed our suitcases and at last made it down the staircase to the place that would be home for the next three weeks.

The staircase was steep, and the basement was indeed dark and creepy. We opened the apartment door and were greeted by twinkling lights, a small decorated tree in the corner, and evergreen boughs, all adorning a newly remodeled, sparkling clean studio. There was modern plumbing and a kitchenette with perfect wiring. There was a tantalizing fruit basket on the table and a big, soft bed covered with the whitest and fluffiest down comforter I'd ever seen. Calvin spontaneously lifted me over the threshold.

"Merry Christmas," I sighed. He set me down, wrapping his arms around me. I wrapped back. We were God's gift to each other.

~Kristi Hemingway

Chicken Soup for the Soul: A Book of Miracles

The Christmas Bonus

And the apostles said to the Lord, "Increase our faith."
~Luke 17:5

My youngest sister called just before Christmas. "Guess what?" she began.

With Jacki I never knew what to guess. I worried about her... her safety in a tiny apartment in a bad part of town, her minimum wage job, her lack of health insurance, and her broken down car. Only four Christmases ago, she was earning hundreds of dollars working in bars, dancing, living a life far apart from mine. Miraculously, God had turned her life around. I was thankful for that, but her faith, still new, seemed fragile.

I braced myself. "What happened?"

"Remember how I told you we were going to get a Christmas bonus?"

I recalled how she had recently scoured the entire floor of the small convenience store where she worked, on her knees with a tiny scrub pad. It took her over a week, but she was so proud of the clean white floor. Even with her seven-dollar-an-hour salary, she was always doing over and above at her job. She even made little doggie treats for customers' pets. She always smiled and customers loved her. Now at Christmas, she really needed money for extra car expenses and just to pay bills.

"Well, I opened my bonus envelope to find three hundred dollars cash!"

"Wow!" I rejoiced with her. "I bet you hollered when you opened that envelope!"

"Yes! And I thanked God for always supplying my needs." She went on to say that she paid her bills and bought a few groceries. She giggled with joy, and I laughed with her.

The next day Jacki called again. This time her voice trembled. "My manager called very upset. She had opened her own bonus envelope to find a cash amount far below what she expected. 'I was supposed to get $300,' she said."

Oh, no, I thought.

My sister continued. "I had a sick feeling. The manager and I have the same first name. What if there was a mistake? What if I got the wrong envelope? And now the money is gone! But I'm still going to call the store owner right away."

"Why don't you wait?" I urged her. "Give it some time. Think about it. The envelope did have your name on it."

"I can't. I prayed about it and I know what I need to do."

"But maybe it wasn't a mistake," I argued. "Maybe you were rewarded for all your extra work." I hated the thought of her talking to the owner, who was known to be a highly critical woman, downright mean at times.

"You deserve the money. I think you should keep it."

She didn't listen to me. Instead, she called the owner.

"You should have known you wouldn't get that much," the owner ranted. "We go by the rules here and low-ranking employees like you don't get extra. Only the managers get extra."

She told my sister that she must return the full amount immediately. There would be no bonus at all for her. What she couldn't pay back would be taken out of her paycheck.

Three hundred dollars… a fortune to Jacki, especially at Christmas. I was sick with anger. How could a person who owns several businesses punish someone who works so hard for almost nothing? I wanted to call the owner, write the newspaper, drive several hundred miles with all my friends to my sister's town and picket!

My sister said no. "I did the extra work for the Lord. And I know I did the right thing by telling," she said. "Besides, God always provides my needs."

Shaking, I hung up the phone. My first thought was to send her $300. I'd always wanted to jump in and fix things for her. I could afford it and I wanted desperately to make it right for her. It wasn't fair. She was still learning to trust God and now this happened.

In my heart, I heard God say, "Then let her trust Me. And you need to trust Me, too."

So I didn't send the money, but it was hard.

I got the call a week later. "Guess what?" Jacki chirped.

"What?" I asked tentatively.

"I bought a lottery ticket."

I groaned. I knew that every once in a while she enjoyed spending a dollar on a lottery ticket. I didn't think money should be used that way but I kept my mouth shut.

"I won something this time!" she exclaimed. "You need to thank God!"

My first thought was, "God would definitely *not* use a lottery ticket."

On the other hand, when my mind got quiet enough, He reminded me that He uses all kinds of things... a rib, a donkey who spoke, the jawbone of an ass, mud in a blind man's eyes, five tiny fish. He loved my sister and He'd reached into her world. Maybe it happened to be a lottery ticket.

"I won three hundred dollars!" she exclaimed.

Of course you did.

~Martha Moore

Chicken Soup for the Soul: Answered Prayers

My Snow Angel

It is not known precisely where angels dwell — whether in the air, the void, or the planets. It has not been God's pleasure that we should be informed of their abode.
~Voltaire

A warm, sunny day in early November, especially in the Sierras, was a nice surprise. One look at the cloudless blue sky was all it took to convince me to drive twenty miles into the valley to do early Christmas shopping. My husband was content to stay home and rake up the last of the fallen leaves. I called out to him before I got in the car, "Call me if you think of something you want me to bring home." He smiled and waved as I drove away.

Temperatures in the valley are between eight and ten degrees higher than in the foothills where we live, so I enjoyed the warmth and sunshine as I walked from store to store. It wasn't until around sunset when I realized I had been shopping for most of the day. I was surprised I hadn't had a call from my husband as he usually thought of something he wanted from town while I was gone.

I rummaged through my purse for my cell phone only to discover it wasn't there. Not all that surprising as it wasn't the first time that had happened. "It's probably on the car seat or on the floor," I said to myself as I hurried to the parking lot. I put the bags in the trunk and got in the car, but the cell phone was nowhere in sight. After a frustrating search I found it under the seat and sighed with relief. Not only to find the cell phone but also to discover the source of the clunking sound every time I had turned a corner on the drive to the valley.

My husband will have a good laugh about that, I thought, as I dialed our home phone number. I didn't get the chance to tell him. I heard the panic in my husband's voice when he answered the phone. "I've been trying to call you. It started snowing up here half an hour ago," he shouted into the phone.

"But the storm wasn't due in until after the weekend," I said.

"I know, I know, but there was a sudden drop in temperature and it switched from fall to winter just like that," he said.

Another surprise from Mother Nature. That's how things happen in the Sierras, which is why I keep a box of emergency supplies in the trunk and carry chains from fall through the end of spring.

"Well, I guess I'll have to stop and put the chains on when I get up there so I can make it home," I sighed. My husband coughed nervously and cleared his throat. "Uh, I forgot to put the chains back in the trunk when I vacuumed the car out yesterday. I saw them in the garage when I finished raking," he said. I resisted the urge to scream. I checked my watch. The two local auto parts stores were closed by now.

"How much snow is on the ground now?" I asked.

"Only an inch or two. I think you can make it home okay if you leave now and drive slowly and follow the tire tracks in the road when you get to the snow."

I hung up and slammed the phone into my purse. I berated myself for not checking the trunk after he cleaned out the car. It was a constant battle with him to put things back where he found them. Usually it was his stuff, but this time I was the victim of his carelessness. I had to let a scream out to release my anger rather than carry it home with me.

Big tufts of white swirled in front of the car headlights when I reached the 1200-foot level. I kept the car in low gear and crept slowly toward the 2600-foot elevation where we lived. I started talking to myself and to God. "Help me get home," became my prayer mantra as I repeated it every few minutes.

My biggest challenge would be to get over the reservoir bridge, then up the hill on the other side. The only way to make it would be to keep the car moving steadily and hope the cars and trucks had displaced enough snow so my tires could get traction. I continued my mantra. The snow was falling harder when I reached the reservoir bridge. I blinked back tears.

A truck was driving across the bridge ahead of me. My hopes soared. Those big tires would make a good path through the snow and help my car tires get enough traction to make it up the hill. The truck slowed as I got closer, then stopped. I slowed the car but had to stop a few feet from the truck. I watched helplessly as the driver got out, swept snow off the truck hood and windshield then got back in and drove off.

My car had lost precious momentum. The path from the truck tires helped until I reached the end of the bridge and started up the hill. The car started to swerve. I turned the wheel to correct each swerve. The tires started spinning and the car started to slide back down the hill toward the sloped side of the reservoir. I was on a direct path into the water.

"God, please, I need help right now," I yelled. The car stopped. I pressed my head against the steering wheel and said, "Thank You." Someone was rapping on the window. I rolled it down to see a young man with dark curly hair and sparkling blue eyes. He smiled. "You'll never make it up this hill without chains. I'll push your car to the side. You can walk up the hill," he said.

The car seemed to float effortlessly to the side of the road. The young man came to the open window and nodded. "Remember to take those Christmas gifts out of the trunk when you leave," he said. How did he know there were Christmas gifts in the trunk?

I grabbed my purse and jumped out of the car so I could thank him for his help. I looked around. No one was there. There were no cars or trucks on the road. I looked for footprints but there were none, only a pristine layer of snow growing deeper by the minute. I reached for my cell phone to call my husband but then remembered that reception at this level was poor even in good weather.

I slipped on rubber boots and a hooded sweatshirt I kept under the spare tire, grabbed the shopping bags and started walking toward the gas station at the top of the hill. When I saw the dim light over the door I knew it was closed. My plan to call my husband was lost in the swirling snow around me. I had to keep walking until I got to a house where I could use a phone.

Just as I turned off the main road, a white truck pulled up next to me and the driver got out and came toward me. "Would you like a ride home?" he asked. I nodded and he opened the door. He smiled when I started giving him directions and said, " I know where you live." I looked at him more closely to see if I recognized him and noticed some dark curly hair sticking out of his knit hat. "Are you the young man who pushed my car off the road on the hill?" I asked. He smiled and nodded.

The truck seemed to glide over the road and I was surprised when it pulled into the driveway to our house in a matter of minutes. It takes about ten minutes to cover that distance in nice weather. I thanked him after he helped me out of the truck and turned to wave, but the truck was gone.

My husband was startled to see me come in the front door instead of coming from the garage. I told him about my trip home from the valley. When I finished, he scrunched up his face and looked at me. "I didn't hear a truck pull into the driveway," he said. After a short discussion he challenged me to show him the tire tracks. We walked out to the driveway.

There were no tire tracks, only a deep, smooth white blanket of snow — except where my footprints started and led to the stairs to the house.

Since that experience the term "Snow Angel" has a special meaning for me.

~L.A. Kennedy

Chicken Soup for the Soul: Angels Among Us

8

Christmas Grace

You are excellent of men and your lips have been
anointed with grace, since God has blessed you forever.
~Psalm 45:2

S now continued its determined onslaught outside the assisted
living facility windows. By late evening, I grew anxious about
how the roads would be when I headed home. It was the
week before Christmas. I should have been on my way home
by now. The evening receptionist who was scheduled to relieve me
had phoned to say she'd been unable to get her car started. Why was
I the unlucky one stuck behind a receptionist's desk when I should
have been home sipping hot cocoa and decorating the Christmas
tree?

The telephone shrilled. Answering a little grouchily, I heard a
man's voice. "Is this Avis rental car?"

I tried to remain calm. "No, I'm afraid our phone number here
at the assisted living facility is one digit different than Avis. Let me
give you that number so you don't have to look it up again." Sighing,
I quickly glanced at the familiar number of the car rental company on
the pad of paper in front of me. I finished giving the gentleman the
number, wishing him a Merry Christmas. Just as I was about to hang
up, I heard his voice in midair.

"Wait a minute please!"

"Yes?"

"I know this must sound insane, but I have to ask: do you believe in miracles?"

I sat straighter in my chair, startled at such a question from a total stranger.

"Definitely; why do you ask?"

"I'll try to make a long story short. My parents recently passed away in a car accident. I have no one left in the world but a grandmother somewhere in Virginia who I haven't seen since I was little. An uncle placed my grandmother in an assisted living facility when he grew too ill to care for her any longer. He's gone on to heaven as well. I have to ask -- do you happen to have a Grace Sheperd at your facility?"

My heart beat faster as I recognized the familiar name. I pictured the gentleman holding his breath on the other end while I listened to the pinging sound of the icy precipitation pelting the window to my right.

"Are you still there?" he asked finally.

"Yes, I'm here. I wish I could give you the information you're after. I'm afraid there's a privacy policy that prohibits me from answering. The director of the facility will be in her office on Monday morning, however."

"I understand your responsibility in protecting the residents." The young man sounded so sad. "Thank you for your time, and Merry Christmas!"

"Wait!"

"Yes?"

"Virginia is a beautiful state to visit at Christmas time! Let me give you our address in case you happen to be traveling through our area any time soon!"

"Bless you!"

Christmas Eve I arrived at work earlier than usual. Christmas lights twinkled on the decorated trees up and down the hallways. Carols drifted from beneath a resident's closed door as I delivered the morning papers.

I was passing Grace Sheperd's room when I suddenly froze in place. Grace sat in her usual rocking chair, her Bible open in her lap.

Seated on the stool directly in front of her was a handsome young man with curly dark hair. His hand gently clasped Grace's as she read *The Christmas Story*.

Suddenly Grace spotted me. "Paul, here's the woman who helped you find me! Mary, please come and meet my grandson, Paul!"

I hurried inside as tears clouded my vision. The young man slowly rose to his feet, taking my hands in his.

"How can I ever thank you for leading me to my grandmother?" Shaking my head, I attempted to talk around the enormous lump in my throat.

"We both know it was a Christmas miracle!"

"Yes it was… Merry Christmas!"

"Merry Christmas, Paul. Merry Christmas, Grace!"

Making my way back to the reception area, I sent a silent prayer heavenward.

"Father, now I know why I was meant to stay late the other night. Thank you for the miracle of Christmas and for your abiding grace…. Paul's Grace too!"

I couldn't help smiling. It was going to be a glorious Christmas!

~Mary Z. Smith

Chicken Soup for the Soul: A Book of Miracles

9

A Gentle Warning

We have two ears and one mouth so that we
can listen twice as much as we speak.
~Epictetus

"Go home," something inside me seemed to say. "You need to leave now." I had no idea where this warning was coming from, but it wouldn't stop. I tried to brush it aside as I stood watching a line of children waiting their turn to sit on Santa's lap at the Sun Valley Mall, a shopping center thirty miles east of San Francisco.

Just two days before Christmas 1985, my husband and I had left our two young children with his parents while we did last minute shopping. First, we'd had dinner at a restaurant adjacent to the mall and then walked over to join the holiday shoppers. A heavy fog settled over the mall but this didn't dampen the spirits of last-minute shoppers. Lighted Christmas trees, carolers, and a Santa's Village set in the center of the mall created the perfect environment to forget one's cares and abandon oneself to the holiday season.

"Let's meet at the Santa village," I told my husband, as we each headed in different directions for shopping.

With people rushing to and fro and carrying overflowing shopping bags, a special magic filled the air. Usually, I savored the hustle and bustle that only Christmas can create, but a nagging sense of danger cast a shadow over my joy.

The thought kept going through my head: *You need to leave now!* I stopped shopping and headed back to the designated spot where my husband and I were to meet. If he didn't come soon, I'd go look for him.

Trying to brush aside the urgent feeling to leave, I watched a line of children patiently waiting to see Santa. Protective parents hovered and clasped tiny hands. Cameras clicked and bulbs flashed. Younger children cried when parents placed them on Santa's lap. Older children smiled and shyly recited their wish lists in the jolly man's ear. I smiled to myself: *Treasured memories to keep for a lifetime.*

I should have brought our children, I thought. *They'd love to see these Sesame Street figures in the display.*

But this was our "date night," a tradition that started after our children were born. Each year, we'd arrive at my husband's parents for Christmas, and they'd insist we leave the children and enjoy an evening together. Usually, this meant an early dinner, some shopping, and a movie.

This year would be no different, if only that sense of impending danger would leave me alone.

When my husband arrived, I said, "We need to leave. I'm not sure why, but I have an uneasy feeling. I can't explain it, but something inside me keeps telling me to leave."

"I thought we were going to a movie," he said.

"No, we need to go home," I said. "I just have a strange feeling."

Fortunately, he didn't argue. As we walked across the packed parking lot, the fog was denser than I'd ever seen. The mall looked like an eerie ghost shrouded in a heavy veil, and lights from the stores almost faded away.

"Are you sure you want to go home?" my husband asked again, as we climbed into the car.

"I feel uneasy being out," I said. "Let's go back to your parents'."

Once we arrived at my in-laws' house, the warning inside my head stopped. A great sense of relief swept over me, yet I didn't know why.

The next morning, my father-in-law greeted us at the breakfast table by holding up the morning newspaper. "Read this," he said.

Splashed across the front page were the words: *Plane Hits Mall; 3 Die, 50 Injured: Bay Area Shoppers Panic as Wreckage Spills Flaming Fuel.*

"This could have been you," he said.

Not only had the plane crashed into the Sun Valley shopping center just moments after we left, but it crashed in the exact spot where I'd been standing — Santa's Village! My heart sank. *What about those poor children? What about the parents?* "Oh, God," I prayed, "please take care of everyone who was injured. Please comfort those who lost loved ones." *How could this have happened just two days before Christmas? How could it have happened at all?*

Only then did I tell my husband and his parents about the sense that kept warning me to leave the mall. "I believe it was the Lord," I said.

"If you had ignored it," my father-in-law said, shaking his head, "you'd probably be dead or seriously injured."

Why I got the warning, I'll never know. But I had no doubt this was divine protection. Five more minutes could have been the difference between life and death.

To this day, I grieve for those who lost loved ones that terrible night. If only they had heard that same gentle warning.

~Jeanne Getz Pallos

Chicken Soup for the Soul: Miracles Happen

10

Silent Night No More

Faith and joy are the ascensive forces of song.
~Edmund Clarence Stedman

I stared at our antique player piano, too afraid to touch the keys. Those keys were now foreign, glaring back at me like eighty-eight black and white teeth, one scale away from taking a bite out of my calm. Three years before this moment I had been enduring ENT and gastroenterology visits, endoscopies and laryngoscopies, speech therapy, and a vague diagnosis of "muscle tension dysphonia" that forced me to walk away from the stage and the college classroom. After twenty-five years of performing and teaching, I was no longer able to sing. I thought my life was over.

Yet after reinventing my career with the use of the written word as my voice, I found myself taking a call from a producer for The Young Americans international performance company. She was assisting with *The Magic of Christmas*, a five-show run in Southern California, and informed me, "Our lead singer has laryngitis. She's trying steam treatments right now but if Jessica can't sing, can you go on for her tonight?" My first instinct was to run. All I could think of was my current Sunday morning attempts to sing from the church congregation, voice cracking frequently and throat sore for the rest of the day. Mondays found me without a voice at all. How could I get through a public performance?

More profoundly, beyond the physical performance, however, I took into account my continuing grief. Only a month earlier, I had a conversation with my husband about how heartbroken I'd been away from the stage these years, not able to share my heart with an audience. I told him, "Being onstage was a precious place for me. I felt beloved there. I don't feel beloved anymore." *What if something went wrong and I had to spend even more years coping with my loss?*

As I contemplated my answer, the lesson from those painful years hit me. It had taught me that when I want to run from what is scaring me, I should lean into the fear and embrace it. So I took a deep breath and said, "I'm available but can you send me the audio file to see if I can even handle it?" The "Ave Maria," Schubert's reverent interpretation of the enduring prayer to the blessed Virgin Mary, was a beast. There would be no faking my way through it.

Now faced with the piano and the alarming task of a simple warm-up, I tentatively depressed the first key, then another and another. Soon I was vocalizing, triad after triad, arpeggio after arpeggio, head voice connecting to mixed and mixed voice to chest until I felt ready. I opened my mouth to try the classical piece and what came forth was decent. It was certainly safer than a singer with laryngitis. I called Tara and told her I could do it if necessary, simultaneously praying for Jessica's total healing before the show. At 2 p.m. I got a text: *You're on.*

I drove to the theater, my pulse racing and my palms sweating. I got a brief walk-through and sound check, then went to my dressing room to get ready for an 8 p.m. show. The stage manager gave me a five-minute call, and I slowly walked to the stage right wing. One hundred and fifty choral voices were already onstage performing an excerpt from Handel's breathtaking "Messiah."

I appealed to the Holy Spirit to blow His breath in me, giving a clear voice to Schubert's musical prayer. Then I walked on. What came forth surprised me. There was a clarity of tone and richness of resonance I had not been able to achieve in three years. I did it! At the close, however, I thought, *Whew, that was nerve-wracking. Now I can't wait to hear Jessica in the next four shows*, having faith she would be in good voice the next day.

God had other plans.

Jessica texted me the next morning that, though she had regained her voice before going to bed the previous night, she couldn't talk at all when she woke up. I received the same text the third day. So I went on again… and again… and again… and again. Five shows total. That glorious Sunday morning driving to the theater, I realized I had been experiencing a miracle. I had been so focused on evaluating my vocal performance and praying that Jessica heal that I hadn't been focused on the gift I was receiving and giving to others with each performance. Many audience members knew of my vocal journey, of my inability to speak or sing for some time. I began to realize, as people approached, hugging me and crying after the show, that they craved a miracle as much as I did. There were overwhelming embraces, comments and tears as people told me they needed the prayer of the "Ave Maria" just as I sang it. I was blown away.

It dawned on me that God had orchestrated an event that I never could have imagined, even down to the song selection. I reflected that I had been praying the "Hail Mary" my whole life, first on my knees each night with my sisters as children, then many times in the rosary at my lowest. I couldn't have been more intimately acquainted with it. I recalled that my beautiful daddy taught Latin in school, and I was graced to be speaking it in song. It had even been my final goodbye to my grandmother at her funeral years earlier. Oh, so many connections and gifts had rained upon me. Most of all, I realized this miracle was giving me the very gift I had so desired. I felt beloved again, and more than anyone, loved by my Beloved. He was letting me know he heard my prayers, heard my needs, heard my sorrows. He gave me a gift that will last me forever.

The following day my throat was sore and my voice hoarse again. I could barely speak. I had not done one thing to prepare for Christmas. Not one gift bought or wrapped. Not one Christmas card addressed or mailed. But none of that mattered. I had been given the gift of singing a tender prayer for my children, my husband, and hundreds more. I had been blessed to sing for so many who needed His presence, many of whom had lifted me up in my years of loss or who had suffered losses of their own. Most importantly, though I had unwittingly forgotten the meaning of Christmas in years past, I realized the wonder I had experienced is exactly what that sacred season has always been about. We are His beloved, and there are miracles all around us every moment of the season and beyond into the New Year. All we have to do is look for them.

~Cynthia McGonagle McGarity

Chicken Soup for the Soul: Hope & Miracles

A New Leash on Life

Dogs bring out the best in us.
~Author Unknown

"Mom! Get your dog off me!" I yelled, two seconds after walking through her door. It was Christmas Eve, one of the few days a year when I dress up. My thirteen-year-old daughter Desirée and I had arrived to pick my mom up for church, and before I even closed the door behind me, my mom's Shih Tzu, Verdell, had gotten her light-gray hair all over my nice black pants.

Instead of pulling Verdell away with both hands and messing up her own clothes, my mom grabbed the dog's collar with her index finger. Verdell was so excited to see us that she spun around in circles trying to free herself. But instead of freeing herself, she twisted the collar around my mother's finger, tightening it more. My mother's finger was stuck and Verdell couldn't breathe.

My mom screamed and got down on her knees. I thought she was screaming in pain but it was more than that. She was trying to unfasten the collar but it wouldn't budge and neither would the dog. Verdell was motionless.

I could see the fear in my mom's eyes as she realized her closest companion couldn't breathe. She tried pulling her finger out but couldn't. There was no time to spin the dog back around to free her. My mom frantically found scissors but I grabbed them away from her, fearing she would nick the dog trying to cut the collar with one hand. I wasn't comfortable cutting it off with both hands but I knew it was our only hope.

My hands shook rapidly as I pushed the blade under Verdell's collar, freeing her and my mom. Verdell's head fell to the floor. I had never seen her still before. I put my ear to her chest to check for a heartbeat. There was nothing. I looked up at my mom, shook my head, and said, "She's gone."

"Noooo! Nooo! Nooo," my mom wailed. My daughter, who grew up with Verdell, ran to the bathroom and locked herself in. I stared at the dog in shock. I couldn't believe Verdell was gone just like that. Only a couple of minutes earlier, she was greeting us at the door. It didn't seem real. The lively little dog, who was never short of energy, lay there lifeless.

My mother's sobs penetrated my heart. I had never heard her cry like that. I thought her grief would kill her. I was never close to Verdell. I'm allergic to dogs, a bit of a germophobe in general and, as if she knew that, Verdell always went after me of all people. Aside from the shedding, she'd drool on me and even manage to slip her tongue into my mouth—a doggie French kiss.

I don't know what happened, but something clicked inside me. I grabbed Verdell's slobbery mouth, took a deep breath, and proceeded to do CPR. I didn't even know if CPR worked on pets or if I would remember all the steps, but it all came back to me. I tilted Verdell's head back, put my mouth over hers, and breathed. Then… I pumped her chest.

"One-one thousand, two-one thousand, three-one thousand," I recited, and then breathed. "One-one thousand, two-one thousand, three-one thousand."

I checked for her breath and heart beat. There was nothing.

"One-one thousand, two-one thousand, three-one thousand," I said, and prayed to myself. *Please Lord. Bring her back for my mom. She can't take this. Verdell's all she has.*

My mom looked on quietly with hope and expectation, as if I knew what I was doing. I listened for Verdell's heartbeat again. It wasn't there.

"One-one thousand, two-one thousand, three-one thousand," I lamented.

I checked Verdell's vitals again. Nothing.

"One-one thousand, two-one thousand, three-one thousand." Now I could barely get the words out.

With tears rolling down my face, I checked Verdell one more time, looked up at my mom, and finally said, "That's it."

My mom burst into tears again, and I along with her. In the background, I could hear my daughter's muffled cry coming from the bathroom. My mom and I looked down at Verdell. I zoned out looking into her eyes. For a second, I thought I saw one of them blink. I shook my head to snap myself out of it.

"Did you see that," my mom asked. "She blinked. There it is again!"

I wondered if we were both wishful seeing.

This can't be, I thought. Then Verdell's tail wagged.

"Look, look, loo loo look… her her tail. Her tail!" my mom jumped up screaming.

"She's alive!" we cheered. "She's alive! She's alive!"

I embraced my mom, not something we normally do in my undemonstrative family, as we watched Verdell slowly come back to life. Her blinking and tail wagging got faster and faster. Then Verdell lifted herself up by her front legs and joined our celebration as she joyfully ran around the house dragging her back legs behind her.

Little by little, Verdell's hind legs regained strength as well and she jumped all over us. I held her in my arms and she attacked my face with kisses. I didn't resist. Verdell ran back and forth between me and my mom like a puppy pleading to play. Then suddenly she stopped dead in her tracks and made a beeline for the bathroom where my daughter remained barricaded. Verdell scratched on the wooden door, but Desirée didn't answer. She couldn't hear anything over her sobs.

"Desirée! Open up," I yelled through the door.

"Nooo!" she yelled back.

"Open the door," I said. "Someone wants to see you."

"No!" she shouted. "I don't want to see anyone right now."

"It's Verdell," I said. "She's alive!"

Desirée opened the door just a crack to peek out but enough for Verdell to push her way in. Desirée looked down at Verdell in shock. And then excitement.

"Verdell, Verdell, Verdell," she screamed, through her strained voice.

Desirée came out with Verdell in her arms. The dog squirmed, wanting to get down and run around some more. We called an emergency veterinarian. He wasn't surprised by our Christmas miracle and said CPR is often used on animals. The vet asked a few questions about Verdell, congratulated me, and said we didn't need to bring her in. I thought it was all too good to be true but he assured us that she was fine.

We never made it to church that evening but Jesus definitely made His way to us. Verdell and I had a special bond after that night, a special connection that only we shared.

~Adrienne A. Aguirre

Chicken Soup for the Soul: The Dog Really Did That?

Chapter
2

A Book of
Christmas
Miracles

Holiday Blessings

Pumpkin Pie

We must not allow the clock and the calendar to blind
us to the fact that each moment of life is a
miracle and mystery.
~H. G. Wells

Christmas morning was my favorite time of the year. Soon our two sons, three daughters, their spouses, and our ten grandchildren would arrive and fill our house with the sounds of ripping paper, squeaking toys, and giggling children. While kids and dogs chased through the rooms, the women would gather in the kitchen drinking coffee and offering advice on everything from preventing migraine headaches to locating a good babysitter. As usual, they'd volunteer to help with the cooking and, as usual, I'd refuse. The men would huddle in front of television sets — my husband and most of the others watching the History Channel in the living room and two sons-in-law cheering for football teams in the bedroom. Occasionally someone would yell, "Quit picking on your little brother," or "Leave those poor goldfish alone."

For now, the elderly calico cat and I were the only ones in the kitchen. With a contented smile, I ran my bare foot across her soft fur.

I loved this quiet time alone, up to my elbows in flour, surrounded by the smells of coffee and cinnamon. Four freshly baked pies lined the counter and two more were in the oven. The turkey was waiting to be stuffed; bread dough was rising. Outdoors, Bing Crosby's dreams were coming true. Wind-driven snow tapped against the windows and drifted across the roads.

The oven timer dinged and I picked up the worn potholders, taking care to avoid the thin spot. Yes, the pumpkin pies were perfect, filling set around the edges, fluted crust brown but not burned. As I set them on the cooling rack, I felt a sudden, overpowering urge to take a pie to our neighbor, nicknamed George.

George, whose real name was Beulah May, had lived around the corner from us since our children were babies. Like me, she felt the best part of the holiday was baking. Normally we compared notes, but this year had been even busier than usual, and I realized I hadn't spoken to her in weeks.

"Take George a pumpkin pie," a voice said. It sounded like a Charlton Heston parting-of-the-clouds, thunderous rumble. Not a voice to be ignored.

"George doesn't need a pie. She probably has more than I do," I said out loud.

The need to give George a pie persisted. "It's snowing out," I said. "I'll feel foolish. I'll fall on the ice and freeze to death." I was full of arguments. Then, without realizing what I was doing, I grabbed a coat, slid into flip-flops, and carried a still-warm pie wrapped in a white dishtowel out my back door and down the street to George's house.

Nine-year-old Annie saw me coming and opened the door. Her grandmother was right behind her, a worried look on her face.

"Come in out of the snow," George said as she pulled me into the house. "Where are your boots? Are you crazy?" I realized with surprise that I had no hat and my feet were all but bare, yet I wasn't cold.

"I brought you a pumpkin pie," I said. "You'll think I'm crazy but I heard this voice telling me you needed one." I could feel a warm blush spread across my cheeks. "You probably have six already."

Instead of laughing at me, George covered her face with her hands and started to cry. "No," she said between sniffles, "no pies at all. I didn't make any this year."

I was stunned. George didn't bake for Christmas? Then I noticed how quiet the house was. "Where is everyone?" I asked. George's holidays always involved at least twenty people packed around her dinner table. I looked out the window. "And where are all the cars?"

George rummaged through her pockets for a handkerchief. "There's no one here but Annie and me. We were planning to go to Sue's. You know, with the new baby they couldn't come home like they usually do. But the weather's really bad in Chicago and our flight has been canceled." She abandoned the handkerchief search and brushed the tears from her cheeks with her fingertips. "Oh, I know it seems silly compared to other people's problems, but everyone's pretty disappointed. This will be the first time we haven't all been together." She stared at the floor, bottom lip quivering. "John's going to Iraq. Who knows when we'll have another chance?"

No family for Christmas? That might not sound like a crisis to some people but I knew what it meant to George.

With a sigh, George took the pie from me and set it on the round kitchen table. "We'll be okay," she said, raising her chin with a determined expression. "Christmas dinner won't be the same but I have a canned ham."

"Come to our house," I said. "You're practically part of the family and, heaven knows, there's plenty of food."

George shook her head. "Thanks but no. Annie wants to watch *The Christmas Story* on TV and the kids are going to call at dinnertime." She took a deep breath and then chuckled a little, trying to make light of the situation. "You know, I told the Lord I could manage if I just had a pumpkin pie."

She paused and grinned at me. "And now I do."

Annie jumped up and down, her dark curls bouncing. "Grandma, your prayers have been answered. Is this a miracle?"

"No, no, not a miracle," I said, embarrassed. After all, why would God pick me to be his messenger?

"Not a miracle," George agreed with a little smile. "Now, if she'd brought whipped cream, then it would be a miracle."

~Mary Vaughn as told to Sally O'Brien

Chicken Soup for the Soul: A Book of Miracles

Dancing Words

*I see dance being used as communication between body
and soul, to express what is too deep to find for words.*
~Ruth St. Denis

As a newly transplanted nursing home administrator in the spring of 1980, I was excited to meet the residents at Phoenix Mountain Nursing Center, a skilled nursing home that had just opened a year earlier. Going from room to room introducing myself and trying to remember each resident's name, I instantly recognized the gentleman I had just met — Mr. Russell Lyon, Sr. I had noticed the large billboards advertising the Russ Lyon Realty Company when house hunting.

I asked if he was a relative, but received a blank stare in return. His nurse confirmed that the well-dressed gentleman I just met was, indeed, the same Mr. Lyon that owned the Russ Lyon Realty Company.

Over the next several months I saw Mr. Lyon daily, usually at lunch or dinner in the dining room. Always impeccably dressed, he never responded to the usual pleasantries of the staff or other residents. The blank stare was always present. Physically, he could walk without assistance and was always compliant with the directions and care provided by the nursing staff.

As Christmas approached, groups came by to sing carols, but the highlight of the holiday season was the evening orchestra presentation a week before Christmas Day. Scheduled almost a year in advance, a well-known orchestra was set to perform in front of a dining room filled to capacity. A thirty-by-thirty-foot dance floor was assembled, wassail and dessert were ready, and families were arriving to take Christmas photos with their loved ones before the show.

The show began with traditional carols, and then the orchestra started playing big band tunes. Mr. Lyon immediately stood, turned to his caregiver, and said, "Would you care to dance?"

The caregiver was astonished but said, "I'd love to." Hand-in-hand they walked to the dance floor and Mr. Lyon began dancing as if he had been practicing just for this event. As he danced he chatted with the staff, said hello, told them that he appreciated the little things that they did for him daily, and that he was frustrated with his inability to communicate with them.

I talked with him during a dance and he told me "I'm still here." While the music played, he danced with all of the nurses and was animated in his discussions — and when the music stopped, the blank stare returned as if a switch had been thrown.

This turn of events was shared with his physician and his family, and we speculated how we could continue to open this channel of communication with Mr. Lyon on a routine basis. A portable cassette player with musical recordings from the 1940s provided the key. Using this method, we were able to continue communicating with Mr. Lyon for another eight months, until the brain cells that controlled that channel of communication for Mr. Lyon quit functioning, too. He died a month later.

Our discovery with Mr. Lyon gave us all a renewed sense of optimism when providing care to others with similar diagnoses because, in our minds, they "were still there," even though normal communication routes were not functioning. Since that time, I have seen similar instances of individuals with Alzheimer's who can communicate through music, art, and, I'm convinced, divine intervention — and I continue to remember what Mr. Lyon said: "I'm still here."

~John White

Chicken Soup for the Soul: Living with Alzheimer's & Other Dementias

14

The Christmas Mouse

Animals are such agreeable friends — they ask no
questions, they pass no criticisms.
~George Eliot

Once upon a time, we lived in part of a massive, hundred-plus-year-old stone building with an interesting past. Located at a fork in the road at the top of a ridge in rural Lockport, New York, it had once been a blacksmith shop; before that, we heard, it had served as a stagecoach stop. Though it resembled a fortress, it was a grand old place and we loved it. It had character and charm — and leaks, drafts and holes. Pipes froze. So did we. Our cats regularly left us tiny, gory gifts, remnants of the house mice that entered as they pleased after we were asleep.

One special Christmas, we had emerged from some difficult times, and I, after the summer's cancer surgery, had a new awareness of the worth of each day, as well as a deeper appreciation of love and family. It was an especially excellent Christmas because all six of our children were with us. Although we didn't know it then, my husband, David, and I would move to Florida the following summer, and never once since that Christmas have we all managed to be gathered in the same place at the same time.

At one end of the big area that served as living room, dining room and kitchen, I was putting dinner together. Things were noisy, what with the Christmas music on the stereo, the clatter in the kitchen corner, and nine young adults horsing around (a few had brought friends).

The cats, in typical cat fashion, had absented themselves upstairs, away from the hullabaloo.

Just then, out of the corner of my eye, I caught a small, unexpected movement and turned to focus on an astonishing sight. There in the midst of all this uproar, smack in the middle of a kitty bowl on the floor, sat a tiny, exquisite deer mouse eating dry cat food. Incredulous, I stared, but didn't say a word. For one thing, I wanted to make sure he wasn't a figment of my imagination; for another, I'll admit, I wanted to keep him to myself for a few minutes. He was very charming.

Up on his haunches he sat, chubby rear firmly planted, little front paws holding a piece of cat food. The pieces were round, with holes in the middle; our mouse firmly clutched his morsel with a hand on each side, looking for all the world like a little fat guy munching a doughnut. When he finished one, he'd help himself to another, turning it about and adjusting it in his small fingers till it was perfectly situated, then he'd start nibbling again.

I squatted down and looked at him, catching his shiny dark eye. We gazed at each other, then he looked away and nonchalantly went on eating. It was time to call in the witnesses.

"Hey!" I softly called to the assembled multitude. "Come and look at this." When eventually I got their attention, I thought it would be all over — he'd run and hide from the mob advancing on him. Not so! He sat right there while eleven bent-over people stood in a circle, gawking (not silently, either) at him. He glanced confidently at the crowd, gave his doughnut a quarter-turn, and kept munching.

We were amazed. He wasn't in the least afraid of us. What made the little guy so brave? Some of us brought cameras into the circle, and while the flashes popped, the mouse proceeded serenely onward with his Christmas feast. From time to time, he paused to regard us with that sparkly, confiding glance, as the pile of food in the bowl grew smaller.

For some time we watched in delight while he, apparently bottomless, stuffed himself with goodies. However, enchanted as I was to entertain him, I was uneasily aware that it was also dinnertime for the resident Predators Two. When the cats appeared on the scene, as they were bound to any minute, our Christmas mouse could be seriously hurt or killed in the ensuing pandemonium, even if we were able to prevent the cats from transforming the diner into dinner (a perfectly appropriate denouement from their point of view).

I leaned closer. "Listen," I murmured, "we have been honored. But now you have to go back outside with the other mice. Good company though you are, your life is in jeopardy here. If you will permit, I will escort you."

With that, I reached into the dish and picked him up. He neither attempted to bite nor gave way to panic, but sat in my hand, calm and comfortable, awaiting developments, front paws resting on my thumb. I had not expected this; I thought there would be fear, protest, a struggle. Instead, he looked at me, a veritable paradigm of the intelligent, friendly fairy-tale mouse, exactly like something out of a Disney movie.

"What are you, really?" I silently inquired. "Are you really a mouse?" The cool, rational part of me jeered at the question, yet there was something undeniably uncanny about this Christmas visitor.

I carried him outdoors, followed by the family. It had grown dark—one of those blue-and-white Northern winter nights with snow on the ground, the air crisp and sharp.

Squatting down near the cover of bushes in back of the house, I released him. He sat on my palm and looked about, taking his time. Then he jumped to my shoulder and for a long moment we sat there, I in the snow and he on my shoulder, woman and mouse together looking out into the night. Finally, with a mighty leap for one so small, he flew through the air, landed in the shadow of the bushes out of sight and was gone. We humans stayed outside for a while, wishing him well and feeling a little lonely.

His visit left us with astonishment that has never diminished, the more so because, as country people, we knew perfectly well that wild mice are terrified of humans. Furthermore, deer mice are particularly timid; unlike common house mice, they avoid inhabited homes. Engaging and winsome they may be (in the wild, they are known to sing), but not with our kind.

These rare, luminous occasions when wild things in their right minds cross the line that separates us leave us full of wonder. We resonate with remembrance of something ancient and beautiful. As all together we surrounded him, his little wild presence silently conveyed joy, peace, trust and wonder. He was a delightful mystery and a tiny miracle.

~Diane M. Smith

Chicken Soup for the Pet Lover's Soul

15

We Are All Jews Now

Growth is never by mere chance; it is the
result of forces working together.
~James Cash Penney

Viewed from high on the Rimrock cliffs that run along the northern edge of Billings, Montana, the city presents an attractive sight, a thriving metropolis nestling within the great open spaces of the American West. Citizens of Billings say it's a good, civilized place to live. They pride themselves on the quality of their schools and their strong family values.

So it came as a shock to many, when in November 1995, a series of hate crimes took place against minority groups in the city.

Whoever was responsible for these acts must have thought that their victims would be easy targets. Billings is predominantly white; Native Americans, African Americans and Jews make up only a small percentage of the population. But there are just enough of them to frighten and harass — or so the haters must have thought.

They mounted a series of nasty attacks. Graves were overturned in a Jewish cemetery. Offensive words and a swastika were scrawled on the house of a Native American woman. People worshipping at a black church were intimidated. A brick was heaved through the window of a Jewish child who displayed a menorah there.

But the white supremacists, or whoever they were, had reckoned without the citizens of Billings, who had an answer for them — and it wasn't what the hate-mongers were expecting. An alliance quickly emerged, spearheaded by churches, labor unions, the media and hundreds of local citizens.

The results were dramatic. Attendance at the black church rose steadily. People of many different ethnic backgrounds and faiths began to attend services there. Their message was clear: "We may be all different, but we are one also. Threaten any one of us and you threaten us all."

A similar spirit propelled volunteers to come together and repaint the house of Dawn Fast Horse, the Native American woman. This happened at amazing speed. Dawn had awoken one morning to see that her house had been defaced. By the evening, after two hundred people showed up to help, the house had been repainted.

When it came to the incident of the brick being thrown through the window of the Jewish child, an interfaith group quickly had a creative idea. They recalled the example of the Danes during World War II. When the Nazis tried to round up Danish Jews into concentration camps for subsequent extermination, the Danish people worked quickly, within a two-week period, to transport almost every Danish Jew to safety in Sweden until the end of the war.

So the people of Billings organized, and a campaign began. Everyone pitched in, including the local newspaper, which printed a Hanukkah page, including a full-color representation of a menorah. Thousands of Billings residents cut the paper menorah out and displayed it in their windows. By late December, driving around Billings was a remarkable experience. Nearly ten thousand people were displaying those paper menorahs in their windows, and the menorahs remained in place throughout the eight days of Hanukkah. It was a brilliant answer to the hate-mongers: A town that had a few Jews was saying with one collective voice, "We are all Jews now."

The story of what happened in Billings quickly spread, inspiring a national movement called "Not in Our Town." That Jewish child who had so innocently displayed her menorah in the window helped set in motion a chain of events that affirmed all over America the liberating principle of unity in diversity.

Not for nothing does a menorah have many candles flickering on a single stand.

~Bryan Aubrey

Chicken Soup for the Jewish Soul

16

Christmas Magic

When we accept tough jobs as a challenge and
wade into them with joy and enthusiasm,
miracles can happen.
~Harry S. Truman

I wish I could tell you that the whole thing happened because I'm caring and unselfish, but that wouldn't be true. It was 1979, and I had just moved back to Wisconsin from Colorado because I missed my family and Denver wages were terrible. I took a job at a hospice in Milwaukee and found my niche working with the patients and families. As the season changed into fall, the schedule for the holidays was posted:

DECEMBER 24 3–11 Barbara
DECEMBER 25 3–11 Barbara

I was devastated. Newly engaged, it was my first Christmas back home with my family after many years. But with no seniority, I had little clout to get Christmas off while my dedicated colleagues worked.

While lamenting my predicament, I came up with an idea. Since I couldn't be with my family, I would bring my family to the hospice. With the patients and their families struggling through their last Christmases together, maybe this gathering would lend support. My family thought it was a wonderful plan, and so did the staff. Several invited their relatives to participate, too.

As we brainstormed ideas for a hospice Christmas, we remembered the annual 11:00 p.m. Christmas Eve Service scheduled in the hospital chapel.

"Why don't we take the patients to church?" I suggested.

"Yes," replied another staff nurse. "It's a beautiful candlelight service with music. I bet the patients would love it."

"Great. And we can have a little party afterwards, with punch, cookies, and small gifts," I added.

Our enthusiasm increased as we planned the details of our hospice Christmas celebration.

Now, it never occurred to me that all these great ideas may not float so well with administration. It never occurred to me that we might have to get permission for each of these activities — until the director called me into her office.

"Uh, Barb, I'm hearing rumors of a Christmas Eve celebration here at the hospice."

"Well, yes," I replied. Eagerly, I outlined all the plans and ideas the staff had developed. Fortunately for my career, she thought involving our families with the unit activities was a wonderful idea, too.

"But," she said, "certainly you are not serious about taking the patients to church. It has never been done."

"Yes, I'm serious. It would mean a lot to the patients and families."

"Very seldom do you see any patients at this service, and if they do go, they are ambulatory and dressed." She shook her head. "Our patients are too sick to go."

"But a number of them have indicated an interest," I argued.

"I cannot authorize the additional staff needed."

"The family members can help."

"What about the liability?"

Now I felt like saying, "What could be the worst thing that could happen — someone dies in church?" But I didn't. I just kept convincing her, until she begrudgingly gave approval.

Christmas Eve arrived. Family members gathered in the lounge and decorated a small tree, complete with wrapped packages. Then we implemented our plan for the staff and families to transport the patients to the chapel. While most of the patients had family members with them, one young girl had no one. At just nineteen, Sandy had terminal liver cancer. Her mother had died of cancer three years previously, and her father stopped coming long ago. Perhaps he couldn't sit by the bedside of another loved one dying so young. So my family "took charge" of Sandy. My sister combed her hair while my mother applied just a hint of lipstick. They laughed and joked like three old friends as my fiancé helped her move to a gurney.

Meanwhile, other nurses hung IVs on poles, put IVACs on battery support and gave last-minute pain meds. Then, with patients in wheelchairs and on gurneys, we paraded our group into the chapel just as they were finishing "Joy to the World," with the organ and bells ringing out in perfect harmony. Silence descended on the congregation as we rolled slowly down the aisle. The minister just stood there with his mouth open, staring. Everyone turned around to look at us. We faltered in our steps, each movement echoing in the large, crowded chapel.

Then the *magic* began.

One by one, people stood up, filed into the aisle and began to help us. They handed patients hymnals and distributed programs. They wheeled patients to the front so they could see well. They handed out candles to be lit for the closing hymn. One woman adjusted Sandy's pillow and stroked her hair. Throughout the service, the congregation catered to our patients, guiding them through the worship.

The beautiful service closed with a candlelight recessional to "Silent Night." Voices rang in disjointed harmony as the congregation assisted us in exiting the chapel and returning our charges to the unit. Many stayed to share punch and cookies and stories.

As I got Sandy ready for bed that late night, she whispered, "This was one of the nicest Christmases I ever had."

When I shared her comments with my family later, we realized the magic that evening was on many levels. The unit had a special climate we'd never experienced before. Sandy had one of the best Christmases she'd ever known. The congregation had shared in a special, caring way. But we also realized that this evening impacted our family as well.

We felt closer, bonded in purpose and spirit.

Since that Christmas of 1979, my family has been blessed with many Christmases together — but I think that one was the best. Like author William Shore, I, too, believe that when you give to others and give to the community, you create something within yourself that is important and lasting. He calls it the "Cathedral Within."

Our family cathedral is a little stronger for the privilege of giving that Christmas.

~Barbara Bartlein

Chicken Soup for the Nurse's Soul

The Little Horse That Heals

*Better to light one small candle than
to curse the darkness.*
~Chinese Proverb

We had just finished unwrapping Christmas gifts on the morning of December 20, 1999, and were ready for our traditional holiday breakfast when I said, "Wait, there is one more gift to see!" December 25th was not only a religious holiday, a world-wide celebration, Santa's big day. It was also my dad Robert's birthday. I had gotten up early this morning and secretly headed over to the stable. Hidden on the side of my residential home were my truck and horse trailer. No one knew what was to come.

With my family assembled in anticipation of another surprise, I carefully led my father's eighty-fourth birthday present into the family room. Red-felt reindeer antlers adorned his head, he sported a handsome green halter and a winter's growth of hair seemed to add fifty pounds to his 31" tall frame. A stunned silence quickly gave way to squeals of delight and laughter. There wasn't a dry eye in the house as I handed the lead line to my father and said, "Happy birthday, Dad!" During the past year, Dad had casually mentioned, "Gee, I would sure like to have one of those miniature horses." This was a significant change... this was doable — the last horse he coveted was a Clydesdale!

His name was Rebel, a moniker certainly bestowed as a joke since his personality and temperament would prove to be anything but. I found Rebel just three days before from an ad in the paper. A kind description of the conditions in which I found him would be a puppy mill. When the owner brought Rebel out for me to see, he literally had a live monkey hanging from his neck and a dead-eyed look of unhappiness and toleration. He was completely uncared for. I took him immediately.

I brought Rebel to the stable of a therapeutic riding program for people with special needs where I am a certified riding instructor. At Horses Help, I got Rebel settled in, had our vet check him over and groomed him until the day of his big debut arrived. It was immediately clear that Rebel had the perfect disposition to be a certified therapy horse. There were bigger things in store for this little guy than being the perfect birthday gift.

Soon it became necessary for Rebel to have a real job and we taught him how to pull a cart. At first, the idea of actually working instead of just eating and looking cute didn't sit well with Rebel, but he eventually took to it easily and joined an eight horse and cart drill team. He now performs all over Arizona at horse shows and fairs in a fifteen-minute program filled with resounding, patriotic music. At Horses Help, Rebel lives among fourteen big horses of all sizes and shapes, and we use him to help children get used to the larger animals by leading and grooming him. Dad comes every Tuesday to visit, delighted to own a horse but have none of the responsibilities of its care.

One of my interests lies in animal-assisted therapy and the elderly, so it wasn't long before Rebel and I became the only miniature horse Delta Pet Partner therapy team in the entire state of Arizona. In two years, we have visited over twenty care centers for the elderly. Rebel's expertise turns out to be patients afflicted with Alzheimer's or dementia. Instinctively, he seems to know that he must spend more time, to wait for a reaction, when he encounters a person with cognitive impairment. Time and time again, he quietly rests his head on a bed or a wheelchair, waiting patiently for a hand to be raised or a voice to be heard, but with someone else, he might allow a quick pat and move on. On one visit to a day-care facility for the elderly, he quickly made his way through the crowd of almost eighty residents. My heart swelled with pride when he hesitated longer with two women, sitting at opposite ends of the room, that were blind and needed more time to "see" with their hands. On another occasion, we visited a woman who was about to die and Rebel gently laid his head near her hand so she could pet him. He somehow knew she needed him in her last few hours of life. We can't teach this, it is simply in a creature's heart. It is a gift and every time I watch my little horse bring a smile to a face or a tear to the eye, I am blessed with the most incredible feeling of joy and pride and fulfillment.

No one told Rebel he isn't the size of a draft horse. If they had, he wouldn't have believed them anyway. He doesn't know he was born premature, abandoned by his mother and, at one point in his life, wasn't very well cared for. From the start, this scrappy little guy just followed his heart as he chased the big horses in the pastures. Rebel still follows his heart as he faithfully clip-clops up the steps, in the elevators and down the halls of hospitals, schools and nursing homes, past noisy respirators to visit his special people. He doesn't know that horses don't usually do that, either.

Rebel doesn't see the Alzheimer's, the hospital beds, the blindness, the wheelchairs, or the fear in the eyes of those who feel unsafe, just like he doesn't see size. But he does see the smiles and the joy. Even dressed up in bright red reindeer antlers, he quietly demonstrates what he's known all along; life is good, people are good. If Rebel could talk, he would probably ask, "What size is positive attitude? How tall is success? How big is love?" This funny little horse doesn't know or even care. He simply goes about his business in a great big way, gently showing every one he touches that none of us is small and everyone counts.

Another Christmas day found Rebel and me at a care center for the elderly that we frequent. I had Rebel loaded up on the trailer, ready to go when down the sidewalk came a woman frantically pushing her husband in a wheelchair. "Did I miss him? Oh dear, did I miss him?" Her face beheld desperation, disappointment and sadness, even panic.

I will never forget that look. Sitting in the wheelchair was a tall man, seemingly unaware of his surroundings, his head cocked to one side and an empty look on his face.

"I was just about to leave. Do you think your husband would like to meet Rebel?" I asked.

"I just don't know anymore," she answered, with so much sadness and loss of hope that my heart broke.

"Let me get Rebel out. Let's try."

I led Rebel over to this shell of a man. As usual, Rebel put his head on the man's lap and just waited. Sure enough, up came a hand, reaching weakly for Rebel's muzzle. Then, the man's head rose and a slight moan escaped from his lips, "Rebel." His wife was in awe. It had been a very long time since her husband had responded to anything or anyone. I could visibly see her despair soften as Rebel continued to visit with her husband.

"Thank you," she said softly, gently stroking her husband's shoulder, "you and Rebel have given me the best Christmas present ever."

~Leslie A. Paradise with Jan Clare

Chicken Soup for the Horse Lover's Soul II

18

Delayed Delivery

They that love beyond the world cannot be separated
by it. Death cannot kill what never dies.
~William Penn

S tella had been prepared for her husband's death. Since the doctor's pronouncement of terminal cancer, they had both faced the inevitable, striving to make the most of their remaining time together. Dave's financial affairs had always been in order. There were no new burdens in her widowed state. It was just the awful aloneness… the lack of purpose to her days.

They had been a childless couple by choice. Their lives had been so full and rich. They had been content with busy careers and with each other. They had many friends. Had. That was the operative word these days. It was bad enough losing the one person you loved with all your heart. But over the past few years, she and Dave repeatedly coped with the deaths of their friends and relations. They were all of an age — an age when human bodies began giving up. Dying. Face it — they were old!

And now, approaching the first Christmas without Dave, Stella was all too aware she was on her own.

With shaky fingers, she lowered the volume of her radio so that the Christmas music faded to a muted background. To her surprise, she saw that the mail had arrived. With the inevitable wince of pain from her arthritis, she bent to retrieve the white envelopes from the floor. She opened them while sitting on the piano bench. They were mostly Christmas cards, and her sad eyes smiled at the familiarity of the traditional scenes and at the loving messages inside. She arranged them among the others on the piano top. In her entire house, they were the only seasonal decoration. The holiday was less than a week away, but she just did not have the heart to put up a silly tree, or even set up the stable that Dave had built with his own hands.

Suddenly engulfed by the loneliness of it all, Stella buried her face in her hands and let the tears come. How would she possibly get through Christmas and the winter beyond it!

The ring of the doorbell was so unexpected that Stella had to stifle a small scream of surprise. Now who could possibly be calling on her? She opened the wooden door and stared through the window of the storm door with consternation. On her front porch stood a strange young man, whose head was barely visible above the large carton in his arms. She peered beyond him to the driveway, but there was nothing about the small car to give a clue as to his identity. Summoning courage, the elderly lady opened the door slightly, and he stepped sideways to speak into the space.

"Mrs. Thornhope?"

She nodded. He continued, "I have a package for you."

Curiosity drove caution from her mind. She pushed the door open, and he entered. Smiling, he placed his burden carefully on the floor and stood to retrieve an envelope that protruded from his pocket. As he handed it to her, a sound came from the box. Stella jumped. The man laughed in apology and bent to straighten up the cardboard flaps, holding them open in an invitation for her to peek inside.

It was a dog! To be more exact, a golden Labrador Retriever puppy. As the young gentleman lifted its squirming body up into his arms, he explained, "This is for you, ma'am." The young pup wiggled in happiness at being released from captivity and thrust ecstatic, wet kisses in the direction of the young man's face. "We were supposed to deliver him on Christmas Eve," he continued with some difficulty, as he strove to rescue his chin from the wet little tongue, "but the staff at the kennels start their holidays tomorrow. Hope you don't mind an early present."

Shock had stolen Stella's ability to think clearly. Unable to form coherent sentences, she stammered, "But... I don't... I mean... who...?"

The young fellow set the animal down on the doormat between them and then reached out a finger to tap the envelope she was still holding.

"There's a letter in there that explains everything, pretty much. The dog was bought while his mother was still pregnant. It was meant to be a Christmas gift."

The stranger turned to go. Desperation forced the words from her lips. "But who . . . who bought it?"

Pausing in the open doorway, he replied, "Your husband, ma'am." And then he was gone.

It was all in the letter. Forgetting the puppy entirely at the sight of the familiar handwriting, Stella walked like a sleepwalker to her chair by the window. She forced her tear-filled eyes to read her husband's words. He had written the letter three weeks before his death and had left it with the kennel owners, to be delivered along with the puppy as his last Christmas gift to her. It was full of love and encouragement and admonishments to be strong. He vowed that he was waiting for the day when she would join him. And he had sent her this young animal to keep her company until then.

Remembering the little creature for the first time, she was surprised to find him quietly looking up at her, his small panting mouth resembling a comic smile. Stella put the pages aside and reached for the bundle of golden fur. She thought that he would be heavier, but he was only the size and weight of a sofa pillow. And so soft and warm. She cradled him in her arms and he licked her jawbone, then cuddled into the hollow of her neck. The tears began anew at this exchange of affection and the dog endured her crying without moving.

Finally, Stella lowered him to her lap, where she regarded him solemnly. She wiped vaguely at her wet cheeks, then somehow mustered a smile.

"Well, little guy, I guess it's you and me." His pink tongue panted in agreement. Stella's smile strengthened, and her gaze shifted sideways to the window. Dusk had fallen. Through fluffy flakes that were now drifting down, she saw the cheery Christmas lights edging the roof lines of her neighbors' homes. The strains of "Joy to the World" floated in from the kitchen.

Suddenly Stella felt the most amazing sensation of peace and benediction wash over her. It was like being enfolded in a loving embrace. Her heart beat painfully, but it was with joy and wonder, not grief or loneliness. She need never feel alone again.

Returning her attention to the dog, she spoke to him. "You know, fella, I have a box in the basement that I think you'd like. There's a tree in it and some decorations and lights that will impress you like crazy! And I think I can find that old stable down there, too. What d'ya say we go hunt it up?"

The puppy barked happily in agreement, as if he understood every word. Stella got up, placed the puppy on the floor and together they went down to the basement, ready to make a Christmas together.

~Cathy Miller

Chicken Soup for the Pet Lover's Soul

19

The Poop that Saved Christmas

Diaper backward spells repaid. Think about it.
~Marshall McLuhan

After I was laid off in mid-October, I faced the loathsome task of informing our seven-year-old. I tried to put it in as positive a light as I could — when the company merged with another company, they had twice as many people without having twice as much work to do. I stressed that I hadn't done anything wrong and that it was nothing personal, but that they no longer had enough work for me, so I was basically finished with my job.

I said nothing about us having been treated more like an acquisition in spite of the fact that our company owned a controlling share of the new stock. I never cast aspersions on how our CEO cut us loose during the worst economic crisis since the Great Depression, nor did I point out that the company's profits had been up by more than eighty percent, which negated any claim that the layoffs were a necessary cost-cutting maneuver.

I figured that was too much for a seven-year-old to swallow, which is why I put on a smile and simply told him I'd be looking for a new job, ignoring the urge to warn him that he might hear weeping sounds coming from Mommy and Daddy's room.

Later came the talk of cutting our own expenses. We knew we'd be able to pay all of our bills through the end of the year, with little extra. Unfortunately, that time span included a period when tradition dictates that a family needs that little extra — Christmas. It's one of the two most important holidays on the Christian liturgical calendar, as well as the season to essentially stick a vacuum cleaner hose in my wallet.

Nevertheless, we switched the vacuum cleaner off, and Christmas was suddenly about religion again. That's also difficult for a seven-year-old to accept, but we figured it might be easier if he had advance notice. Hence came Part Two of The Talk, in which I explained that fortunately we'd bought a few small gifts for him and his brother before I'd lost my job, my money and my self-worth. This meant they'd get something for Christmas, but not nearly as much as in past years.

He took the news remarkably well; in fact, he even put a positive spin on it: "That's okay, Dad — at least Santa Claus will still bring us the big gifts."

After removing that dagger from my heart, I slunk to my computer to see if there was any possible excess in the budget I'd worked up. That Santa! He's always upstaging me. The budget review indicated that even Santa had no chance of scoring with the big gifts.

There's another aspect of the holidays that was affected by the layoff — travel. We needed to visit my parents, especially since my mom had a stroke in October. By the way, the news of Mom's stroke was the third bad thing to happen in that October week that included my layoff and the death of a long-time pet.

So we knew we should go visit my parents in Virginia for Thanksgiving, but for us to get there would have cost more than we had between the cost of the gas and the hotel room we needed because I was allergic to their dog.

Not so with my in-laws. Which is how we found ourselves driving to their home the weekend before Thanksgiving. They live a little closer, so the gas cost is better, but the big difference is in being able to sleep in their house instead of a hotel.

Halfway there, I started feeling guilty about my own parents. But my thoughts were interrupted by a more urgent problem.

"I needa go poo-poo," our toddler said.

"Okay, hold on. We need to find an exit. Will you sit on the potty at a gas station?"

"No."

Sigh. We've been fifty percent successful with his potty training. He mostly wears "big boy unnerwear" and is able to keep them dry, but when it comes to Number Two, he's been defiantly resistant. He warns us when it's on its way, but refuses to sit on a potty. Instead, we have to take off his pants and underwear, put on a Pull-Up, and let him do his business as if he's still in diapers.

So we pulled up behind the closest gas station/convenience store, and made ready for the deed. My wife was willing to do the hard part while I stood in the 20-degree night air, waiting for her to roll down the window and hand me a sealed freezer bag containing a soiled Pull-Up and wipes. My job was to throw it away while she changed him back into his big boy underwear.

When I finally took possession of the freezer bag, I had to walk around to the front of the store to find a trashcan for it. I had a hard time finding one, and briefly considered keeping the bag, so I could later mail it to my former CEO.

But I was resolute, and my search eventually took me inside the convenience store. I forgot all about the freezer bag once I noticed the glitzy display of lottery scratchers at the cash register. When I remembered my own lottery rules—including the increased likelihood of winning when a ticket is purchased in a nasty store in the middle of nowhere—I knew I had to buy one.

So I sidled up to the counter and asked for one of the scratchers, fishing in my pocket for money with one hand while I clutched the dirty freezer bag behind my back with the other. I glanced at the cashier's nametag: "Virginia." Ouch. Let the parent-related guilt continue.

We arrived at my in-laws in our usual flurry of chaos, the boys hyped on chocolate and excited about seeing their grandparents, me unloading our luggage as quickly as possible in order to minimize my risk of hypothermia. It wasn't until the next morning that I remembered the scratcher. I found a penny, and began the anticipatory scratching ritual. I won $200 on the first space, and was ecstatic. I figured no more prizes would be revealed, but continued scratching. Nothing. Nothing. Then another $100 — the holidays were suddenly looking up!

Next space, nothing. Then $100 again. Then a third $100. Was this really a $500 winner, or was I reading the numbers wrong? Next two spaces, nothing. Then another $200. Whoa. They don't make $700 winners, do they? Nope — next space, another $200! Nothing, nothing, then $100 in the last space.

When I told my wife we'd just won $1,000, she asked, "How is that possible?" That's when I had to admit I'd been frivolous and bought a lottery ticket. She asked where I'd bought the ticket, and that's when it hit me — I had no idea. Neither one of us could remember the exit number, the town, the highway, the gas station, or the store name. It was supposed to have been nothing but a poop stop, but suddenly my son had presented us with the richest poop in town. Courtesy of a cashier named… Virginia.

"Sweetie, I think we should go to my parents' place during the holidays, after all. We can stay in a hotel for one night. And maybe we should buy a couple more Christmas presents for the boys. And what the heck? Why not make a mortgage payment, while we're at it?"

Most importantly, while I was full of holiday spirit, I finally threw away that freezer bag before I could find my ex-CEO's address.

~Dan Bain

Chicken Soup for the Soul: Count Your Blessings

20

Left Behind

Don't be dismayed at goodbyes. A farewell is necessary
before you can meet again. And meeting again,
after moments or lifetimes, is certain for
those who are friends.
~Richard Bach

I stared at the wall in front of me, then turned to look out the window at the people walking along the street. This was my daily routine now, silently sitting in my husband's armchair, listlessly moving my eyes around the room, then going back to bed to try to sleep away my despair.

A month ago, on an October morning, my husband Art, my best friend, had suddenly passed away. We had often talked of growing old together, but something had gone wrong and I was left behind.

Like a robot, I had arranged a memorial service. "Life will go on. You will feel better soon," well-meaning friends tried to encourage me. But I shrugged them off. How could they know the hopelessness I was facing? I was alone. Alone with my grief, my pain, and my agonizing thoughts. Art and I had just moved to this town three months earlier. I had not yet had an opportunity to make friends. I didn't even know my neighbors.

A few days after Art's death, I called one of our best friends. Even though Gina and Ron lived an hour away, they came right over. "Please, help me pack Art's stuff," I sobbed. "And would you take it with you? Keep what you would like and give the rest away."

"Why don't you wait until you feel a bit better," Gina advised. "It's too soon to give his things away."

"No, No! I can't face looking at it. It hurts too much," I pleaded. There was no way I wanted to let them know that I also wanted to give my stuff away since my life was over too. After Gina and Ron left, I slumped into an armchair next to a side table where Art's photo was prominently displayed. Pain shot through my heart as I stared at it. Then, ever so slowly, I turned the picture over. I could not tolerate the pain of seeing his smiling face when I had no hope of ever seeing him alive again.

One day I decided that I should go down to the beach. At least I would see people instead of sitting alone at home. Slowly I trudged the ten minutes down the hill and began walking along the promenade. People passed me, arm in arm, hand in hand, talking, laughing, enjoying themselves. Everyone seemed to have someone. Everyone except me. So, with a wounded heart, I quickly fled back home.

Another day I went to the mall to buy some groceries. There my heart took another dive. The stores were decorated for Christmas and there were shoppers everywhere. *How could I face Christmas without my beloved Art? Why even bother to put up a tree?*

Then Ron and Gina invited me to spend Christmas Day with them. "Please," they urged. "We'd love to have you." I quickly declined. Joining in their Christmas festivities without Art would tear my heart apart even more. I would not tell them that I was slowly dying inside, and probably in a few weeks there would be another memorial service. Mine.

However, Christmas Day changed my life forever. That morning I awoke with a start. There stood my Art in the doorway of our bedroom: whole, healthy, alive. "Inga!" he called, looking at me tenderly. Overjoyed to see him again, I bolted upright, ready to jump into his arms. But at that precise moment, Art disappeared, leaving me wide-eyed in wonder and shock.

Was he real? Was it a vision? I sank back into the pillow in despair, my eyes filling with tears, dreading the new day. How I missed him! Just then a Bible verse I had read came to me. "I am the resurrection and the life. He who believes in me will live, even though he dies; and whoever lives and believes in me will never die" (John 11:25-26 NIV).

Suddenly it felt like a curtain was removed from my eyes. *Art was alive in the beyond, waiting for me to join him when my time was up.* A wave of hope washed over my anguished spirit, raising me from the grave of grief. *I would see Art again in Heaven.* Yet I sensed another message Art was bringing me. "Until we meet again, get involved in life," he seemed to say. Right away I sought activities I would enjoy. I joined the local walking club, a Bible study, and the widows' club that met weekly for lunch. Life became bearable again, especially when I made several new friends.

I savored the message of hope Art had brought me. God had not forsaken me. I was not alone. The Lord was with me even in the midst of tragedy. Yes, life would go on and I was left behind to fulfill God's purpose for me on earth. Today, I look forward to each new day's challenges and blessings because God sent Art to me, even though for only a second, to let me know He cared and that someday I would spend eternity with my beloved Art and with the Lord.

~Inga Dore

Chicken Soup for the Soul: Miraculous Messages from Heaven

21

Chicken Soup for the Soul

The Spirit of the Season

The most vivid memories of Christmases past are
usually not of gifts given or received, but of the spirit
of love, the special warmth of Christmas worship,
the cherished little habits of home.
~Lois Rand

I t was my first Christmas in Los Angeles, and somewhere between the strangeness of the weather and the fact that I had never spent Christmas alone before, the holiday blues were setting in, in a big way. I spent my days behind a cosmetics counter, explaining the difference between various moisturizers and why night cream is so important. Just after Thanksgiving, we received a shipment of beautiful three-tiered silk moiré jewelry boxes our cosmetics company put out as a last-minute promotion. They had only sent three, and for a good reason. They retailed for about seventy-five dollars apiece, putting them far out of reach for most of our customers.

Having worked in retail for many years, I was used to merchandise coming and going, and rarely if ever wanted much, but the minute I saw the jewelry boxes, I wanted one desperately. I wanted it for a combination of reasons, the first being that it was absolutely beautiful. A deep, emerald green, it was full of the company's best products, meant to be used so that the box could later hold jewelry. Secondly, I was scrimping and saving every cent just to get by, and this was one of the most decadent, extravagant things I'd ever seen. I walked or took buses in a city in which everyone has a car, brought my own lunch every day rather than eat at the expensive mall food court, and clipped every imaginable coupon. The idea of not only owning, but buying something like this just seemed so unbelievably out of my reach. Finally, I was still very much a stranger in a strange land. Everything that year seemed challenging, and I suppose I needed something to just be easy and even, perhaps to make me feel as though this was truly Christmas time. The thought of just being able to buy the jewelry box seemed like a way to accomplish both.

The jewelry boxes sat on the counter for two weeks and were admired and examined by almost every woman who came by, each one saying how much she'd like to have it. Although none actually purchased one, every time someone looked as though she might, my heart always sank. The idea of someone walking away with one of my boxes was more than I could take.

The week before Christmas, a man of about fifty came up to the counter, clearly overwhelmed by the thought of having to pick something out.

"Can I help you?" I asked.

"I hope so," he said. "I need a couple of presents, and I don't know where to start. This stuff mystifies me."

"Well, what are you looking for?" I asked.

"I have absolutely no idea, and I'm in a little bit of a hurry. What would you want if someone were buying something for you?"

This question presented a moral dilemma for me. There was no question what I would want, but I didn't want to tell him. He might buy it, and then we would only have two left.

"Well, honestly, I would probably buy this." I walked him over to the box and proceeded to extol all its virtues, demonstrating every drawer, every hidden compartment, all the while hoping silently that he wouldn't buy it.

"I don't know," he said, looking at it pensively. "Seventy-five dollars seems like a lot."

I elaborated, explaining that any woman would be thrilled to have it.

"Well, all right. Can you wrap it for me?" he asked.

"No problem," I said, not sure if I had really wanted him to say yes.

When I came back to the counter from the stockroom, he said he wanted a second box. A little confused about why someone who was so ambivalent about buying one suddenly wanted two, I returned to the stockroom. When I returned, he said he wanted a third, wanted them all wrapped and would be back later with a credit card.

Forty minutes later, he came back to the counter.

"Did you get them wrapped?" he said, clearly ready to get his shopping finished.

"Yes, I did," I answered. "Would you like to put that on your charge?"

"Yes, but first, do you have gift cards?"

"Watch him," I whispered to my manager. "I'm starting to worry that he's going to take those boxes and run."

I returned with the cards, now getting a little angry, and more important, concerned that he had no intention of paying.

"Here," I said, handing him three cards and envelopes. "Why don't I ring this up for you?"

He handed me his credit card and took a seat at the counter, suddenly taking his time to fill out the cards.

To my surprise — and to a certain degree, my dismay — his card went through. My dream of having the jewelry box was over.

"Here you go," I said, handing him the sales slip to sign.

He signed it, and then took one of the gift cards and put it in an envelope.

"Just a minute," he said.

He took one of the wrapped boxes out of its bag, put it on the counter with the card and said, "Thanks for all your help. Have a great holiday," and walked away with the box still on the counter.

I was dumbfounded. Instinctively, I opened the card. It read:

Merry Christmas, Courtney.
Love, Santa

In the midst of all the Christmas chaos, in a town in which acquiring things is a blood sport, this man did something that stayed with me for the rest of my life: He gave me hope that even when things seem dark, someone will come along and make everything just a little easier.

~C. L. Robinson

Chicken Soup for the Shopper's Soul

22

Christmas Ice Storm

Having a place to go — is a home.
Having someone to love — is a family.
Having both — is a blessing.
~Donna Hedges

My sister and I had already put up our Christmas tree, trimming it with strings of colourful lights, glass ornaments, and tinsel. My parents and my brother had decorated our home with outdoor festive lights and garlands, and had placed a Christmas wreath on our front door. The neighbourhood was decked out for the holidays as Christmas approached.

Then, on Saturday December 21st, we were hit by a severe ice storm in southern Ontario. The freezing rain fell continuously, and the ice began to build up everywhere. On Saturday night, somewhere in the distance, I heard the frightful sound of electrical transformers exploding. The lights flickered on and off, but I was relieved each time the power came back on. My mother went to the basement to find candles and flashlights in case we needed them. When my sister returned home from work that evening, she was soaking wet, and really cold. "The roads and the sidewalks are covered with ice," she exclaimed. "It's a miracle I didn't fall." My brother, who was visiting, decided to stay overnight, fearing the roads were too dangerous to drive home to his own apartment.

When I awoke the next morning the house was eerily silent. I realized the furnace had gone off, and we had lost power. We had no lights, no heat, and of course our electric stove did not work. The house was already cold, and we had no way to boil water or make coffee to warm up.

Outside, the trees and streets were covered with a thick layer of ice. It looked like the kind of winter landscape you see depicted on a Christmas card, with rooftops shimmering and trees encased in sparkling ice. However, the reality wasn't as pretty as the picture. As the freezing rain continued to fall, the temperature dropped steadily in our home. As the hours went by we waited, hoping for the power to be restored. A neighbour came by to help us scrape the large build-up of ice from our driveway and walkway. Another neighbour, who had a gas stove, came over to offer my mother a kettle full of tea. "This will help warm you up," she said.

With no radio or TV, we had no news about the extent of the damage, or when the power might be restored. My sister was scheduled to work that afternoon, but the slick, ice-covered sidewalks had grown even more treacherous overnight. She wasn't sure she could get there, so my brother offered to drive her.

It was now early afternoon. With no power to make a hot lunch, we settled for making sandwiches. As we were preparing them, my brother returned with some good news. He had passed by his own apartment and discovered that his building had power!

"You can't stay here — it's too cold," he said. "We'll have lunch at my place." We quickly packed up the sandwiches we had prepared, and left. When I opened the back door to my brother's car, a sheet of ice fell to the ground. As we drove through the city, there were fallen tree branches lying in the middle of roads and hanging dangerously from power lines. Some streets were closed with yellow police tape blocking off the sections made dangerous by fallen trees or electric wires. It was a strange combination. There was the frightful scene of downed power lines and branches and, at the same time, a picturesque scene of sparkling trees and glittering rooftops.

When we arrived at my brother's apartment we turned on the television and learned that the power outages were far more widespread than we'd thought. Hundreds of thousands of people were without power, we learned, and it might be several days before it would be restored. It was only three days before Christmas, and no one was sure if people would be able to return to their homes by Christmas Day. When I heard this, my heart sank.

From the beginning, Hydro workers worked day and night to restore power. Others came from all over Ontario and then from all over Canada, sacrificing their own Christmas at home with their family and friends to help Ontarians through this crisis. They worked fourteen to sixteen hours a day in cold and freezing rain to get the power back on in homes.

That evening we returned to our own home to see if the power had been restored. But it was still dark. There were no streetlights on in our neighbourhood, and there was no warmth in our dark, silent house. Using flashlights and candles, we gathered together some overnight supplies. We let the water run to prevent the pipes from freezing. To our surprise a glass of water which my mother had left on the kitchen table already had ice in it.

On our way out, my mother saw our neighbour outside. He had decided not to leave his home despite the loss of power. They had a gas stove, and were able to at least prepare hot food and drinks. His little granddaughter was at a relative's house, however, because her lips had turned blue in the cold.

"I wish I didn't have to leave," my mother sighed. "I've never had to leave my home before, especially at Christmas." She gave him a box of chocolates as a Christmas gift and asked him, "Please watch over our home, and call me if you see anything." He smiled when he saw the chocolates, knowing they would cheer up his granddaughter. "Don't worry," he said. "I'll let you know if I see anything."

When Christmas Eve arrived there was still no power in our neighbourhood. But we were all at my brother's, preparing our traditional Italian Christmas Eve dinner, a special meal made up of fish and pasta dishes. Despite the difficulties, we were all together and that was the most important thing. Just as we were about to sit down to dinner the phone rang. It was our neighbour announcing that the lights had come back on. We were ecstatic! Those hard working Hydro workers had restored power to our neighbourhood, and we could go home.

When we returned home, we immediately turned on the Christmas lights. As our neighbourhood quickly sprang to life, those lights seemed to shine more brightly that Christmas Eve than ever before. The Christmas of 2013 will forever be remembered in Toronto as the Christmas of the Great Ice Storm. Filled with Christmas spirit, everyone worked together to help bring about a Christmas miracle.

~Nada Mazzei

Chicken Soup for the Soul: The Spirit of Canada

Chapter
3

A Book of
Christmas
Miracles

Christmas Spirit

23

Christmas Eve Service

Gratitude can transform common days into
thanksgivings, turn routine jobs into joy, and change
ordinary opportunities into blessings.
~William Arthur Ward

"Merry Christmas!" Annie called out as soon as I entered the Fellowship Hall. When she saw the cookies I carried, she angled her head toward the kitchen. "You can drop those off with Gary."

Every church, synagogue or house of worship has an Annie and Gary. They're the couple who help without being asked, step forward when others step back, and make congregational life run smoothly. But there's a twist to Annie and Gary's volunteering: Annie chairs committees, organizes fundraisers and takes center stage. Just as warm, but quieter, Gary supervises coffee hour and washes dishes after potlucks. This might be common among my peers, but not in the previous generation. I wondered — did Gary mind doing "domestic" chores?

"I like being back here," he said, standing at the oversized kitchen sink. Wearing a chef's apron, he rinsed and loaded dirty cups and plates onto racks and ran them through the church's heavy-duty commercial dishwasher. Sleeves rolled up, hands soapy, face pink from the steamy hot water, Gary seemed happy. "This is my calling. This is the best way I know of serving people. The work is spiritual, especially when there's a full congregation worshiping upstairs and you're all alone down here."

He made it sound so easy and serene, but it wasn't. Week after week, Gary handled the many tasks associated with coffee hour: operating the industrial-sized coffee machine, laying out the snacks for kids and adults, setting up tables and chairs so people could linger after the service—a service Gary rarely got to attend in its entirety. He either came in late, slipped out early, or never made it upstairs at all.

Until I got to know Gary I took his labors for granted. Like other parents with young children, I volunteered in Sunday school and felt that was enough. As my girls got older and could manage for themselves, I began helping out with coffee hour. Eventually I learned my way around the kitchen and grew to enjoy the quiet Gary talked about. Missing a service now and then was fine, but not Christmas. Never Christmas. I couldn't imagine missing a Christmas Eve service.

Except the reception following Christmas Eve service was the church's most crucial coffee-hour event. Attendance doubled, and the tradition of members dropping off home-baked cookies, cakes and treats meant someone had to stay downstairs to receive the goodies. Then there was the long to-do list: make the holiday punch; lay out linens and napkins; cut up the coffeecakes, fruit cakes, rum cakes; arrange slices and cookies for serving; and brew coffee.

The reception volunteer missed out on all that made Christmas Eve special—the carol sing-along; ringing the jingle bells as the children paraded around the sanctuary; passing the light during the "Silent Night" candle ritual; seeing the darkened sanctuary lit by the glow of two hundred dancing flames. Missing these traditions would mean missing Christmas, I thought. Not me. I wouldn't.

Fortunately, I was never asked to make that sacrifice. You can guess who did it.

But not even Gary could be two places at once. The year my husband was president of the congregation, Gary announced he'd be out of town Christmas Eve. Jim explained the jam he was in. I listened stony-faced with arms crossed. Finally, he just said it: "Would you organize the cookie reception?"

My look would have dimmed even Rudolph's shining nose. "You're kidding, right?"

"I can't ask anybody else. You know what's involved. And I bet your mother would be willing to help."

"But the service ends at eight, and there'll be people in the Fellowship Hall until nine. It'll take at least forty-five minutes to get everything cleaned up and put away. And my mother can't drive after dark; I'll have to take her home. That means I won't get home until close to eleven. I'll miss Christmas Eve with the girls."

"I'll pick your mother up before church. And I'll get the girls to bed and help them set out milk and cookies for Santa. I really need your help."

I felt aggrieved and put-upon as I arrived at church an hour early on Christmas Eve. Not wanting my mother to miss out too, I shooed her away as the service started. "I need you up there to make sure the girls don't get burned by hot wax," I told her. "You have to help them with their candles during 'Silent Night.'"

Alone, I somehow felt better. The music filtered down from above, setting a steady rhythm for the work ahead. I rinsed out the punch bowl and poured in lemon-lime soda, fruit juice and sherbet. I draped three banquet tables with colorful tablecloths, then artfully arranged Christmas-themed paper napkins. I moved evergreen boughs from the windows to the tables and nestled votive candleholders among them. When the coffee machine's ready-to-brew light went on, I put the big industrial filters into the metal baskets and filled them with ground coffee.

Each simple kitchen task, familiar to me after years of volunteering, took on the majesty of ritual. I began to understand what Gary meant about service to others being spiritual.

The rumble of footsteps in the stairwell broke my reverie. The Fellowship Hall was soon standing-room-only. Mounds of cookies and sweets were reduced to a few scattered crumbs on empty plates. The large room echoed with holiday spirit, the joy of fellowship and community. I felt an unexpected ownership of this moment, as if this were my home and I was responsible for everyone's good cheer.

The reception came to a close and a steady stream of members and friends filed into the kitchen to drop their glasses and cups into a sink topped with soapsuds. I'd hoped to get a head start on the dishes, but I kept needing to stop and dry my hands to receive hugs, thanks and praise.

An hour later I locked up the church and drove my mother home, giddy with success and relief. We exclaimed over the holiday light displays we passed, and I added a few extra turns to the trip to see the most spectacular houses. After dropping her off, I followed my usual route for the twenty-minute crosstown drive from her house to mine. Yet tonight, the roads I'd taken hundreds of times before were completely transformed.

Every street was lined with glowing paper bag luminarias. I'd never been in this part of town on Christmas Eve and had forgotten the neighborhood's longstanding tradition of lighting the way in the spirit of the season. This was a magical moment I'd never witnessed because I'd never ventured outside my usual routine.

I drove home filled with the joy of a different kind of Christmas Eve service — not the service that I'd missed, but the service I'd offered to others — and how it had made this night the most memorable Christmas Eve of all.

~Linda Lowen

Chicken Soup for the Soul: Volunteering & Giving Back

24

Christmas Spirit Regained

*Just as you have the ability to change your mind, you
also have the ability to change the state of your mind.
Happiness and joy are states of mind to be
enjoyed any time you want.*
~Author Unknown

As a child I didn't really have fond memories of Christmas, so as an adult, Christmas became a time I just wanted to avoid. I particularly had trouble with all the Christmas music, which seems to be just about everywhere. I guess that was why I volunteered to work that Christmas Eve. The retail store where I worked in downtown Toronto was one of the few that didn't play Christmas music. But that year I was given the best gift ever — a stranger came along and rekindled my Christmas spirit.

It was the Christmas of 1992 and I was working at my sales job during the busiest season of the year. It's a time when customers become difficult to please, as tempers and patience seem to be lost in the crowds. Few people are nice to salespeople during this time and working in a store becomes a major challenge.

I was relieved that my shift was over and I could go home to avoid the rest of Christmas. I entered a subway car at the College Park subway station and found a single seat at the back of it, as far from others as possible. I just wanted to get home and be rid of my bad mood.

I hadn't noticed which station we were in when the stranger with the homeless appearance and boisterous voice entered the subway car. When he started to chat with the other passengers, I purposefully turned my attention to something else. I wanted to make it clear I had no interest in talking to this guy. Then the train was delayed in the tunnel for ten minutes. As we sat there motionless, I was becoming more and more aggravated.

When the stranger started singing "Jingle Bells" I knew I'd had enough, but I was trapped. Then, slowly the other passengers joined in, and soon everyone sang with him. Then, to my shock, I found myself singing as well!

Well, with that guy leading, we sang every Christmas song I remembered from my childhood. When the train finally got going, we continued singing. As we stopped at other subway stations, passengers from other cars ran to join us. The thought of our car filling up with singing people while others were empty made me laugh. Never in my life had I witnessed so many strangers joining together like this to sing.

The subway train reached its last stop on the line and every one stopped to look around at each other. And then the boisterous voice of the stranger cried, "Merry Christmas" to each passenger as they left the train. As I ran to catch my bus, I could still hear people singing as they headed home for Christmas Eve.

Though none of us had ever met each other before that night, and never saw each other again, I felt we'd shared a special and unique bond of Christmas spirit. Since then I carry that spirit with me. I've never lost the spirit that I gained that Christmas Eve. I look forward to Christmas now, and when the music starts to play, I remember that special night.

You never know what you might learn from a stranger.

~Judith Smith

Chicken Soup for the Soul: O Canada The Wonders of Winter

25

Gift of the Shepherd

Mirth can be a major tool for insight,
changing "ha-ha" to "aha."
~Author Unknown

As I completed one holiday chore after another, my neck and shoulders began to ache from stress. I heard music drifting out of every store at the mall. A male voice crooned "chestnuts roasting on an open fire..." The holiday spirit filled my heart, but my body needed a hot soak in the tub.

My fingertips read the Braille list that I pulled from my pocket. I visualized mountainous displays of clothes and toys to our left and right. With my guide dog Misty leading the way, the mall madness did seem a bit more manageable. Still, shoppers asked if they could pet my German Shepherd, even though her harness sign read, *Please do not pet me. I'm working.* She eased me between the crowds, while I imagined their outstretched hands. Finally, my list grew shorter as the bags grew heavier.

Back home, some chores disappeared from the list while new chores were added. My husband Don and I had decorated our tree. The lights and ornaments were spaced perfectly—no "Charlie Brown" tree for us. Why were we so obsessed with our decorations? We dressed the tree as though Martha Stewart would stop by. Don and I had wrapped the presents and placed them beneath the tree. For each purchase, we had gone over budget, hoping we chose just the right gift.

The next day, ingredients lined our kitchen counter for cookie baking. My guide dog flitted at my feet. Normally, at this time of day, we would be returning from our daily walk. Then she loved being brushed. But her grooming routine needed to wait along with a walk. Once again, I felt her cold nose nuzzle my skirt, so my floured hand waved her away. She brought in her favorite toy and dropped it. I tossed the rubber ring into the next room to keep her out of the kitchen. *Who wants dog hair in their cookies?* Within minutes, cinnamon and vanilla perfumed our kitchen. I pulled out the first tray of cookies and turned to put them on the table. Our cookie baking reminded me of a factory. My husband, without hesitation, had the next batch going into the oven. The kitchen mess reminded me that we still didn't have any time to relax.

A bunch of stamped Christmas cards sat on the table. I still needed to Braille a message in each card sent to blind friends. *Would I have the time or energy?*

"After this last batch of cookies, I'm going to play with her," I told Don. Suddenly, I could not ignore a loud sound nearby. "Crunch!" Misty had swiped a cookie off the cooling tray. I used a firm tone of voice: "No." The success of our partnership depended on praise and gentle correction from me. Like a child's cry for attention, Misty's mischievous behavior announced her boredom. A few minutes later, I felt guilty for ignoring her. "Here's a biscuit, girl," I said, using the treat as a peace offering instead of praise.

Then, Misty was oddly absent from the kitchen, after being underfoot all morning. I searched the house. When I called her name, I followed the sound of her thumping tail. Her body stretched full-length beneath the Christmas tree. As I reached to pet her, my hand felt her dog biscuit. Misty had placed her treat in the manger scene next to the figurine of the Christ child. For the first time that day, I laughed.

Misty's gift to me fit perfectly, was suitable for my age, the price was just right, and I did not have to exchange it. Misty reminded me to "stop and smell the pine boughs." The blessing of the season, I learned from my furry pal, is sharing time with those we love.

~Carol Chiodo Fleischman

Chicken Soup for the Soul: The Dog Did What?

26

The Power of Giving

Christmas is the spirit of giving without a thought of getting. It is happiness because we see joy in people. It is forgetting self and finding time for others.
~Thomas S. Monson

The e-mail came from a friend who is always doing something interesting, unusual or rewarding. This time, it was an invitation to participate in a Christmas Day visit to a Lutheran assisted-living facility in our community. The mission: help the staff in whatever way we could because, as Jewish families, we don't celebrate Christmas ourselves.

Christmas can, in fact, be a somewhat odd day for those of us who are Jewish. Most years, the formula is familiar: a newly released movie and Chinese food.

We almost said no. We'd already made plans, and this suggestion sounded a bit daunting, as the unfamiliar often does.

But after some conversation, my husband and I decided to take on the three-hour shift together at the familiar building on our town's Main Street, a building we'd walked past often.

Of course, the motivation was not only that we could be of help to the staff; we also could hopefully interact with some of the lonely souls who were not slated to have visitors on Christmas Day.

My husband always had the gift of easy communication and connection. As a long-time writer I, however, had been shielded behind the written word.

I'm a tad shy, and I was more than a tad nervous about this Christmas Day visit.

"These are strangers," I reminded my easygoing husband. "We're Jewish. We don't even celebrate Christmas. What will we talk about?"

Vic made short shrift of my anxiety. "We're human!" he said. "Humans find ways to communicate."

We got our first challenge at the entrance to the Lutheran home, where a lone elderly man sat in a wheelchair. We greeted him with the standard "Hi," but got no response.

He seemed so alone, and what touched us so much was that he was holding a small American flag in his hand. There he sat, on Christmas Day with his flag. But after several attempts at conversation, it struck us: He had lost the gift of speech. A stroke, perhaps, or some other infirmity.

I don't know what made me do it, but I stepped up close to his wheelchair, smiled and pointed to the flag. And I gave it a thumbs-up.

Suddenly, a smile as radiant as the sun spread across an old soldier's face.

Mind you, we don't know that he was one, but he seemed straight out of Central Casting as a World War II vet.

In that moment I knew we'd made a very good decision.

All around us were people in wheelchairs — some surrounded by families, some alone. There were staffers bustling around, leaning over to whisper something sweet or funny or just friendly. These are the amazing men and women who sacrifice their own Christmas Days to be there for the forgotten or the needy.

Suddenly, religion didn't matter a bit. Nor did shyness. All that mattered was the privilege of being a part of this day.

To pause to say "Merry Christmas!" To shake a hand. To offer a cookie.

But there was so much more to come.

We were ultimately assigned to the area where the Alzheimer's and dementia residents were finishing lunch, many of them slumped in their wheelchairs, a few with some small spark of awareness.

We'd been advised to meet these residents at eye level, to approach them from the front, never from behind, and to expect anything from total indifference to anger to a blank stare.

We got some of each.

But gradually, as we knelt down to try to connect — as we smiled, patted a shoulder, held a hand — there was a glimmer of something.

Eye contact. A hesitant smile. A word or two.

In some ways, that was a most difficult, even exhausting experience. But oh, the amazing rewards.

There was the tiny lady whose sweet face showed delight when we wished her a Merry Christmas. Her nails had been polished, her white sweater was clearly for special occasions, and her ability to connect and respond was in there somewhere.

So we talked without words. And yes, that's not just possible — it's amazing.

I handed her two soft little plush teddy bears that were available to these residents to have and to hold. She cuddled them close to her heart.

We repeated this again and again with men and women who didn't care what religion we were or why we were there, as long as we let them know that they were worthy of a smile or a touch.

And then we discovered the lady with a cap of silver hair who began to call us "Mommy" and "Poppy," and reminded us that we used to make Christmas pudding together. She was, she told us, seventeen years old.

Good for her! Maybe that's how she felt on this Christmas Day in her late senior years.

Our most astounding moments came with her.

The background music piped into the activity room was Christmas music, and almost instinctively my husband began singing along to the words of "I'm Dreaming of a White Christmas." Then I, the world's most self-conscious singer, joined in.

Then, suddenly, there was a third voice. Our silver-haired lady friend was singing every word of "Jingle Bells," and then of "Silent Night."

There we sat, two Jewish Christmas visitors and a sweet woman with a voice like an angel, singing together on Christmas Day.

Unlikely? Definitely.

Uplifting? Absolutely.

Meaningful? Certainly for us.

Hopefully also for the residents of this place, five blocks — and light years — removed from our lives.

When we tiptoed away, we noticed that our new friend had fallen into a peaceful sleep, with just a hint of a smile on her lips.

We left knowing that we'd just experienced our very own beautiful, wonderful Christmas miracle.

~Sally Friedman

Chicken Soup for the Soul: Volunteering & Giving Back

27

Welcoming a Stranger

Fun fact: The smallest breed of cat is the Singapura.
Females may weigh as little as four pounds.

When we bought our ten-acre "mini-farm" back in 1991, our family inherited Snagglepuss, a flame-orange barn cat that the sellers had adopted. She was joined the following year by a cat of similar appearance, but very different temperament, that someone dumped by the side of the road near our house late one autumn night.

My sister had been visiting, and in the wee hours she heard a car slow down, then one of its doors slam before it drove away. She didn't think any more about it until our daughter found the cat in the morning when she was starting to walk to school. After listening to some teary-eyed gushing from her about how adorable he was and how Snagglepuss needed a friend, we told her we would keep him if no one came to claim him. Of course, no one did.

Our daughter may have honestly thought Snagglepuss would like having a friend, but the older cat quickly made it clear she had other ideas. She disliked the new cat at first sight, hissing at him whenever he got too close or tried to play with her always-twitching tail. Even worse, she seemed to hold him in contempt because he was lazy and a terrible "mouser." Those qualities, along with his golden-orange coloring, gave us the idea for his name: Goldbrick.

One of the few things those two barn cats agreed on was that no other cats belonged in the territory they shared begrudgingly with each other. There was a small tiger-gray feral cat living under a fallen tree along the creek bank, and both our cats chased the poor little stray away at every opportunity. Though our fields surely had enough mice to feed an army of cats, they weren't willing to share a single one of them with the interloper if they could prevent it.

With that as the backstory, I couldn't have been more surprised at what I found when I went out to the barn on Christmas morning to give the kitties a treat. Our barn cats were a bit spoiled, with a long table set up with a comfortable arrangement of crates and blankets to keep them warm. They also had a heat lamp designed for poultry overhead. Since it was bitter cold that was where I found them — under the heat lamp. But as they stood up and stretched, I saw that I was going to need to split their plate of sausage and eggs three ways instead of two. The little gray stray was nestled between them, out of the cold and snow. I had never before seen or heard of cats — especially barn cats — with so much "Christmas spirit!"

After that week's cold snap was over, our cats also snapped out of their holiday mood and began chasing the stray away as before. But when the stray had been in danger of freezing to death, they seemed to sense that it was no time for being territorial and selfish, and were moved to something as close to pity as cats are capable of feeling.

Animal behavior has been studied a great deal, but the animals themselves still have a lot to teach us.

~Mary L. Hickey

Chicken Soup for the Soul: My Very Good, Very Bad Cat

A Closed Highway Opened Hearts

The everyday kindness of the back roads more than
makes up for the acts of greed in the headlines.
~Charles Kuralt

several years ago, our family of five began its annual Christmas trek to Grandma's house. As we traveled from Wisconsin to Indiana on Christmas Eve day, the weather became increasingly worse. Heavy snow continued to fall, and high winds, which swept across the flat farmlands, whipped up the snow and dumped it into drifts across the highway, slowing traffic to a crawl. All movement came to a complete halt near an off-ramp when we encountered snowplows parked sideways across the road to block the highway. Their bundled-up operators, who stood beside the plows in the road, slogged to our car to inform us, "The highway's closed. This is as far as you can go."

"But what can we do?" we asked.

They replied, "There is a small church just down the road. They have opened its doors to stranded travelers." Creeping carefully down the off-ramp, we caught sight of a white wooden building with a spire that became our inn for Christmas Eve night.

We entered the church and discovered a couple of hundred fellow travelers who had taken shelter. The refugees ran the gamut in age from babies to old folks, representing all humanity. Even a few dogs huddled next to their masters. The church's young pastor evidently started a calling chain among his parishioners, asking for their help. They responded quickly by braving the bitter cold and deep snow to bring us blankets, pillows, cookies, and cakes. Then a contingent stayed on to turn the fellowship hall into an impromptu restaurant by preparing hot chili, cocoa, and coffee for their disconsolate guests.

We sat around in small groups, disappointed that our anticipated plans with our loved ones had been ruined. As there were no cell phones in those days, there was a continuous long line of people impatiently waiting to use the church's wall phone to alert relatives to their safety, to tell them where they were, and that they would not be getting home for Christmas.

Our daughter Deb brought her guitar with her. She took it out of its case and, while sitting on the gym floor, began to softly sing Christmas carols. Soon, a small group gathered around to join their voices with hers. They were to become "our group" for the rest of the time. Deb played quietly far into the night, as people began to seek out pews, hallways, or floors on which to sleep. The young minister and his wife stayed at the church with us all night. When Christmas morning dawned, he led our rumpled, dispossessed group in our own private worship service.

As the sun announced the arrival of the new day, a different batch of church members left their own Christmas preparations and plodded through the snow, bringing pancake mix, juice, and eggs to make us breakfast. Many of the dispirited visitors' thoughts traveled to the destination their bodies could not reach, and they envisioned blazing Christmas trees surrounded by piles of unopened presents. Since our new acquaintances replaced the families we could not be with, we spent the morning comparing stories. When noontime found us still snowbound, a second crew arrived to fix lunch. A mechanic left his warm home and family to work outside in the zero weather, jumping cars that had frozen overnight. A filling station owner interrupted his Christmas celebration to open his station so we could have gas in our tanks in case the roads became passable.

Late in the afternoon, word arrived that one lane of a road had been cleared, so our family decided to try completing the journey to Indianapolis. After a harrowing six-hour drive on slippery roads, we arrived at our grandparents' home late Christmas night. Although it was not the holiday we had planned, we all knew it was one we would remember when all the other ones were forgotten. We received a gift that could not fit under a tree, wrapped in the caring compassion of those church members. They put aside their own comfort and traditions to welcome us at their "inn," not just with food, but with cheer and loving concern. We witnessed the true spirit of Christmas, of giving instead of receiving, by a congregation who set their own celebrations and enjoyment aside to care for strangers in their tiny town of Morocco, Indiana.

~Martha Ajango

A Chicken Soup for the Soul Christmas

29

A Different Kind of Christmas

Christmas is most truly Christmas when we celebrate it by giving the light of love to those who need it most.
~Ruth Carter Stapleton

I didn't have a plan. And that was painful. It was Christmas Day, our first in California after having moved from Austria due to my husband's work, and we had no family to share it with. We hadn't met enough people yet to invite them for dinner. We thought about Christmas back home in Austria, with the magical fragrance of fresh cookies in the air, snow blanketing everything outside in silence and the mysterious anticipation about what the Christkind (the Austrian version of Santa) would bring this year.

Typically there had always been lots of presents. Not because we parents overwhelmed the kids with them, but simply because many people came together that day and everybody wanted to give something. That certainly wouldn't be the case this year because we hadn't made enough contacts yet. Of course we had been exchanging good wishes in the days and weeks leading up to the big day, but on Christmas Day itself? That would surely be a family affair; a day when people would withdraw to enjoy privacy with their own loved ones!

But that is not what happened on this day! Somebody must have sensed our situation and thought about how they could put a smile on our faces that day. They must have wondered what the best time would be, how old each of our children was, and what would give them the most joy. And they had also decided that it would be a complete surprise and they would remain anonymous.

We were just about to open the presents when a loud whoop of excitement went through the house. Ten-year-old Esther had just opened the front door and couldn't believe what she was seeing. Right in front of her was a pile of presents as tall as she was! Every single one of them beautifully wrapped in green, red and gold! She looked at each of them from the bottom of the pile to the top and then, stretching up, she discovered a note way up on top. A Santa Claus was drawn on it along with a message: *For the three Austrian girls! Have a wonderful Christmas!*

The others ran quickly to see what was going on and couldn't believe their eyes. A small present would have been "realistic" but such a high pile? They had never seen anything like it in their entire lives! What a surprise!

The rest of the day was saved and not just that, the entire Christmas holiday was marvelous. It turned out that our three girls had received many, many board games. They were not new, as our experienced parents' eyes quickly detected. But somebody must have thought of us and knew how much joy these gifts would bring us. And this somebody took the effort to pick a special occasion, wrap each present individually, and add a personal note. The timing of the gift and the loving wrapping were worth so much more than money! A pure act of thinking about us without even expecting a thank-you.

Our kids tried of course to guess who the presents were from but they just could not work it out, so they drew a huge picture of Santa Claus with chalk in the middle of the street with the words "Thank you Santa!" As it doesn't rain very often in California the picture stayed there for a long time and I am wondering how often the picture must have put a smile on the face of our mysterious giver!

Later that day a neighbor dropped by and gave each of the girls a ten-dollar voucher for a local bookshop.

It wasn't the financial value that made that Christmas so special. In fact it was probably the lowest-cost Christmas that we had ever had as a family. And yet it was the most valuable in many ways, especially for me as a mother. I was given many presents that day that had nothing to do with money: There was the gift of not having to manage a beautiful feast and yet see a wonderful outcome. The gift of being given so much without the expectancy of having to give anything in return. The gift of getting a present totally unexpected, far away from home. The gift of being made part of a community. It was a real feast of love, of unearned love.

Did I ever find out who played Santa Claus for us that day? Maybe, but that is a different story....

~Sandra Wright

Chicken Soup for the Soul: Random Acts of Kindness

30

A Christmas Story

*Christmas is not a time or a season but a state of
mind. To cherish peace and good will, to be plenteous
in mercy, is to have the real spirit of Christmas.*
~Calvin Coolidge

I t was just a few more days until Christmas in San Francisco, and the shopping downtown was starting to get to us. I remember crowds of people waiting impatiently for slow-moving buses and streetcars on those little cement islands in the middle of the street. Most of us were loaded down with packages, and it looked like many of us were beginning to wonder if all those countless friends and relatives actually *deserved* so many gifts in the first place. This was not the Christmas spirit I'd been raised with.

When I finally found myself virtually shoved up the steps of a jammed streetcar, the idea of standing there packed like a sardine the whole way home was almost more than I could take. What I would have given for a seat! I must have been in some kind of exhausted daze because as people gradually got off, it took me a while to notice that there was room to breathe again.

Then I saw something out of the corner of my eye. A small, dark-skinned boy — he couldn't have been more than five or six — tugged on a woman's sleeve and asked, "Would you like a seat?" He quietly led her to the closest free seat he could find. Then he set out to find another tired person. As soon as each rare, new seat became available, he would quickly move through the crowd in search of another burdened woman who desperately needed to rest her feet.

When I finally felt the tug on my own sleeve, I was absolutely dazzled by the beauty in this little boy's eyes. He took my hand, saying, "Come with me," and I think I'll remember that smile as long as I live. As I happily placed my heavy load of packages on the floor, the little emissary of love immediately turned to help his next subject.

The people on the streetcar, as usual, had been studiously avoiding each other's eyes, but now they began to exchange shy glances and smiles. A businessman offered a section of newspaper to the stranger next to him; three people stooped to return a gift that had tumbled to the floor. And now people were speaking to one another. That little boy had tangibly changed something—we all relaxed into a subtle feeling of warmth and actually enjoyed the trip through the final stops along the route.

I didn't notice when the child got off. I looked up at one point and he was gone. When I reached my stop I practically floated off that streetcar, wishing the driver a happy holiday, noticing the sparkling Christmas lights on my street in a fresh, new way. Or maybe I was seeing them in an old way, with the same open wonder I felt when *I* was five or six. I thought, *So that's what they mean by And a little child shall lead them....*

~Beverly M. Bartlett

Chicken Soup for the Woman's Soul

31

The Year the Animals Brought Christmas

The best remedy for those who are afraid, lonely or
unhappy is to go outside, somewhere where they can be
quiet, alone with the heavens and nature.
~Anne Frank

It was Christmas Eve of my fifty-eighth year. I lived by myself on a small farm in the hills above British Columbia's Fraser Valley. My mood was melancholy, for tomorrow would be my first Christmas morning without overflowing stockings, explosions of brightly wrapped packages, or the comforting laughter of excited family members. I was bereft of Christmas spirit despite the falling snow that transformed my land into the perfect Canadian Christmas card.

I was not completely alone, however, for I shared my space with four old rescue dogs, a cat, an abandoned alpaca, and a family of twelve potbellied pigs. The boar and very pregnant sow had been brought to me, a few months earlier, to be fostered after being seized in an animal cruelty case; their ten babies were born two weeks later.

As the snowfall finally eased to a few drifting flakes, I trekked out to the barn to check on the animals one last time, the dogs by my side. The snow was well over their heads, and our kindly neighbour had once again plowed the drive so we could move with some freedom if we stayed on the path. But of course, as dogs are wont to do, they bounded off into the deepest parts and surfaced with frosty, happy faces.

I stepped into the dark interior of my rustic, dilapidated barn. The snow reflected through the windows, casting a soft light over the old wood. The potbellied pigs were nestled deep in the straw; they raised their snouts high as I peered over the stall gate to check that all were warm and safe. I breathed in the scent of weathered timbers and fresh shavings, of wet dogs and healthy pigs, loving the feel of the barn and the silence of the night. I tucked a wool blanket over the oldest pig, and fed the youngsters a flake or two of hay, singing softly.

The oldest pig, Scotch, loved to be sung to. During his first weeks here, when he and his mate, Soda, were scared and unsure of themselves, I often sat in the stall with them at night, singing and humming and letting them get used to my scent and sound. I sang lullabies, children's songs, old campfire favourites. Scotch particularly liked "You Are My Sunshine." Whenever I sang it, he would softly grunt, lay his head on or near my lap, and roll over on his side to let me stroke his belly. It soothed both of us — me, a new foster mama to pigs, and Scotch, a finally safe piggy who was learning about the big world beyond a much-too-small and filthy wire cage.

And so, that Christmas Eve, I curled up in the straw beside him, my head on his back, and sang to him once more. He grunted and hummed along with me, and soon I felt another warm piggy body stretching out alongside my back — Whisper, one of the young piglets, had come to join us. Then I felt a nudge at my hand as another piglet let me know he, too, wanted contact.

Soon I was joined by another, and another, and another, until all the piggies were nestled around me, in straw and blankets, some touching me, each touching another. For a few moments in time, I was just one of the herd.

When they were all asleep, I slipped quietly from their stall, whispered good night, closed the big barn door and made my way across the pasture to the alpaca's stable. Martin was bedded down on his straw, well protected from the weather. In the dark of night, with only my small flashlight to provide a warm glow, I saw before me an image of a long-ago nativity scene: Martin, so like his camel kin who carried the three wise men to Bethlehem; the manger filled with soft hay, such as provided a crib for the child born long ago; and the snow sparkling like the brilliant star that shone in the East. I heard Martin softly acknowledge my presence with his low uhn-uhn-uhn, and smiled as I thought how those sounds would have filled the stable that first Christmas Eve.

I believe there is a reason why the animals figure so prominently in the Christmas story. Unconditional love, a sense of purpose, courage to go on, faith in tomorrow — lessons that the person called Jesus taught in his lifetime — are modeled for us best by the animals around us.

I whistled for the dogs and headed back to the house, back to the modern world of computers and microwaves, televisions and electric lights. Within me, I carried a sense of peace and reverence and awe, the Christmas spirit, found where Christmas first began — outdoors, in a crude and humble shelter, surrounded by the animals on a dark silent night.

~Jean F. Ballard

Chicken Soup for the Soul: O Canada The Wonders of Winter

A Heart Full of Questions

The important thing is not to stop questioning.
Curiosity has its own reason for existing. One cannot
help but be in awe when he contemplates the mysteries
of eternity, of life, of the marvelous structure of reality.
~Albert Einstein

My family's assorted Christmas decorations sparked my first big inquiry into faith. The scent of Douglas fir filled the air while we unpacked ornaments in the living room by the tree. My brother retrieved his favorite decoration from a cardboard box. Perched atop a world globe sat a silver biplane flown by none other than Santa. But it was me who always set out our tiny nativity.

It looked like a three-sided horse stall made of brown plastic dusted in gold glitter. The people and animals stood no bigger than my pinky. Each December when I unwrapped the nativity, a feeling of peace and hope swept over me.

My first attempt to push open that doorway to faith came when I asked my mom, "What does the little stall with the people have to do with Christmas?"

"It's just a thing we do," she said. Her nervous response clued me in that she did not want to talk about it, or maybe she didn't know the answer, either.

The second question arose during summer vacation from school.

"What religion are you?" my nine-year-old friend, Becky, asked me as she looked over the rim of her glass of Hawaiian Punch. Janice crunched into a Snickerdoodle and stared. I looked at the tiled kitchen floor and shuffled my feet, not sure what to say. An uncomfortable silence hung between us while my neighborhood playmates waited. Then I smiled, stood up straight, pulled back my shoulders and pronounced, "I'm Irish."

Janice gave Becky a weird look and stared back at me.

"No," Becky said. "I mean, are you Baptist, or Lutheran, or Catholic?" All words I had never heard in my nine years of living.

"I don't know anything about those," I said. "All I know is Mom's Irish and Daddy's French." They gave each other a puzzled look and shrugged, and we ran back outside to play.

The question gnawed at me all afternoon. *What did Becky mean by religion?* When I returned home later that day, I asked Mom what my friends meant.

"How rude. Don't those girls have better manners?" she said. "If they ask you again, you tell them you're Episcopalian."

I stumbled over the foreign word, trying to repeat it. "What's that?" I asked.

"That's what your dad's family is, so you tell them you're Episcopalian," she snapped.

Startled by her response, I grew quiet and thought it best to never bring up the subject again. "Okay," I said, unsure of what I was agreeing to. And the door slammed shut on any further discussion.

My friends didn't ask me any more about religion. And with nowhere to find answers, the questions piled up in my head.

Fall came, and I went back to school, my mind occupied with fractions, world geography, and U.S. history. That is, until Halloween arrived.

Dressed like a scarecrow, I raced across my friend Lenora's yard and onto her front porch. The house stood dark. To the left of the door, a bowl of apples sat on a table with a note that read: *Gone to church. Please help yourself.*

I paused for a moment in the glow of a single porch light. *Why didn't Lenora and her brothers dress up and trick-or-treat like the rest of the neighborhood kids?* Instead, they went to church. I didn't get it. Wasn't church just for weddings and funerals? Each question that lingered was like another swipe at a cobweb that veiled me from the truth.

The one constant was Christmas, that magical season of flying reindeer, Santa and his elves. Each year, like welcoming an old friend, I reached into the boxes of decorations to reclaim a wad of aged tissue sparkled with gold and unwrapped the nativity. My brother set out his flying Santa. Elves dressed in red and green felt took their usual place as sentries on the console stereo. And alone in the background sat my beloved decoration. However, it just didn't seem to fit with the rest of my family's Christmas theme. Year after year, my heart stirred with more questions about the brown plastic stall that I felt so drawn to and loved so much. Maybe it was the couple looking at the baby, or maybe it was the animals gathered around them. I didn't know or understand the significance of the manger or the Savior it represented. I only knew how the scene made me feel, and because of that I treasured it. The plastic people and animals told a story, one I wanted to know.

The mystery lived tucked away in my heart until a boyfriend invited me to church when I was in high school. I wasn't sure about all the God talk, but my curiosity was piqued. When Christmas came, we attended the children's program. I watched while the elementary kids took their places on the stage. The lights dimmed, and a spotlight shone on a young couple. As the play continued, the children formed the same scene that was in my nativity. In awe, I leaned forward on my chair and listened to every child's line. It was as if the door had been flung open, and I finally understood.

My stall was a stable, the couple was Mary and Joseph, and the shepherds had received a special invitation from heaven's angels to come and worship the new baby. And the baby had a name: Jesus. The Prince of Peace. Emmanuel. God with us.

Now I knew the reason for the peace and hope that washed over my soul each year. God wanted a relationship with me, to be an active part of my life, and He was extending to me a special invitation to be His child forever.

That Christmas, I accepted God's invitation. I not only discovered my faith, but years of questions were wiped away, and I finally knew the story behind my treasured Christmas decoration.

~Kathleen Kohler

Chicken Soup for the Soul: Finding My Faith

Chapter
4

A Book of
Christmas
Miracles

Holiday Angels

All That We Can Give

*As we express our gratitude, we must never forget
that the highest appreciation is not to utter
words but to live by them.*
~John F. Kennedy

On Thanksgiving Day I awoke on the mattress that I shared with my two young children and tumbled into despair. At the time I was twenty-five and recently divorced. It was three days to payday and there was no money left. I had a job, but was only making $300 a month, and that month's entire paycheck had already gone to pay for the apartment and food for my little boys. I had swallowed my pride and applied for food stamps, but had been turned down — because I made two dollars over the monthly limit.

On that Thanksgiving Day, there was nothing left to eat in the house but three hot dogs.

Perhaps hardest of all was my feeling of isolation. There were no friends to help. No one had invited us to share the holiday dinner. The loneliness was worse than the ever-present hunger.

But it was Thanksgiving, and for the sake of the children, I knew I had to make the best of the day.

"Come on, boys," I said. "Today's a special day. We're having a picnic!"

Together the three of us went to the park and cooked the hot dogs on the grill. We played happily together until late in the afternoon.

But on the way home, the boys asked for more food. The single hot dog they had eaten did not come close to being a decent meal. I knew they were hungrier even than they let on.

I tried to joke about it with them, but inside I was very, very scared. I didn't know where our next meal was going to come from. I'd reached the end of my rope.

As we entered our apartment building, an old woman I'd never seen before stepped directly into our path. She was a tiny thing wearing a simple print dress, her wispy white hair pulled up in a bun. With her smile of greeting, she looked like a kindhearted tutu, an island grandmother.

"Oh, Honey," the old lady said as the boys and I started to walk past. "I've been waiting for you. You left this morning before I could catch you. I've got Thanksgiving dinner ready for your family."

Caught by surprise, I thought that I shouldn't accept such an offer from a complete stranger. With a word of thanks, I started to brush past.

"Oh," said the old lady, "but it's Thanksgiving. You have to come."

I looked at my boys. Their hunger tore at me. Even though it was against my better judgment, I accepted.

The old lady's apartment was on the ground floor. When she opened the door, we saw a beautiful table set for four. It was the perfect Thanksgiving meal with all the traditional trimmings. The candles were lit and it was obvious that guests were expected. We were expected.

Gradually I began to relax. We all sat down together to enjoy the meal. Somehow, I found myself talking freely of my loneliness, the difficulty of raising two small boys by myself and of the challenges I was facing. The grandmotherly woman listened with compassion and understanding. I remember I felt that for that time, at least, we were home.

As the evening ended, I wondered how I could possibly express my thanks for such incredible kindness. Eyes brimming, I simply said, "Thank you. I know that now I can go on." A complete stranger had reached out and given our little family such an important gift. The boys were grinning from ear to ear as the elderly lady loaded them down with Tupperware bowls full of leftovers.

We left her apartment that evening bubbling with joy, the boys joking and laughing. For the first time in a long time, I felt certain that I could face what had to be faced. I was a different person from the scared girl I had been that morning. I'd somehow been transformed. We all had.

Early the next day, in a happy mood, I went back to visit my new friend and to return the borrowed bowls. I knocked, but there was no answer. I looked through an open window.

What I saw shocked me. The apartment was completely empty. There wasn't a stick of furniture. There wasn't anything.

I hurried down to the manager's apartment. "What happened to the elderly lady in apartment three?" I asked.

He gave me a look and said, "What lady? That apartment's been vacant for the past ten or twelve weeks. Nobody lives there."

"But I had Thanksgiving dinner last night with the lady who lives there," I told the manager. "Here are her bowls."

The manager gave me a strange look and turned away.

For many years, I didn't tell anyone the story of that special Thanksgiving. Finally, in 1989, I felt compelled to speak out.

By then, I had become the wife of the Kahu Doug Olson, Pastor of Calvary by the Sea Church on O'ahu.

I went before the congregation and told them of my dream: to establish a program to help women in Hawai'i who find themselves in a situation similar to the one I had faced so many years ago.

Now, over a decade later, the Network has helped over 1,400 homeless, single mothers and their children to get back on their feet. After "graduation," a remarkable 93 percent of the families continue to support themselves. Last year's budget, which is funded by state, church and private monies, was $700,000.

I really surprised myself by telling the congregation my entire story that day, but I think it was meant to be. In the end, helping the homeless with money and food is only secondary.

What I learned on that Thanksgiving Day is that an hour of being loved unconditionally can truly change a life. In the end, it is all that we can give.

And the name of the organization?
Angel Network Charities, of course.

~Ivy Olson

Chicken Soup from the Soul of Hawai'i

34

A Christmas Gift

Never worry about numbers. Help one person at a
time, and always start with the person nearest you.
~Mother Teresa

It was a half-hour before midnight on December 24, 1989. I was a ticket-counter supervisor for a major airline and was looking forward to the end of my shift at Stapleton International Airport in Denver, Colorado. My wife was waiting up for me so we could exchange gifts, as was our tradition on Christmas Eve.

A very frantic and worried gentleman approached me. He asked how he could get home to Cheyenne, Wyoming. He had just arrived from Philadelphia and missed his connecting flight. I pointed him to the ground transportation area. There he could either hire a limousine or rent a car from the various agencies.

He told me that it was extremely important for him to be in Cheyenne for Christmas. I wished him well, and he went on his way. I called my wife to let her know I would be home shortly.

About fifteen minutes later, the same gentleman returned and informed me that all the buses were full and there were no cars or limousines available. Again he asked if I had any suggestions. The most logical option was to offer him a room in a hotel for the night and get him on the first flight to Cheyenne in the morning. When I suggested this, tears starting running down his cheeks.

He explained that his son was seventeen years old and weighed forty pounds. He had spina bifida and was not expected to live another year. He expected that this would likely be the last Christmas with his son and the thought that he would not be there to greet him on Christmas morning was unbearable.

"What's your name, Sir?" I asked.

"Harris, Tom Harris," he replied, his face filled with desperation.

I contacted all of the ground transportation providers and the car rental agencies. Nothing. What was I to do? There was no other choice.

I told Tom to go to the claim area, collect his luggage and wait for me. I called my wife Kathy and told her not to wait up for me. I was driving to Cheyenne, and I would explain everything in the morning. Something had come up that was more important than our exchanging gifts on Christmas Eve.

The drive to Cheyenne was quiet, thoughtful. Tom offered to compensate me for my time and the fuel. I appreciated his gesture, but it wasn't necessary.

We arrived at the airport in Cheyenne around 2:30 a.m. I helped Tom unload his luggage and wished him a Merry Christmas. His wife was meeting him and had not yet arrived.

We shook hands. As I got into my car, I looked back at him. He was the only customer in the airport. I noticed how peaceful and quiet this was compared to the hectic, crowded airport in Denver. Pulling away, I waved goodbye and he waved back. He looked tired and relieved. I wondered how long he would have to wait for his wife to pick him up. She was driving quite a distance.

Kathy was waiting up for me. Before we went to bed, we traded gifts and then our conversation concerned Tom. We imagined his family on Christmas morning as Tom and his wife watched their son open his last Christmas presents. For Kathy and me, there was no question that driving Tom to Cheyenne was the only option. She would have done the same thing.

A couple of days later, I received a Christmas card with a picture of Tom and his family. In it, Tom thanked me for the special gift he had received that holiday season, but I knew the best gift was mine.

~Bob White

Chicken Soup for the Traveler's Soul

35

Nurse Puss 'n Boots

Do all things with love.
~Og Mandino

It was Christmastime in 1979, and I lay recovering from "female surgery" in a hospital in Virginia. To make matters worse I got stuck with a wacky nurse. And she was mean as a viper. Her short, chubby body waltzed into my room each morning, waking me and shouting, "Time to get up, Missy! Get up and get outta that bed before you catch pneumonia. You've got to move about, or else!"

I didn't like her much, and I let it be known. Besides, it was plain she didn't like me. She frequently quipped, "I'm just doing my job, and I intend to do it by the book, Missy. By the book."

Outside the snowfall piled higher and higher and half of the nursing staff was unable to get to work. But of course Nurse Puss 'n Boots made it. I called her that because she came in every afternoon with her white boots on, covered with snow and stomped around in them all day. I could see her from my window trotting through the white flakes every day at 2:30 on the dot. *What was it about this particular nurse that intrigued me so?* I wondered.

I was sure she didn't have a life outside the hospital. She was domineering and mean and always eager to start her shift, as if it was so wonderful to be stuck in a hospital with sick people every evening. Sullenly I asked God, *Must Christmas come this year? And must I spend it with this gruff nurse?*

Christmas Eve came and I was devastated that my husband and baby boy were stranded at home, an hour from the hospital. There was no way they could drive through the snow-packed interstate. I lay in my bed in a deep state of melancholy imagining how little "Bradley Boy" would look when he opened his train.

To make matters worse, Puss 'n Boots came marching in and noticed my sadness. "Well, Missy. You'll just have to do better than this. You'll have to take what comes," she insisted. I made a face at her when she turned and walked out the door. I could hear her at the nurse's station. "That's right — by the book, always by the book." I groaned and covered my head with my pillow.

At seven o'clock sharp, I heard Christmas carolers in the hallway, singing "O Holy Night." I smiled in spite of myself and walked to open my door. Shocked, I stammered, "I'm dreaming! Ol' Puss 'n Boots put something in my ginger ale."

"Nope. No dream," my husband beamed. "Thanks to your nurse, I'm staying in the hotel one block away." Nurse Puss 'n Boots had arranged for her husband to drive his Jeep to our town the day before and pick up my husband. Not only did she bring him to me, but she paid for his hotel room for a few days, until I could be discharged. I stood gazing at the mean nurse, now turned heroine. She even smiled at me, as I stood with my jaw dropped open in marvel.

I learned this extraordinary nurse and her wealthy husband did generous deeds for many people. She didn't even have to work, but chose to fulfill her life with nursing. My husband adored her. "She's tough, like my old drill sergeant," he said. "We need more nurses like her."

Today, as a nurse, I trot through snow in the hospital parking lot wearing white boots in honor of my favorite nurse. I called her hospital to inquire about Puss 'n Boots and to tell her how she had inspired me. They said she had passed away in her sleep at home — her generous heart stopped beating.

If I know Nurse Puss 'n Boots, she's standing at the gates of heaven right beside St. Peter with her ink pen and chart. She's grabbing each lost soul who tries to slip through the cracks, saying, "By the book, Missy! By the book!"

~J. C. Pinkerton

Chicken Soup for the Nurse's Soul

36

Thanks for the Giving

Thanksgiving, after all, is a word of action.
~W.J. Cameron

My heart sank as I heard the familiar clicking sound of the electricity being shut off. It was two days before Thanksgiving. I poured a drink and sat in my room to wallow in self-pity. I had been unemployed for months, and my daughter and I were barely surviving. I grabbed my purse in a desperate attempt to fix the problem. As I did, moths flew out of it as if I were living in a cartoon. I gathered all the change that I could, but $1.75 was not going to solve our problem. How was I going to explain this situation to my daughter?

We were months behind on the rent, to the point that eviction notices were being posted on our door daily. Now we were not only going to be forced out of the only home that she had known, but we were going to make that move in the dark and cold.

I tried to be positive and look for the silver lining, but all I did was become angry as I thought through the list of all the people who had lived in my house or at least slept on my couch in the past decade — for free. I stopped counting after I hit fifty. Then I ran to the bathroom and got sick. After I washed my face, I looked in the mirror and said to myself, "You suck and Thanksgiving is ruined." I was giving up.

Just then my daughter got home from school. "Is the electricity off again?" she asked with an accusatory tone.

"Yes," was all that I could muster as I hung my head in shame.

"Mom, are we poor?"

"Only financially," I responded, choking back the tears.

At that moment, I felt a burst of energy. I had to do everything I could to make sure that Thanksgiving happened. After all, it would be our last one in our home.

During my childhood, Thanksgiving was rarely celebrated. In my family it was just another Thursday. There had been a family fight between my mom and uncle on the holiday before I was even born, so we didn't celebrate it. Instead, I usually spent the day eating frozen pizza and listening to my mother cry. When I moved out on my own, the tradition continued. It was me, alone, watching bad television, while all my friends were off with their families.

One year I decided to make my own tradition. I couldn't be the only one feeling so alone on this holiday. I started an "Orphan Thanksgiving." Those with nowhere to go were welcome. I was bound and determined to make sure no one felt alone on such a meaningful day.

As the years passed, it became my favorite time of year. I knew I would see people that I loved, if for no other reason than my grandma's famous pumpkin muffin recipe. I would cook for days to prepare for the dozens of friends and family members who would come through the front door. Now, with an eviction notice and no electricity, how would I make my fifteenth Orphan Thanksgiving a reality?

I was a woman on a mission. I had to call in favors, but slowly I was getting things done. The people living next door were generous enough to throw an extension cord over the back fence so I could charge my phone and computer. We gathered candles. I even put out an announcement that it would be the last Thanksgiving at my house. A friend who lived down the street was going out of town for the weekend, but gave me a key to use her stove and oven. All that was left was to find the money to buy food for a Thanksgiving meal.

That night, I sat in my candlelit bedroom with my daughter sleeping soundly next to me. I held my grandmother's gold locket in my hand for what felt like a lifetime. She was the woman who taught me to cook when I could barely walk. She grew up during the Depression, and she had told me many stories of hardship. I reasoned that she would have wanted me to give to those less fortunate. She would have approved. So, the next morning I sold the locket to put food on the table for one last holiday. And then I rushed to the store to buy a turkey with all the trimmings.

I spent the day traveling back and forth from the oven a block away. By the time guests started to arrive, I am sure that I looked as exhausted as I felt. But the candles were lit, the food prepared and smiles were on faces. This had become my best turnout in history. Despite the lack of heat or light, everyone was enjoying dinner and conversation. My daughter proudly announced that the thing she was thankful for was her mommy, which brought tears to my eyes. It truly was a day for which to be thankful.

As the sun came up the next morning, I had enough light to begin the cleanup of the previous night's festivities. In the darkness I had missed the suitcase sitting on my living room floor until I tripped over it. On top was a note that read simply "Thanks for the giving." Inside were cards, notes and encouragement from all of the attendees from the previous evening; plus others that I hadn't heard from in years. All with thanks for what I had done for them. More than that, inside was money. I cried, mouth agape, while counting the total. There was even information about an account that had been opened so that friends could wire money from all over the country.

To this day, I do not know who orchestrated this miracle. It was enough to get my electricity back and save me from being evicted. My daughter and I still live in the same house, with my new husband. The twentieth anniversary of "Orphan Thanksgiving" comes up this year. I am living proof that the good things that you put out to the world will come back to you, sometimes when you least expect it.

~Jodi Renee Thomas

Chicken Soup for the Soul: The Power of Gratitude

37

Twelve Days of Kindness

If compassion was the motivating factor behind
all of our decisions, would our world not be a
completely different place?
~Sheryl Crow

Twinkling Christmas lights on our Charlie Brown Christmas tree reflected off the shiny ornaments, throwing flashes of light on the wall. Outside a few snowflakes drifted down as the grey Sunday afternoon sky darkened. My mood was as dark as the sky. Although it was less than two weeks before Christmas, I found it difficult to be in a festive mood. We had immigrated to Canada from south of the border, and holidays were difficult for us because we missed our family in Minnesota.

Our family was also going through a very difficult year, with major health issues, a serious work-related problem for my husband, and trouble with our rebellious teenage son. I made a half-hearted effort to put up a few decorations around the house, but my heart just wasn't in it.

"Mom, I wish we could spend Christmas with Grandpa and Grandma in Minnesota," said my fifteen-year old daughter, Rachel. She was sitting on the floor, wrapping a small gift for one of her friends.

A wave of homesickness swept over me. How could I encourage my daughter when I was also struggling? "I know you'd like to spend Christmas in Minnesota, Rachel. So would I." I looked up from the notes I was writing on my printed Christmas letters. "But Minnesota is 2,000 kilometres from Calgary. You remember how hard it was to drive in that snowstorm two years ago? And then the temperature dropped to −30 on the way back?"

"I remember," she sighed. "Tim and I almost froze our feet when the heater didn't work well." She shivered just thinking of it.

We had concluded driving to Minnesota for Christmas was simply too risky and buying airline tickets for four people was totally out of the question. No one was coming over for Christmas either; I just didn't have the energy to invite anyone. We would be spending Christmas alone.

I was startled when the doorbell rang. It was dark outside, and we weren't expecting anyone. Rachel went to open the door, and then said, "Mom, there's a box on the doorstep — with presents… and nobody is out here!"

Who could have left it? It was indeed a mystery. The box contained numerous packages wrapped in bright Christmas paper. Each had a typewritten tag: Open Dec. 14, Open Dec.15. There were a total of twelve — the "Twelve Days of Christmas."

It was December 14th, and the tag for that day was attached to a turkey still wrapped in the plastic from the store — so we wouldn't miss the fact that it needed to be put into the freezer immediately, and not get placed under the tree by mistake! The tag read:

> *Our LOVE is given anonymously, so enjoy fun with*
> *your family, but don't tell anyone please.*

I put the turkey in the freezer and the rest of the gifts under the tree. After that, we gathered each day as a family to open one more gift. Each one had a clever little note. We would try to guess what each package contained. It became a game for us. Even our son joined us on occasion. As the days passed we discovered potatoes, sweet potatoes, a package of marshmallows, cranberries, packages of gelatine, pickles, olives, cans of green beans, corn, mints, ginger ale and nuts.

All together the packages made a complete Christmas dinner for four people. As we opened each package, we realized an unknown

Canadian friend was thinking of us, loving us, wishing us a wonderful Christmas — someone who wished to remain anonymous.

We opened the 12th package on December 25th. But it turned out we didn't need to use our packages of food on Christmas Day because a family from work kindly invited us over for Christmas dinner. We wouldn't be spending Christmas alone after all! Instead we used those food packages for our New Year's Day dinner. We felt so blessed, and were so thankful to be loved!

Now, two decades later, that difficult year is a distant memory. We never found out who gave us the anonymous Christmas gift. At first I wanted to know, but later it became unimportant. I'm thankful for the Canadian spirit of kindness and generosity that came at a time we desperately needed to know we were not alone after all.

~Janet Seever

Chicken Soup for the Soul: The Spirit of Canada

38

From Gloomy to Grateful

This is the message of Christmas: We are never alone.
~Taylor Caldwell

A family of six living paycheck to paycheck usually means a pretty skimpy Christmas. But in 2014, it finally felt like we were going to have more than one or two presents under the tree. I had a list, a budget and a plan. It was going to work!

Then our dryer broke. A family of six creates a full load of laundry every day. Since it was the middle of winter, hanging laundry outside to dry wasn't an option. I had one dryer rack because that was all I had room for in my house. Going to a laundromat was out of the question—I would have to live there to get it done. Then the brakes on our van started squeaking, signaling that it was time to replace the brake pads. It was one thing after another. In one week, we went through nearly all the money we had set aside for Christmas.

The night I had planned on ordering the presents for the kids, I stared glumly at the lists I had made. I crossed off the most expensive gifts first, feeling a pang of sadness when the remote control tractor that scoops had to come off my older son's list. It was the one thing he had asked for over and over. I kept telling myself that Christmas isn't about the presents and that the kids were still young enough to not really care about how many presents they didn't get. It didn't work. All I felt was frustration that the same thing seemed to happen all the time, not just at Christmas. We would finally get just a little bit ahead and then something would happen.

I cried to God that night, telling Him how I was so tired of feeling so hopeless. I wailed that it wasn't fair — that I didn't want to be a millionaire, but I just wanted to know what it feels like not to worry about money. I just wanted to give my kids a nice Christmas, for crying out loud! What's so wrong about that?

The next day, I went to the gas station to fill up the car. I knew we only had twenty dollars to spend on fuel until my husband got paid the next day. There wasn't enough fuel in the car for him to get to work, so that was where our last twenty was going. I went to the cashier to pay and she said, "Someone just came and put twenty dollars on every pump, so go ahead and pick one!" I walked back to my car, stunned. I had heard of this kind of thing happening and thought it was awesome, but I never expected it to happen to me.

The day after that, there was a knock on our front door. It was the local leader of our church. He handed me an envelope, wished me a Merry Christmas, and walked away. Inside were gift cards worth one hundred and fifty dollars.

A week later, my husband was at the store buying some diapers and other necessities. There was a lady in front of him and he noticed that before she left, she handed the cashier an envelope. The cashier rang up his purchases, he paid for them and then was handed the envelope the previous customer had left behind. Inside was a one-hundred-dollar bill. The stranger had told the cashier to give it to my husband as a Christmas gift. When he came home and handed me the money, I couldn't stop crying. I've been the receiver of kind deeds before and I had always been grateful for them — but these deeds were coming at a time when I really needed them.

I thought money towards gas, gift cards and a random one-hundred-dollar bill were more than enough to prove to me the generosity of people's hearts. I was to be proven wrong. The same night that we were anonymously given the one hundred dollars, there was a quiet knock on the door. I was in the middle of changing a diaper and it was so quiet that I wasn't even sure I heard it. I called out; "Just a second!"

in case there really was someone there, hurried with the diaper, and then went to the door. All four of my little ones were right at my heels. When I opened it, I discovered two big boxes full of wrapped presents. Tears began to sting at my eyes. Of course, there was no person standing there for me to thank. I yelled out, "Thank you!" and then brought the boxes inside.

The kids saw the packages and knew they were for them. I couldn't stop them from unwrapping them, even if I had wanted to. They were each labeled by name for the kids, so whoever our anonymous gift giver was, they knew us and we knew them. There was a sled and some books for our older son, a play doctor's kit and doctor's dress-up outfit and crayons for our older daughter. A baby and a stroller and dress-up dress for our younger daughter, some balls and puzzles for our baby boy. Presents that were immediately loved, hugged, and played with.

It wasn't until after I had gotten the wrapping paper cleared away that I saw the envelope. It was sitting at the bottom of one of the boxes with the names Josh and Nicole on it. I picked it up, hoping there would be a name of our gift giver. What I found inside left me in tears.

There was a note, but it wasn't signed. It said simply:

Joshua and Nicole
We were given a gift when our budget was tight. Now we are happy to pay it forward. You are an inspiration!

Inside the envelope — not one, not two, not three — but TEN one-hundred-dollar bills — one thousand dollars. I think I quit breathing for a few seconds. When my husband got home from work and I showed him what had been given to us, I thought I was going to have to administer CPR. He too, was completely speechless.

We still didn't have a huge Christmas by any means. It was very tempting to go out on a major shopping spree, but I remembered my pleas to God just a few weeks before of wanting to know what it would feel like not to have to live paycheck to paycheck. This completely unexpected money was an answer to those pleas. It wasn't enough to meet all of our obligations — but it was enough that not every single cent from my husband's next paycheck would have to go to bills. It was just enough. It was exactly what I wanted for Christmas.

~Nicole Webster

Chicken Soup for the Soul: Random Acts of Kindness

39

Filled with Kindness

The cheerful heart has a continual feast.
~Proverb 15:15

O ur monthly military pay never stretched to the end of the month. We were young newlyweds, expecting our first baby, and living in an old mobile home in Delta Junction, a rural, wilderness town at the end of the Alaska Highway. Large, wild animals roamed freely, and a closet-sized post office and equally small bank bookended the one general store in town.

I shopped on post at the Army commissary once a month, and because of our tight budget, I had to become a very creative cook. We purchased twenty pounds of ground meat, which I shoved into our built-in, dorm-sized fridge with a tiny, ice-crusted freezer.

I learned to prepare hamburger dishes thirty different ways. Often, I made one-pan meals of chili or soups and stews. Rarely did we have poultry or fish, unless you consider cans of no-name, smelly tuna packed in greasy oil a meal.

Mainly, we ate lots of pasta and carb-loaded meals with little meat and lots of tomato sauce. Most goods had to be trucked in from the lower forty-eight states. Dairy products, fruits and vegetables, prescribed as a healthy part of a prenatal diet, were especially costly and out of our price range. I was homesick, not only for my mom, but also for the variety of stores and farmers' markets back in Missouri, and the accessibility and affordability of fresh fruits and veggies.

Eighteen-hour days of winter darkness arrived in November. On our monthly shopping trip to the commissary, I planned ahead for our Thanksgiving dinner. I bought less ground beef and purchased one fat roasting chicken, which I stuffed into our tiny freezer. I also purchased a package of Pepperidge Farm dry stuffing mix and a can of cranberry sauce for our big meal. We invited our neighbors, Karen and Bob, a young military couple from Oregon.

All month long, I eagerly awaited our Thanksgiving get-together.

I rose early on Thanksgiving morning, pried the frozen poultry from the freezer, and thawed it. I washed and salted the hollow cavity and stuffed it with sage dressing. I smeared butter on the breast of the roasting hen and popped it into our twenty-inch, propane-fueled oven.

Half an hour into the baking, I peeked in. The light bulb illuminated a raw chicken in a barely lukewarm oven. I fiddled with the knobs and called my husband, who went outdoors to check the twenty-pound propane tank.

I knew before he announced it that the tank was empty. We didn't have enough money to refill it. Our friends and neighbors were as impoverished as we were, so borrowing money was out of the question. I dug deep into the bottom of my purse and rummaged through the couch cushions. Together, we came up with ninety-seven cents — not even a dollar. Three days before payday and flat broke, we drove to the service station on the main highway and asked the owner, an older gray-haired man who hustled out to greet probably his only customers, if he could please fill our small cylinder with just under a dollar's worth of propane.

"You kids stationed at Fort Greely? How long have you been up here? This your first Thanksgiving?" His exhaled words crystallized in mid-air, and he rubbed his hands together to warm them. The town's population was just over 500, and any newcomer was usually a military family. Many were young newlyweds, as we were, a year out of high school, and unfamiliar with the hazards of the large, free-roaming wild animals and the deep-freeze climate conditions. Spouses who joined their soldiers at the top of the world were required to take a survival training class on how to prevent frostbite and avoid serious situations.

At that moment, though, our most serious situation was having no way to cook our Thanksgiving meal.

The man tugged his fur-lined cap out of his pocket and pulled it down around his ears. He lifted our small propane tank from the trunk and said, "Hold on there a minute. See what I can do for you. Just under a dollar will get you through to payday, you say?"

I was so thrilled that I clapped my hands. "Oh, thank you, sir. I have the bird in the oven, and the oven went cold." I was too embarrassed to tell him our bird weighed less than five pounds and was a chicken, not a turkey.

He walked to the propane tank to dispense fuel. I watched the gauge register fifty cents, sixty-five cents, and when it surpassed a dollar, I panicked. "Tell him to stop filling!"

Before we could get the window rolled back down, the man turned to put our tank in the car. I dropped ninety-seven cents into his calloused hand and said, "I'm sorry, sir. You filled it, but we don't even have a dollar to pay you." I expected he would remove the small tank because there was no way to return the unpaid fuel.

With a genuine smile on his kind face, he said, "You kids have a nice Thanksgiving, and don't worry about it." If I had been outdoors, my tears would have frozen on my cheeks.

We thanked him for his generosity and promised to bring four dollars and three cents on payday to repay our debt. He waved us on our way.

I baked that chicken to a golden brown, whipped up instant mashed potatoes, opened cans of green beans and cranberry sauce, and proudly served a feast. As Bob, Karen, my husband and I bowed our heads to say grace, I was especially thankful for the generosity of a stranger with a heart of gold. I am forever grateful for his unexpected kindness as he demonstrated the true meaning of Thanksgiving.

~Linda O'Connell

Chicken Soup for the Soul: My Kind (of) America

40

No Random Act

Remember there's no such thing as a small act
of kindness. Every act creates a ripple
with no logical end.
~Scott Adams

I peeked out from under the covers to check the time. The clock read 4:00. I rolled onto my back and stared at the ceiling. It was 4 p.m., not 4 a.m., and I had managed to waste away another entire day in bed.

It was a week and a half before Christmas and despite all the pep talks I had given myself I was having a really hard time staying positive. In a few days I would be facing the anniversary of my daughter Kyley's death, followed by her birthday on December 23rd. I had always looked forward to this time of year and now I just prayed for it to hurry up and be over.

I sat up and let my feet dangle over the edge of the bed. I had put off my Christmas shopping long enough. I decided to head to a neighboring town to find the perfect gift for my husband Joey. I wrapped my long hair up in a messy bun, skipped the make-up, and did nothing about the ratty old sweats I was wearing.

I made it into town and stopped by a few local boutiques, festive with holiday music and bright Christmas décor. Shoppers hurried from display to display, eagerly picking out the perfect gift for their loved ones. I left empty-handed but not completely discouraged. I still had two more stops and I was determined to find something, anything, before I headed home.

I suspected the local trading post would have a few good "guy gifts." I headed that way and arrived at 6:04 p.m. The sign on the locked gate showed I had missed them by four minutes! I took a deep breath. The thought of having to go out another day and do this all over again was overwhelming. I shook my head. It wouldn't come to that because my next stop was a huge, multi-level specialty store where I knew I would find the perfect gift for my husband.

I arrived and was pleasantly surprised that the parking lot wasn't all that crowded. Great! I started walking toward the front door when I noticed a lady who had come out of the building. She was looking at me with that "look." You know the one, the "I know something you don't know look." I recognized it and stopped. "Are they closed?" I asked her.

"Yes ma'am. We close at 6:00," she pleasantly replied.

My shoulders slumped as my head fell forward. I felt defeated. This was a huge store. It was the holidays. How could they be closed? I could sense that she was walking toward me. She stopped in front of me and asked that fateful question: "Are you okay?" Now, if you are a woman and you've ever had a really bad day, you know what happens when someone asks if you are okay. Yep, you cry… a lot, and you spill the beans about whatever it is that has got you down. And that's exactly what I did. I told her about Kyley, about the anniversary date, about her upcoming birthday, and how I just wanted to buy a present for my husband. I was pitiful.

The lady told me to wait there. I watched as she rushed back toward the building, knocked on the locked door, and disappeared inside. She reappeared a minute later and motioned for me to come to her. She was excited as she told me that the manager had agreed to open the store for me. I protested, now feeling rather embarrassed, but she set her purse and car keys on a nearby counter and asked what I was looking for. She led me to the back of the store and showed me where I could find the perfect gift for Joey.

"I don't want you to feel like I'm hovering over you, rushing you, so I'm going to go stand right over there." She pointed to a nearby display a couple of aisles over. "You take your time and if you need help, don't hesitate to ask." She smiled sweetly before walking away.

I stood there looking at the huge empty space that was normally filled with hundreds of people and I knew this woman had already helped me.

That night I had needed to be heard. I needed someone to know I was hurting and to acknowledge that pain, and although I didn't realize it at the time, I needed someone to unlock the doors of a major department store after hours and let me in. I walked to where she was standing and asked her what time the store opened the next morning. I thanked her and told her I would never dream of keeping her and the others who had volunteered to stay behind for me from their families. I would return the next day during their regular business hours. I hugged her goodbye and told her I would see her the next morning.

The following morning I woke up, got dressed, and made the drive back to the store. I walked down the main aisle and immediately recognized the woman coming toward me. I asked her name and told her I wanted to thank her again for what she had done for me the night before. She looked puzzled. I smiled and told her I was the crying lady in the parking lot.

"Oh, my! You look so different! I didn't even recognize you!" she said.

It is pretty amazing what sleep, a new day, hair and make-up, and just a little bit of kindness from a stranger will do for a girl.

I shared with her how much her act of kindness truly meant to me. I found my husband the perfect gift and I was on my way.

You hear lots about "random acts of kindness" but I got the distinct impression that this was no random act on this lady's part. I do believe that I captured a glimpse of how this woman, Carol Roberson, lives her life every single day. Wow, what a wonderful world it would be if it were filled with people like Carol.

~Melissa Wootan

Chicken Soup for the Soul: Random Acts of Kindness

41

Stranded

*Not all of us can do great things. But we
can do small things with great love.*
~Mother Teresa

My mind started wandering. I had been driving on I-79
North in our newly acquired used Jeep Cherokee with
my pregnant wife through the mountains of West
Virginia for nearly two hours. No radio. No cell phone
service. No stop lights. No rest areas. No vehicles on the road other
than ours. The only noise we heard was the slow drone of the wiper
blades moving back and forth, reminding me of the metronome my
fifth grade piano instructor used to keep me on tempo. The slushy
mix of snow, rain, and sleet started picking up, making it harder and
harder to focus on the seemingly endless road before us.

It was the night before Christmas Eve and we were making the
long trek home to rural Pennsylvania. I was attending graduate school
in Kentucky and our winter break had finally arrived. My wife and
I had to work earlier in the day so we got off to a later start than we
would have liked — forcing us to drive in utter darkness the entire
trip home. We didn't really mind the drive though, knowing that in
eight hours we would be enjoying eggnog in front of a warm fireplace
with our family.

BOOM!!!

"Did you hear that?" I asked my wife.

"Yes. What happened?"

"I must have hit something," I said.

I pulled the vehicle off to the side of the road to check out the damage. I grabbed the flashlight from under my seat.

"We got a flat!" I yelled. "I'm going to put on the doughnut."

One by one I grabbed our Christmas presents, placing them on the sloppy ground. I finally made it the bottom of the pile, grabbing the jack, our only source of hope on this wintry night.

"Great, just our luck, it's broken! The car dealer sold us a vehicle with a broken jack! Now what?"

One by one I placed the saturated Christmas gifts back into the vehicle, replaying in my head how I could have made such a mistake. I returned to my seat and started wondering what our next move might be. We took a moment to assess the situation and offer up a quick prayer.

We laid out our options:

Option 1 — It looked like there was a house way off in the distance. I could ring their doorbell.

Option 2 — The next exit was fifteen miles. I could walk to the exit and my wife could stay in the car until I returned.

Option 3 — We could wait it out in the warmth of our car until the gas ran out — hoping that another vehicle would stop and perform a modern-day Good Samaritan deed on our behalf (even though we hadn't seen another car on the road for nearly two hours).

Neither one of us liked options one or two, considering the fact that we were in the middle of nowhere in West Virginia — so we decided on option three.

I reclined in my seat, not expecting to see another vehicle for several hours, if at all. I shut off the wiper blades so I could have a normal conversation with my wife. But before I uttered the first sentence, I heard what sounded like sirens. I looked in the rearview mirror and shouted as if I had just won the lottery: "A police car!"

The policeman pulled alongside our vehicle, asking us how he could be of service, telling us that his name was Officer Anderson.

I told him about the flat tire and that we didn't have a working jack or cell phone service. Without hesitation, Officer Anderson hopped out of his vehicle, grabbed the jack from his car, plopped down on the soggy grass, and started changing the tire. He then told us to stay inside where it was warm while he found us a mechanic. He eventually found us one, but it was forty-five miles away. He told us that he would follow behind us until we made it to our destination. So for the next hour and half, Officer Anderson followed behind our vehicle, even though it was way out of his jurisdiction.

When we finally arrived at our exit, Officer Anderson told us to follow him to the mechanic and that he would give us a ride to a hotel. Before he left, I felt compelled to ask him for his police station address so I could send him a proper thank you, and to ask him a question that I had been mulling over since the moment he stopped to help us several hours before:

"So why did you stop?"

After a long pause, he looked me directly in the eyes and said:

"I stopped to help you and your family because someone stopped and helped me and my family when we were in need many years ago."

Officer Anderson's words have been reverberating in my heart and mind ever since that night. His words (and actions) have provided me with much hope in my life when we have been in difficult situations and needed help—and there have been many. His words have also been the driving force behind my mission in this life—to reach out and help those who are in need, to those who are hurting, to those who need compassion, to those who need someone to help carry their burdens.

The truth of the matter is that we all need an Officer Anderson from time to time. Life gets challenging—a flat tire, a broken relationship, an unforeseen illness, a sudden job loss, or an unexpected bill to pay. But like Officer Anderson mentioned, he stopped and helped us because someone stopped to help him first.

The day after Christmas I decided to contact the police station to properly thank Officer Anderson for his service. The police chief answered and I started recounting the amazing act of kindness we had received from one of his officers. The police chief responded, "I'm very glad you received the help you needed the other night but there isn't an Officer Anderson at our station."

To this day I'm not sure if there really is an Officer Anderson who roams the mountains of West Virginia on I-79 north or if he is simply an angel, but I do know that this amazing act of kindness has drastically changed the course of my life.

~Tom Kaden

Chicken Soup for the Soul: Angels Among Us

42

Glorious Groceries

I am convinced that these heavenly beings exist and
that they provide unseen aid on our behalf.
~Billy Graham

In the summer of 2004, I had moved to a new area in the Colorado Rockies for a change of pace and to enjoy the clean mountain air. I had lived in California for many years and always dreamed of a simple life in the mountains.

Although my new town was beautiful, I had a difficult time finding work. Opportunities were limited for professionals in the resort-like area, and my intended job fell through. I ran out of money trying to find a job after several months. I was alone and stranded.

In October, I became very ill with a rare intestinal infection. It was the beginning of my first winter in central Colorado, and I wasn't accustomed to the harsh weather. I had no job, no health insurance, and few friends in my new town. I was sleeping on the floor of a new friend's vacant rental property. Despite the challenges I faced, I had no choice but to get up every day and pull myself together for job interviews.

Toward Christmastime, I secured a part-time job in a mall store and made enough money to put gas in my car, pay a few bills, and eat at least one meal every day. It was life changing to see people spending money on Christmas gifts when I could barely afford a meal. Some days I didn't eat much at all. Since I needed strength to regain my health, I sat in my car in the parking lot after work one evening and prayed.

I prayed deeply and specifically. I asked the angels, my guides, and the loving higher power to hear my request for food. "I need to eat a decent meal, Lord God and Angels on High," I prayed. "I need food so that I can get well and go on with my purpose for being here. I can help no one when I am this low. Please hear me." When I drove back home that night, I was driving on pure faith.

Twenty minutes later, I pulled into the driveway. The snow crunched under my tires, and the wipers strained to push the ice from my windshield. Although the car window was foggy, I noticed something on the porch. I blinked a few times and slowly exited my car, looking all around for any sign of someone who might have paid me a visit. I saw no one, but there on my dimly lit porch sat two brown bags filled with groceries.

My mind raced. *Who could have left me this glorious gift of food?* I'd been private about the depth of my financial crisis, even to my family back east. No one, including my family, knew where I lived. It could have only been a neighbor or the woman who owned the rental property. There was no other possibility. I knocked on my neighbors' doors to ask about the food. No one had knowledge of it. Then I called the owner of the rental. She said, "I wish it had been me, but it wasn't. I'm stuck here and couldn't have made it down there in this weather."

The most amazing aspect of the mystery groceries is that they included some of my favorite foods. If I had been given fifty dollars to buy myself groceries that night, I'd have purchased many of the same items that were left clandestinely on my porch. To this day, no one has taken credit for the gift. In a way, those two bags of groceries saved my life. I had good food to eat. I became stronger and got better physically. After the gift of the groceries, my faith was strengthened, and my spiritual vigor increased. It was only a few weeks later that I was offered a good job in my profession, and able to move into a healthy environment within two months. You might say that the groceries were a most miraculous Christmas gift, because they were the injection of positive energy I needed to go on.

Of course, many logical explanations went through my mind. Perhaps someone ordered groceries from a nearby store and they were delivered to my porch by mistake. Maybe an acquaintance left them anonymously, so as to avoid hurting my pride. Or, maybe a local nonprofit organization or shelter heard about my plight and sent the groceries. Although I researched these possibilities, I only reached dead ends. I came to accept that there might not be a logical explanation for the gift, and I made peace with the fact that I had received a Christmas miracle.

Who was listening to my prayer on that cold winter night in Colorado? And who was it that had the power to deliver bags of groceries, a tangible gift to my doorstep? I am thankful to the angels for the priceless Christmas gift they quietly gave to me that year.

~Karena D. Bailey

Chicken Soup for the Soul: Miracles Happen

43

Miracle on Clark Street

Sometimes being a brother is even better
than being a superhero.
~Marc Brown

Explaining death to a young child is never easy. When my brother suffered a massive coronary while riding the Metro to work and died suddenly, I struggled with what to say to my young son about his Uncle Bobby. Spencer thought the sun rose and set around superheroes like Spider-Man till the day Uncle Bobby hoisted him up on his shoulders in one swoop and carried him through the streets of Washington, D.C., high above the crowd. That day, Uncle Bobby, not Spider-Man, was the strongest man in the universe. When I explained that Uncle Bobby's heart just stopped working, Spencer thought for a moment and then sighed, "Gee, I wish we could have gotten him a heart like Ironman's."

"Me too," I sighed, as I fought back tears and hugged Spencer. I kept the message in as simple terms as possible, and after our talk, Spencer said, "So Uncle Bobby is in Heaven?"

"Yes, and he'll still watch over all of us and take care of us just like always."

"Okay," Spencer said happily with a reassured smile as he hopped off the couch and went about his eight-year-old day.

At that moment I wished my own heart could have been as easily comforted. But I knew that my only brother was gone forever, and there were things I would never be able to tell him. Like how I measured every boy I dated against Bobby's character, or how, when he taught me to ride a bike, he also taught me how to pick myself up after I fell. I would never again hear his voice on my birthday when he would call me and, for that brief moment, make me feel like he had nothing more important to do than talk with his baby sister. How would he ever know now how much I loved and adored him? No, my sadness was not as quickly comforted with the simple knowledge that my brother was in Heaven.

A few weeks later we were in church, kneeling in silent prayer before mass, when Spencer started giggling. When I looked his way to give him the standard mom, stern "time-to-be-quiet-and-stop-playing-with-your-brother-look," I noticed he was staring up at a corner of the church. "What are you looking at?" I whispered.

"Uncle Bobby," he whispered back matter-of-factly, his gaze never leaving the spot. "He says to tell you 'Hi.'"

To say I was surprised or shocked by his response would not be true. Spencer has always been a "special" boy, and truthfully, this is not the first dead person with whom he's conversed. When he was three years old, he proudly announced at my niece's wedding that "Ra Ra" (a beloved family friend who had passed away a few months before), was standing next to the bride.

So on this day, I simply whispered back, "Tell Uncle Bobby Mom says 'Hi' and that we miss and love him."

"He said he knows that, Mom. He said to tell you he loves all of younz and it's pretty warm here."

The "pretty warm" comment was one thing, but the "younz" gave me the real pause. That's a Western Pennsylvania term that my family uses for "you all," but I quit using upon moving to Wisconsin fifteen years earlier.

"Oh," Spencer quickly added, "I mean it's pretty AND warm here."

I immediately smiled and shook my head. "Thanks for clarifying your location, Bob," I said to myself.

Spencer continued to giggle, and when I asked why he was laughing, he whispered, "Mom, it's Uncle Bobby. You know he always makes me laugh."

I could not argue with that. Bobby's laughter was infectious. His trademark smirk was so permanently fixed on his face that even the funeral director could not make him look sad. This little exchange in church brought me back to my own youth and the many stern looks I got from my mom as a result of my brother's sense of humor, which was apparently still contagious, even in death.

"Did Uncle Bobby like comic books?" Spencer asked me one day as we drove to his favorite place in the world, Galaxy Comics on Clark Street.

"Yep! He liked Archie Comics and Mad Libs when he was a kid, and we watched the old *Batman* series on television every week."

"Cool," Spencer said, feeling his bond to his Uncle Bobby was still intact.

On December 26, 2012 the last book in the Spiderman comic book series (#700) was released. Galaxy is a block from my office, and I intended to go during my lunch hour to pick it up for Spencer, but work got in the way. It was after five when I finally arrived at the store. I looked on the shelf, but did not see anything with the number 700 on it. It was then that I learned from the laughing store clerk that they sold out within thirty minutes of opening the store. He told me to tell Spencer not to be too disappointed, as the new "Superior" series would be starting soon. I went back to the shelf intending to find something else to hold him over till then, when something with #700 on it caught my eye. I picked it up and asked the clerk, "Is this the one he wanted?"

Stunned, the clerk replied, "That's impossible! I know I sold the last one early this morning. I've been telling people all day we sold out. I have no idea where this came from!"

For a brief moment I thought I heard the distinct hearty chuckle of my brother behind me and then I smiled. "Don't worry," I said to the clerk, "I know where it came from." I whispered a grateful thank you to my brother.

I now have no doubt Bobby does look out for our happiness, and my heart is a bit more consoled. Even though it was December

26th, in the eyes of a ten-year-old boy, it was a true Christmas miracle, confirming Uncle Bobby's status as a superhero in all our hearts.

~Jodi Iachini Severson

Chicken Soup for the Soul: Miraculous Messages from Heaven

Chapter
5

A Book of
Christmas
Miracles

The Joy of Giving

44

Drawn to the Warmth

There is no exercise better for the heart than
reaching down and lifting people up.
~John Holmes

Factoring in the wind chill, I knew the temperature was below zero. The bitter cold cut through my Californian sensibilities, as well as my enthusiasm as a tourist, so I ducked through the nearest door for warmth... and found myself in Washington, D.C.'s Union Station.

I settled onto one of the public benches with a steaming cup of coffee — waiting for feeling to return to my fingers and toes — and relaxed to engage in some serious people watching.

Several tables of diners spilled out into the great hall from the upscale American Restaurant, and heavenly aromas tempted me to consider an early dinner. I observed a man seated nearby and, from the longing in his eyes, realized that he, too, noticed the tantalizing food. His gaunt body, wind-chapped hands and tattered clothes nearly shouted, "Homeless, homeless!"

I wondered how long it had been since he had eaten.

Half expecting him to approach me for a handout, I almost welcomed such a plea. He never did. The longer I took in the scene, the crueler his plight seemed. My head and heart waged a silent war, the one telling me to mind my own business, the other urging a trip to the food court on his behalf.

While my internal debate raged on, a well-dressed young couple approached him. "Excuse me, sir," the husband began. "My wife and I just finished eating, and our appetites weren't as big as we thought. We hate to waste good food. Can you help us out and put this to use?" He extended a large Styrofoam container.

"God bless you both. Merry Christmas," came the grateful reply.

Pleased, yet dismayed by my own lack of action, I continued to watch. The man scrutinized his newfound bounty, rearranged the soup crackers, inspected the club sandwich and stirred the salad dressing — obviously prolonging this miracle meal. Then, with a slow deliberateness, he lifted the soup lid and, cupping his hands around the steaming warm bowl, inhaled. At last, he unwrapped the plastic spoon, filled it to overflowing, lifted it toward his mouth and — with a suddenness that stunned me — stopped short.

I turned my head to follow his narrow-eyed gaze.

Entering the hall and shuffling in our direction was a new arrival. Hatless and gloveless, the elderly man was clad in lightweight pants, a threadbare jacket and open shoes. His hands were raw, and his face had a bluish tint. I wasn't alone in gasping aloud at this sad sight, but my needy neighbor was the only one doing anything about it.

Setting aside his meal, he leaped up and guided the elderly man to an adjacent seat. He took his icy hands and rubbed them briskly in his own. With a final tenderness, he draped his worn jacket over the older man's shoulders.

"Pop, my name's Jack," he said, "and one of God's angels brought me this meal. I just finished eating and hate to waste good food. Can you help me out?"

He placed the still-warm bowl of soup in the stranger's hands without waiting for an answer. But he got one.

"Sure, son, but only if you go halfway with me on that sandwich. It's too much for a man my age."

It wasn't easy making my way to the food court with tears blurring my vision, but I soon returned with large containers of coffee and a big assortment of pastries. "Excuse me, gentlemen, but…"

I left Union Station that day feeling warmer than I had ever thought possible.

~Marion Smith

Chicken Soup for the Soul: The Book of Christmas Virtues

Working Christmas Day

If a man loves the labor of his trade, apart from any
questions of success or fame, the gods have called him.
~Robert Louis Stevenson

It was an unusually quiet day in the emergency room on December 25th. Quiet, that is, except for the nurses who were standing around the nurses' station grumbling about having to work Christmas Day.

I was triage nurse that day and had just been out to the waiting room to clean up. Since there were no patients waiting to be seen at the time, I came back to the nurses' station for a cup of hot cider from the crockpot someone had brought in for Christmas. Just then an admitting clerk came back and told me I had five patients waiting to be evaluated.

I whined, "Five, how did I get five? I was just out there and no one was in the waiting room."

"Well, there are five signed in." So I went straight out and called the first name. Five bodies showed up at my triage desk, a pale petite woman and four small children in somewhat rumpled clothing.

"Are you all sick?" I asked suspiciously.

"Yes," she said weakly and lowered her head.

"Okay," I replied, unconvinced, "who's first?" One by one they sat down, and I asked the usual preliminary questions. When it came to descriptions of their presenting problems, things got a little vague. Two of the children had headaches, but the headaches weren't accompanied by the normal body language of holding the head or trying to keep it still or squinting or grimacing. Two children had earaches, but only one could tell me which ear was affected. The mother complained of a cough but seemed to work to produce it.

Something was wrong with the picture. Our hospital policy, however, was not to turn away any patient, so we would see them. When I explained to the mother that it might be a little while before a doctor saw her because, even though the waiting room was empty, ambulances had brought in several, more critical patients, in the back, she responded, "Take your time; it's warm in here." She turned and, with a smile, guided her brood into the waiting room.

On a hunch (call it nursing judgment), I checked the chart after the admitting clerk had finished registering the family. No address—they were homeless. The waiting room was warm.

I looked out at the family huddled by the Christmas tree. The littlest one was pointing at the television and exclaiming something to her mother. The oldest one was looking at her reflection in an ornament on the Christmas tree.

I went back to the nurses' station and mentioned we had a homeless family in the waiting room—a mother and four children between four and ten years of age. The nurses, grumbling about working Christmas, turned to compassion for a family just trying to get warm on Christmas. The team went into action, much as we do when there's a medical emergency. But this one was a Christmas emergency.

We were all offered a free meal in the hospital cafeteria on Christmas Day, so we claimed that meal and prepared a banquet for our Christmas guests.

We needed presents. We put together oranges and apples in a basket one of our vendors had brought the department for Christmas. We made little goodie bags of stickers we borrowed from the X-ray department, candy that one of the doctors had brought the nurses, crayons the hospital had from a recent coloring contest, nurse bear buttons the hospital had given the nurses at annual training day and little fuzzy bears that nurses clipped onto their stethoscopes. We also found a mug, a package of powdered cocoa and a few other odds and ends. We pulled ribbon and wrapping paper and bells off the department's decorations that we had all contributed to. As seriously as we met the physical needs of the patients that came to us that day, our team worked to meet the needs, and exceed the expectations, of a family who just wanted to be warm on Christmas Day.

We took turns joining the Christmas party in the waiting room. Each nurse took his or her lunch break with the family, choosing to spend his or her "off-duty" time with these people whose laughter and delightful chatter became quite contagious.

When it was my turn, I sat with them at the little banquet table we had created in the waiting room. We talked for a while about dreams. The four children were telling me about what they wanted to be when they grow up. The six-year-old started the conversation. "I want to be a nurse and help people," she declared.

After the four children had shared their dreams, I looked at the mom. She smiled and said, "I just want my family to be safe, warm and content — just like they are right now."

The "party" lasted most of the shift, before we were able to locate a shelter that would take the family in on Christmas Day. The mother had asked that their charts be pulled, so these patients were not seen that day in the emergency department. But they were treated.

As they walked to the door to leave, the four-year-old came running back, gave me a hug and whispered, "Thanks for being our angels today." As she ran back to join her family, they all waved one more time before the door closed. I turned around slowly to get back to work, a little embarrassed for the tears in my eyes. There stood a group of my co-workers, one with a box of tissues, which she passed around to each nurse who worked a Christmas Day she will never forget.

~Victoria Schlintz

Chicken Soup for the Nurse's Soul

The Cry of a Woman's Heart

Life is short and we have never too much time for
gladdening the hearts of those who are traveling
the dark journey with us. Oh, be swift to
love; make haste to be kind.
~Henri Frederic Amiel

The underprivileged children who attended our church-sponsored Christmas party feasted on Christmas goodies, enjoyed a puppet show and received gifts from Santa. When the last carload of children had gone, we breathed a collective sigh of relief, tinged with fatigue and gratitude.

Pointing to the extra gifts left in Santa's black bag, Jean asked, "What are we going to do with all these toys?"

As we deliberated, Bobbie said, "Remember the three sisters who were at the party? Why don't we deliver the toys to their house on Monday while the girls are in school?"

Everyone agreed. Since I lived closest to the three little girls, I volunteered to deliver the gifts. On Monday, I drove to their home, confident their mother would be there. As I got out of my car, a small dog appeared. He barked ferociously and followed dangerously close to my ankles as I hurried to the front porch. Keeping the dog at bay with one immense bag of toys, I knocked on the door. No one answered. I knocked repeatedly for several minutes. Still no answer.

Exasperated, I said under my breath, "Okay, now what am I supposed to do? I can't haul these presents around all day!"

Managing to stay a few steps ahead of the yapping dog, I returned to the safety of my car. After I calmed down a bit I remembered hearing one of the ladies at the church mention some needy children she had transported to the party. The children lived in a frame house not far from where I sat.

As I approached that location, I saw three run-down frame houses side by side. "Oh, no," I muttered. "How am I supposed to know which house is the right one?" I turned into the large dirt yard that was shared by all three families. As I unbuckled my seat belt, I sighed. "Oh, well, I'll try the middle one first."

I knocked on the door. As I prepared to knock again, the door opened halfway. "Yes?" A tired-looking young woman with reddened eyes stood in the doorway. My guess was she had been crying for some time.

Feeling embarrassed, but remembering my purpose, I proceeded. "Sorry for the intrusion. I'm Johnnie from Glen Forest on Old Alabama Road. We hosted a Christmas party on Saturday, and I wondered if your children attended?"

"No," she answered, shaking her head despondently.

"Well, I happen to have a trunk full of extra presents that I need to give to some willing recipients. If you have children who need toys, I'd be delighted to leave them with you."

The woman began to cry. After several minutes, she regained her composure. Between sobs she explained. "I was just sitting here crying… wondering how I was going to buy gifts for my children this Christmas… and here you are… standing at my front door."

She helped me carry the gifts inside. As tears trickled down her cheeks, she smiled and said, "Thank you… thank you so much."

"No need to thank me," I said gently. "I'm merely the delivery person. Your Heavenly Father arranged for you to have these gifts."

Now, more than twenty years later, I still cannot explain God's mysterious ways, but I can recount the joy of being the one he used to respond to the cry of the woman's heart.

~Johnnie Ann Gaskill

Chicken Soup for the Volunteer's Soul

The Least We Can Do

Human kindness has never weakened the stamina
or softened the fiber of a free people.
~Franklin D. Roosevelt

The young soldier in line two customers behind us looked tired. His pregnant wife played hide-and-seek with a small boy buried under their purchases like a merry troll. While my husband, Dan, hummed along to "Jingle Bells" on the intercom, I watched the serviceman and his family.

Insignias on the chest and sleeve of the camouflage uniform identified the man as an enlisted National Guardsman. He bent and spoke to his little son, who giggled and dove behind a box of Frosted Flakes. Both parents laughed.

Growing up as a Navy brat, I knew firsthand the sacrifices required by military people and their dependents in defense of freedom. I remembered the frequent moves and the long stretches of time without my father. I still recalled the ache in my stomach every time he deployed.

My husband broke my reverie by speaking directly to the soldier. "Thank you for your service."

Startled, the man replied over the head of the woman between us. "It's my privilege," he said — exactly what my father used to say when someone thanked him.

"Are you home for a while?" my husband asked.

"Yes, sir, through the holidays. I ship out again in the new year."

His wife and son glanced up from their game, and their smiles faded.

Dan touched the tips of his thumb and his fingers together, making a circle like a pirate's telescope with his hand. He peered through it at the boy in the cart. "You be the man of the house when your dad's away."

The troll grinned and lifted his fist to look back at us through his own telescope.

"Be safe," my husband said to the soldier. "And thank you again."

I pushed our empty cart out into the lobby while Dan paid the bill for our few items. We met by the entrance, and he passed me the receipt to record when we got home.

As I tucked it into my purse, the total caught my eye — nearly two hundred and fifty dollars. I stopped midway through the automated doors, and the cold air rushed around us. "Dan! There's been some mistake. This can't be our bill."

He took my elbow and steered me toward the parking lot. The bags he carried bumped against the back of my legs. "There's no mistake. I'll explain in the car."

I waited impatiently while Dan opened my door, crossed to the driver's side and got in. He dropped the sacks on the floor behind me. As he fastened his seatbelt and started the vehicle, my husband confessed what he had done.

"I paid for their groceries," he said.

"What? For the Guardsman's family? How did you do that? They were two behind us in the line!"

"I told the cashier to ring up an extra two hundred dollars on our credit card for the cost of their purchase and to give the change to the serviceman. I asked her to tell him someone said, 'Merry Christmas.'"

My mouth hung open, and I stared at the man I married.

"I've been doing this for several years," he said. "When I see a military person in line somewhere, I try to pick up the tab. Most of the time, they never know it's me."

"You big elf!" I punched him lightly on the arm. "What a great gesture."

Dan's face flushed a warm, pink color. "It's no big deal. And please don't tell anyone."

He turned to look over his shoulder through the rear window. As he backed the car out of the parking space, he spoke again softly.

"It's the least we can do."

~Lynn Yates

Chicken Soup for the Soul: My Kind (of) America

48

A Special Breakfast

For it is in giving that we receive.
~Saint Francis of Assisi

Until last year, the greatest sorrow of my life was that my wife Alice and I couldn't have any children. To make up for this in a small way, we always invited all the children on our street to our house each Christmas morning for breakfast.

We would decorate the house with snowflakes and angels in the windows, a nativity scene and a Christmas tree in the living room, and other ornaments that we hoped would appeal to the children. When our young guests arrived — there were usually ten or fifteen of them — we said grace and served them such delicacies as orange juice garnished with a candy cane. And after the meal we gave each of the youngsters a wrapped toy or game. We used to look forward to these breakfasts with the joyful impatience of children.

But last year, about six weeks before Christmas, Alice died. I could not concentrate at work. I could not force myself to cook anything but the simplest dishes. Sometimes I would sit for hours without moving, and then suddenly find myself crying for no apparent reason.

I decided not to invite the children over for the traditional Christmas breakfast. But Kathy and Peter, my next door neighbors, asked me to join them and their three children for dinner on Christmas Eve. As soon as I arrived and had my coat off, Kathy asked me, "Do you have any milk at your house?"

"Yes," I replied. "If you need some, I'll go right away."

"Oh, that's all right. Come and sit down. The kids have been waiting for you. Just give Peter your keys."

So I sat down, prepared for a nice chat with eight-year-old Beth and six-year-old Jimmy. (Their little sister was upstairs sleeping.) But my words wouldn't come. What if Beth and Jimmy should ask me about my Christmas breakfast? How could I explain to them? Would they think I was just selfish or self-pitying? I began to think they would. Worse, I began to think they would be right.

But neither of them mentioned the breakfast. At first I felt relieved, but then I started to wonder if they remembered it or cared about it. As they prattled on about their toys, their friends and Christmas, I thought they would be reminded of our breakfast tradition, and yet they said nothing. This was strange, I thought, but the more we talked, the more I became convinced that they remembered the breakfast but didn't want to embarrass Grandpa Melowski (as they called me) by bringing it up.

Dinner was soon ready and afterward we all went to late Mass. After Mass, the Zacks let me out of their car in front of my house. I thanked them and wished them all merry Christmas as I walked toward my front door. Only then did I notice that Peter had left a light on when he borrowed the milk — and that someone had decorated my windows with snowflakes and angels!

When I opened the door, I saw that the whole house had been transformed with a Christmas tree, a nativity scene, candles and all the other decorations of the season. On the dining room table was Alice's green Christmas tablecloth and her pinecone centerpiece. What a kind gesture! At that moment, I wished that I could still put on the breakfast, but I had made no preparations.

Early the next morning, a five-year-old with a package of sweet rolls rang my bell. Before I could ask him what was going on, he was joined by two of his friends, one with a pound of bacon, the other with a pitcher of orange juice. Within fifteen minutes, my house was alive with all the children on my street, and I had all the food I needed for the usual festive breakfast. I was tremendously pleased, although in the back of my mind I still feared that I would disappoint my guests. I knew my spur-of-the-moment party was missing one important ingredient.

At about nine-thirty, though, I had another surprise. Kathy Zack came to my back door.

"How's the breakfast?" she asked.

"I'm having the time of my life," I answered.

"I brought something for you," she said, setting a shopping bag on the counter.

"More food?"

"No," she said. "Take a look."

Inside the bag were individually wrapped packages, each bearing the name of one of the children and signed, "Merry Christmas from Grandpa Melowski."

My happiness was complete. It was more than just knowing that the children would receive their customary gifts and wouldn't be disappointed; it was the feeling that everyone cared.

I like to think it's significant that I received a gift of love on the same day that the world received a sign of God's love two thousand years ago in Bethlehem. I never found out who to thank for my Christmas present. I said my "Thank you" in my prayers that night—and that spoke of my gratitude more than anything I could ever say to my neighbors.

—Harold Melowski as told to Alan Struthers, Jr.

Chicken Soup for the Christian Family Soul

49

The Angel Project

*As an additional safeguard against self-pity in our
home, Mama kept several charity boxes that were
marked "For the poor." We gave regularly.
It made us feel rich.*
~Sam Levenson

I held onto the hand of my shivering granddaughter as we waited
our turn to enter the huge barn-like building. The length of the
line-up meant we couldn't see inside, so we passed the time
watching the outside line-ups.

At the head of one line, volunteers were busily placing frozen
turkeys into bags, and in the other, families and individuals were
receiving milk.

On the street outside the already full parking lot, a line of cars and
trucks were waiting to enter. Strangely, though vehicles were blocked,
no one honked or seemed impatient. It all seemed a bit surreal, as if
we were in a parallel universe.

Finally our line had moved enough that we could see into the
building. I was overcome with emotion when I noticed hundreds of
overflowing boxes. Some were filled with food for empty stomachs.
Others contained brand new toys for children who might otherwise
go without. Each box, filled with loving care, represented not only
hours of time on the part of volunteers, but the generosity and caring

of hundreds of anonymous individuals from throughout the town and area. This was the "Angel Project" in action.

Touched by this enormous expression of kindness I was I suddenly aware of tears flowing freely down my cheeks. Feeling a bit self-conscious I turned away from the crowds of people to wipe them away, and as I did I saw everything through a mist, causing the area to take on a kind of glowing appearance. "How fitting," I thought, "to see the Angel Project in this way."

It was four days before Christmas and today marked the climax of the Angel Project, an annual event in Calgary. This was the day that families in need could pick up food hampers and toys. Everything here had been donated through the generosity of strangers.

The people in this room had dropped everything in order to sort, label and number boxes, and then hand out delivery addresses to other volunteers so they could deliver boxes to those who had no transportation.

When it was finally our turn at the table, I found it difficult to speak past the lump in my throat. I was overwhelmed by all that was happening around me. Every box in that massive room represented the love of others. Every toy had been carefully selected to be given away, yet the receiver and the sender would never meet.

I felt something extraordinary there in that building. It wasn't quite definable but there was something special — a love that went beyond friendliness. I felt very privileged to be there and be part of it all. You see, my granddaughter and I were on the delivery crew! Jani was visiting me, and earlier that day, when I had suggested that we participate as volunteers, she grinned and said, "Yes, let's do it."

People helped us pack the trunk and back seat of my car with food and toys. I was given two addresses and we set off to make our delivery to the first family. I felt blessed to have a tank full of gas and the opportunity to be doing this.

Whatever it was I expected, I was simply not prepared for the greeting we received when we arrived at the first drop-off location. I found a basement suite and rang the bell, but when no one answered I ventured down a set of steps and called out, "Hello, is anyone home?"

A woman opened the door. As soon as I introduced myself and explained why I was there, she was so overjoyed she shouted to someone we couldn't yet see. She ran ahead of me back up the stairs, while calling out to a neighbour, "They're here! They're here! The Angel people are here!"

Wearing only socks on her feet, she ran out through the snow to the car and began thanking us over and over again. She continued to thank us with each box we unpacked.

"We are just the delivery people," I gently explained. "These boxes are gifts from people all over the area." However, she could not contain her joy, and continued thanking us again and again.

At the second house there were young children, and after we introduced ourselves and explained why we were there, the children were sent upstairs and admonished not to peek. I knew then that what we were about to unload might very well be the total sum of their Christmas presents.

Jani carried in the teddy bears, the huge craft set and the two other toys, all of which had been specifically chosen by Angel Project volunteers for these children. The mother helped me with the heavier food boxes, and I knew this abundant supply would last a number of days.

Before we left we exchanged "Merry Christmas" greetings. Just before the door closed, the woman paused and looked directly at me, and with misty eyes she said, "Thank you so much."

When I climbed back in my car I fought back tears and a choked up feeling. A giant surge of emotion burst inside me as I pictured those children on Christmas morning opening the wonderful gifts chosen by strangers. I could see tummies filled with the holiday food we had delivered. All this because generous individuals opened their hearts and purse strings for people they did not know.

As for Jani and me? Well, we got to spend a very special day together being a part of something beautiful and unforgettable. And though we were the delivery people that day, I drove away feeling as though I was the one who had received the gift.

~Ellie Braun-Haley

Chicken Soup for the Soul: O Canada The Wonders of Winter

50

Making Christmas Hope

Christmas is the one day of the year that carries real
hope and promise for all mankind.
~Edgar Guest

The holiday season was approaching, and our economy was still in a downward spiral. For several months, I had been attending a new church. Reverend Lori's messages were of everyday spirituality, and humanity to our fellow people, and hope, especially in these trying times. Her messages always inspired me and I wanted to follow up and make a difference in someone's life.

So many people this past year had lost faith and, more importantly, hope for a brighter future. People were feeling desperate. The streets were becoming more dangerous. I was thinking about the homeless, how they continued to find strength to go on, and how they would spend Christmas this year.

Across from my church was a park, and as fall came and went, I noticed a larger number of homeless people making their home there. I wanted to make their Christmas special this year, and hopefully remind them of Christmas pasts with their family and friends before hard times came their way. Yes, food and cash would help, but they could receive those any given day, and I wanted to make Christmas Day different.

I bought some Christmas gift bags in bright colors with Santa's face and "Ho-Ho-Ho" written across the front. Wanting to be practical yet capture the spirit of the holiday, I purchased Santa candy, peppermint candy canes, individual bags of nuts, cookies, and bright red tissue paper. Okay, this was a start, yet it wasn't special enough in my mind. Then I saw the fluffy little brown and white teddy bears with red bows around their necks.

Most of the homeless at this park were grown men. *Would they like my gifts?* My friends Marlene, Jerry, Ken and I assembled the bags. Christmas music playing loudly in the background, our hearts felt open and right about our mission. Placing the sparkly red tissue paper inside each bag first, followed by the candy and snacks, the cuddly bear, and a couple of dollars as a gift, we twisted the tissue paper sealing all the treats inside. Early Christmas morning, we set out to the park, stopping at a local Dunkin' Donuts to pick up coffee and doughnuts for the men too.

Never having done this kind of community outreach before, we were not sure how we would be received. The next hour was beyond our wildest expectations. As we approached the park, we saw a few more people than we anticipated, and we said to each other, "I hope we have enough bags." We were then spotted, and twenty or more people approached our car slowly, some walking, some limping, some jogging, still not knowing what to expect as we opened the door. They looked so tired as their eyes scanned the huge bag carrying all our goodies.

We had expected to hand out bags to everyone right there by the car and leave, but the men walked us over to a pavilion where most of them gathered to eat, sleep and just hang out for the day. Once there, we started to pour hot coffee and pass out doughnuts.

No one asked what was inside the bags. Everyone was patient as they took a cup of coffee and a doughnut, sitting down, savoring every sip and bite. As we said "Merry Christmas" to each, their responses of "Merry Christmas" back to us began to strengthen. They started to smile and their eyes brightened. We started to hand out the bags. Some got two bags by mistake and they turned and gave their extra to someone else, saying "Merry Christmas," happy to share their treats.

One younger man, seeing the teddy bear, looked up and said, "I have myself a teddy now." He put it inside his shirt pocket and patted it gently, his eyes gleaming.

Their resilience inspired me that morning — how they put aside their hardship for a couple of hours, opening their hearts, forgetting their troubles as they shared what they had. As we drove away, our own hearts were filled with gratitude and hope for brighter days ahead, and as we looked back, the group gathered under the pavilion waved until we were out of sight.

~Paula Maugiri Tindall

Chicken Soup for the Soul: Count Your Blessings

51

The Little Black Book

Kindness in words creates confidence.
Kindness in thinking creates profoundness.
Kindness in giving creates love.
~Lao Tzu

Many years ago I worked for a man whom today I call a great American funeral director. His lifelong motto was "Families first, no matter what," and he lived this with a consistency that few men ever achieve.

The funerals he conducted were flawless, and people genuinely admired and respected him. He was a grand person. However, one of the most interesting mysteries which accompanied this man was his "little black book." It was a small black book with a lock on the cover. It looked as if it was very old, and it was his constant companion.

If you went to his office, you would see it lying on his desk. At funerals, he would pull the black book out and scribble brief notations in it. If you picked up his suit coat, you could feel the black book in his coat pocket.

You can imagine the gossip by the staff and speculation around the funeral home coffee room as to precisely what was in the black book. I remember on the first day I worked, I very seriously asked the embalmer what the book was for, and he responded with a very mysterious glance, "What do you think is in the book?"

I was not the sharpest knife in the drawer and very innocently I said, "I have no idea."

"Oh, come on, farm boy," the embalmer replied. "He keeps his list of girlfriends in there." I was stunned!

Later I asked the receptionist about the black book. Her response was that it was where he kept the list of the horses he bet on at the race track. Again, I was stunned. My employer was a womanizing gambler! I could not believe it.

For nearly three years the mysterious saga of the little black book continued — all the time, the stories, gossip and intrigue getting more and more spectacular and ridiculous.

Then suddenly one day, while conducting a funeral, my boss, this great funeral director, had a massive heart attack and died.

Four days later, we had a grand funeral for him — he was laid out in a solid bronze casket, flowers were everywhere, and when we took him to the church, the place was packed and the governor was in the front row.

I was standing in the back of the church protecting the church truck (that was my job), sobbing as the minister went on about what a great man my boss was and how just knowing him made us all better people. I couldn't have agreed with the minister more.

Then the minister asked my boss's widow to come up and talk about her husband's character. I thought, "Now this will be beautiful," as she rose to walk to the pulpit. It was then I saw she was carrying his little black book! My tears of grief instantaneously turned to sweats of terror.

She walked to the pulpit, stood with complete dignity, looked at the assembly and said, "Thank you all for being here today. I want to share with you a secret about my husband's character."

I thought, "Oh God, here it comes!"

She continued, "You see this small book. Most of you know he carried it with him constantly. I would like to read to you the first entry of the book dated April 17, 1920 — Mary Flannery, she is all alone. The next entry August 8, 1920 — Frederick W. Pritchard, he is all alone. The next entry November 15, 1920 — Frieda M. Gale, she is all alone. You see when he made funeral arrangements or saw somebody at a funeral that he knew was all alone, he would write their names in this book. Then, every Christmas Eve, he would call each person and invite them to share a wonderful Christmas dinner at our house. I want you all to know that this was the true character of my husband; he was concerned, compassionate and caring. This is what the little black book is all about, and I also want you to know that this being 1971, he did this for fifty Christmases."

There was not a dry eye in the church.

Now almost a quarter of a century after his death, I look back at the inner spirit that motivated this funeral director to do what he did. May this spirit of warmth and compassion guide each of us in this great profession. Just think of the humanitarian possibilities if every member of the funeral profession developed our own little black books. The results of human kindness would be staggering.

~Todd W. Van Beck

Chicken Soup for the Christian Family Soul

52

Warmth on a Winter's Day

Teach this triple truth to all: A generous heart, kind speech, and a life of service and compassion are the things which renew humanity.
~Buddha

I was the assistant director of a local social service agency and I had just overseen our client holiday party. Two hundred volunteers had prepared and staffed a holiday dinner for nearly 1,000 guests. For many of the agency's elderly and physically challenged clients, this was their only holiday celebration, enjoying hot meals, camaraderie and seasonal entertainment as part of an extended family. For parents, it was a chance to enjoy festive, hot meals with their children, who got to open gifts that would have been otherwise unattainable. For just a little while, our guests could set aside their daily struggles and enjoy the holiday season.

Despite the party, I was feeling glum. My own children were now in their twenties and would not be coming home for the holidays. My dearest friend was in the hospital again, having suffered a health setback. I had no plans for the holidays, other than watching old movies and dining on Chinese take-out alone. Nonetheless, I had put on a happy face for the party. That was the least I could do for our guests, who had so little, yet never wallowed in self-pity. I had so much for which to be grateful and I needed to adjust my attitude accordingly.

The party had gone smoothly and a joyous time was had by all. The volunteers had hastily cleaned up, put away the leftover food and refolded tables and chairs. After saying goodbyes and thanking each one for their extra effort on this wintry day, I found myself locking up alone. The sun would set in less than an hour and I wanted to make it home before dark.

A foot of powdery snow had fallen overnight, adding to the two feet already hemming in the Chicago sidewalks. The glistening sunshine was blinding but did little to ease the single-digit temperature and the whipping winds.

I pulled my furry hat down low on my forehead and wrapped my heavy red wool scarf around my face. With my car key in hand, I trudged slowly through the uneven path of ice and snow, struggling to maintain my balance. I pulled my car door open, turned on the ignition and waited a few minutes for the car to warm up. The street was deserted and I prayed that I wouldn't get stuck in the unplowed roadway.

As I approached the first stoplight, I noticed a man standing at the corner with two young girls. He was tall, with short black hair and no hat. His well-worn parka seemed like it had been through many a winter. The man had a brown paper shopping bag in his right hand, keeping his left hand hidden in his jacket pocket. The two children were bundled in pink jackets and matching hats, their brown eyes peeking out over the tops of their scarves. Their white boots were hidden beneath a layer of dirty slush. I wondered where they could be headed on such a chilly, gray day.

I pulled over and asked, "Are you waiting for the Main Street bus?"

"Yes, Ma'am. We've been here nearly thirty minutes so I'm hoping it will be around soon," he replied politely.

I had overheard a conversation about the Main Street bus at the holiday party. Clients were discussing the inconvenience created by the recent Sunday service elimination. Many rode this route regularly and had to find other means of transportation. Few had cars and walking was brutal on these winter days.

"It doesn't run on Sundays anymore," I told him as I got out of my car to avoid shouting. "Where are you headed?"

"Well that explains the wait. I'll have to call a cab. Thank you," he said. "We're heading home, about four miles. We were at Grandma's house helping her with holiday preparations."

For a brief moment, I heard my mother's voice in my head, reminding me to never speak to strangers and especially never, ever to offer a ride to a stranger. However, seeing this young family shivering in the cold, I felt the only option was to lend a hand and get them out of the cruel weather.

"I'm headed that way, too. Please, let me drive you," I instinctively replied. "It's too cold for anyone to be out here, and I'd be happy to have the company." I pulled out a business card and handed it to him as a way of introducing myself and establishing credibility.

"Are you sure? I don't want to put you out. Now that I know there's no bus, I can just call a cab," he replied.

"No, really, it would be my pleasure. Please. I'm going that way anyway and you'll get there faster," I insisted.

"Okay, if you're sure. Thank you, thank you so much," he said with a smile as the girls climbed into the back seat. "I'm Joshua and these are my daughters, Tanya and Toni."

"Nice to meet all of you," I mumbled. "Make sure your seat belts are on."

"You are like an angel from heaven," Joshua said. "It is so bitterly cold out there, and we were starting to lose feeling in our fingers and toes. We were able to get a ride here, but I didn't know the bus wouldn't be running today. I would like to repay your kindness in some way, but I only have our bus passes and a few holiday decorations in this bag."

"Thank you, but there is no need. I'm glad I came by at this exact time and was able to help," I replied. "After all, we are all here just to take care of each other, right?"

Slowly and carefully, I made my way through the treacherous streets. The girls chatted about the day at Grandma's and shared their Santa wish lists. Much like the clients I had served earlier in the day, I hoped Joshua and his family would enjoy a warm, joyous holiday season.

I insisted on dropping my passengers off as close to their destination as possible. The girls thanked me and gleefully called out "Merry Christmas" as they stomped up the walkway to their house. "Thank you again for being our angel. I hope kindness finds its way back to you," Joshua said as he closed the car door.

What he didn't realize was that it already had. I was blessed with an impromptu human connection, lifted spirits and a warmed heart.

~Cara Rifkin

Chicken Soup for the Soul: Random Acts of Kindness

Chapter
6

A Book of
Christmas
Miracles

Family Matters

53

Pop-Up Thanksgiving

One of the very nicest things about life is the way we
must regularly stop whatever it is we are doing and
devote our attention to eating.
~Luciano Pavarotti and William Wright,
Pavarotti, My Own Story

What a year it had been! Our twelve-year-old daughter Sally had been diagnosed with leukemia in early winter, and we had all been thrown into a world that we did not know even existed: one filled with chemotherapy, complications, and hospitalizations.

When Sally developed a fever the week before Thanksgiving, we were all disappointed to go back to the hospital, but hopeful that she'd be home for the big feast we had planned. Her grandmother would be flying in from California and the menu had been developed and debated and amended on the phone by everyone in the family: Broccoli casserole or green bean casserole? How about both? Cranberry sauce with whole berries or jellied? Apples in the stuffing? Now the menu was on hold as we headed back to the pediatric ward.

The detour was easier to accept when Sally's hospital friend Mary, unlucky enough to have a fever of her own, was admitted to the room across the hall. Both girls were out of danger but needed to be monitored.

As the holiday got closer we could smell the homemade desserts in our minds, and picture the table laden with food and family, but going home seemed less likely. Then, on Thanksgiving morning, the doctors gave us great news: they would give Sally and Mary a "day pass" to David's House, the home-away-from-home for sick children and their families, next to the hospital. This felt like a "Get Out of Jail Free" card to all of us. Our two families hurried out in teams to the grocery store and to check out the cooking facilities.

David's House is a warm, welcoming place, and the kitchen is a cook's dream, with multiple ovens, range tops, refrigerators, and surfaces to prepare food, all in a light-filled space. Mary's parents and sister, my husband, and Sally's sister Kathleen pitched in to make the best meal ever. My mother arrived to the sounds of pots and pans and running water, and the smell of chopped onions and minced garlic, followed by the delicious scent of turkey just beginning to roast.

While the food cooked, I went to my car and pulled out all the decorations that had been planned for our home and had been riding around in my trunk since I bought them. Sally, Mary, and I set up multiple elegant tables to fit us all.

With so many handy cooks, the food all came out at the same time and we arranged it as a gorgeous buffet on the long counters. It looked like something from a magazine layout: the huge turkey with the crisp golden skin as the centerpiece, the roasted fall vegetables in beautiful shades of orange and yellow, the creamy gravy, and what seemed like every kind of cranberry sauce there is. What was even better was how it smelled — like home! The warmth and gratitude of this celebration that we had pulled out of nowhere seemed to mix with the rich smells of the food that we prepared all that afternoon.

Just then, the front door opened and an older couple and a younger man walked in, each wearing a look of shock and exhaustion. The young man explained that his wife had gone into early labor with their twins and needed to be hospitalized unexpectedly. He and his wife's parents had been directed to David's House as a place to stay for the night. Their plans had been to check in before going out to find a turkey sandwich somewhere. We led them into the kitchen where, to their great surprise, our beautiful homemade banquet was ready and hot. "Welcome!" we said, "to Thanksgiving!"

The three families sat down together for a meal that we would all remember long after Sally and Mary were cured. It was not the Thanksgiving that we had planned or expected, but it was one that we would never forget.

~Jane Brzozowski

Chicken Soup for the Soul: Food and Love

54

The Ultimate Gift

The pain of parting is nothing to
the joy of meeting again.
~Charles Dickens

A nother Christmas was approaching, and the dull ache of loss that was always with me began to increase. At the age of thirteen, my son, my only child, had died in a tragic accident. It had left my husband Tony and me with a sadness that was never far away and always amplified at this time of year. But this year, the Christmas of 2006 — brought a kind of healing — a holiday miracle just waiting to be unwrapped.

It began in late November when I received a phone call from my cousin, Mary-Gail, our family genealogy expert.

"Gail," she said excitedly, "I have some wonderful news for you! I've just received some information that is simply astonishing! There is no other way to put this," she continued. "I believe you have a brother."

I listened quietly while she breathlessly recited all the details. Apparently my mother had given birth to a boy before I was born, and we had the same father. We were full siblings! She had his name, his address in Mississauga, and his phone number. *But how had this happened? Why had he been adopted out? I had so many questions.*

As a small child, each Christmas my wish list had comprised only one thing. "Can I please have an older brother?" Every year I would ask, and every year I was devastated when my special gift did not arrive. As I grew older and realized that my request for an older brother was genetically impossible, I still persisted in my quest for a sibling. Although I had a much older half-sister, I craved the companionship that only a brother could bring. I desperately wanted to put an end to the loneliness I experienced as an only child.

Still a little unbelieving, I was very anxious as I prepared to make this call. After fortifying myself with a healthy glass of wine, with trembling fingers I dialed his number. Listening to the phone ring at the other end, I could hardly contain my excitement. If this were really true, it would be the answer to my long awaited prayer and heart's desire.

A recorded message answered — a deep, pleasant male voice somewhat reminiscent of a radio announcer. *Could this really be my brother?* After leaving my name and number I hung up and, filled with anxious anticipation, sat down to wait.

The shrill ringing of the phone interrupted my thoughts. "Gail? This is Fred… I'm so excited to hear your voice." For the next three hours we got to know each other and exchanged family information. I learned he had a wife and two grown daughters. By the time I hung up I was convinced he was, in fact, my brother. We arranged to meet a few days later at his home, and I got off the phone in a kind of euphoric daze.

Meeting my brother for the first time could best be described as winning an emotional lottery. After the warmest greeting you can imagine, with my body shaking and my voice quivering, I called Fred my brother for the very first time. His wife, Janet, had prepared a lovely lunch, but I was far too excited to do it justice.

Almost immediately Janet noticed our similar characteristics and gestures. I could clearly see my brother's resemblance to our mother, both physically, and in his gentle caring nature. Fred told me he'd always been mystified by his life-long desire to be a pilot. He was amazed to learn that his half-sister and his father had both been pilots. His father had actually flown in the 1st World War with Billy Bishop.

Just before we parted, Fred said, "How would you and Tony like to spend Christmas with my family and me?"

With my world still reeling from the mindboggling events that were unfolding, I could only enthusiastically nod my head as I joyfully wrapped my arms around his waist.

Christmas Eve greeted us with just the right blend of falling snow. As I skipped up the path leading to his home I could barely contain my excitement. I could hardly comprehend that I was spending Christmas with my brother. With my *older* brother! Even after having repeated those words countless times, I was still overwhelmed by their significance.

At the door, Tony and I were warmly welcomed by my beaming big brother, a loving sister-in-law and two beautiful adult nieces. Suddenly, I was acutely aware of a sensation of family I'd not experienced since my parents' passing. I felt a tiny tear trickle down my check as I hungrily drank in the experience of the moment. At last, I was HOME!

To be home was just beautiful. Gathered around the living room we exchanged stories and pictures, and marvelled at the love that our parents had had for each other. It turned out that Fred's adoptive parents had provided him with a liberal amount of information about his background, and he was now able to share with me the part of our parents' story I never knew.

"Mother and Dad fell in love when she worked for him," he revealed. "But he was married to someone else and was simply unable to leave. When I was born," he continued, "Dad did care for us both and helped Mom out as much as he could. But it was 1938, and an unmarried woman with a child out of wedlock was simply not accepted. Mother's overbearing father insisted she could not keep her young son, and she gave in to that pressure. I was placed with my adoptive family when I was about six months old and, some time after that, Mother and Father went their separate ways."

"I know she loved me," he continued, "as she made me all kinds of knitted things, and came to visit me often before the adoption was final."

Through my tears I gently reassured him, "Our mother was a gentle, kind soul. Giving you up must have been the hardest decision she ever made."

"What's even more incredible," I continued, "is that several years later they met again by chance in Toronto. Dad was now a widower and free to marry. Mom was engaged to someone else, but immediately broke it off to be with Dad. After a short engagement they were married and, three years later, I was born. And it was the strangest thing," I shared. "When I was little, every Christmas I kept asking them for a big brother. It's almost like I knew...."

Gently Fred placed his hand in mine and said, "Gail, I always hoped that one day I would have a picture of my parents, but today you have given me so much more. It means the world to me to know they got married and loved each other enough to build a life together."

Christmas 2006 was a lot more than an exchange of gifts, a glass of wine and a wonderful meal. It was a priceless opportunity to embrace life in a way I never envisioned possible. I was able to hug my niece and thank her, for it was she who had made that initial call to my cousin.

I could feel the familiar cape of depression I had worn so close to my body since the devastating death of my son lifting. It turned out that in addition to being a loving wife and stepmother to three wonderful people, I was now a sister, an aunt and a sister-in-law to an incredible family.

My dad always said there was one special gift to treasure each Christmas. He called it the thrill of Christmas. I knew in my heart I would cherish the special thrill of this Christmas — my Christmas miracle — for the rest of my life.

~Gail Sellers

Chicken Soup for the Soul: O Canada The Wonders of Winter

He's My Brother

Life is too short to hold a grudge, also too long.
~Robert Brault

Like the Christmas before, we didn't send Christmas cards; we called my family in Canada. Ginny and I talked to my mom. We spoke to my uncles and aunts. I hadn't seen any of them in seven years and Ginny hadn't met them yet, but she hoped to one day.

Those calls were completed, but I couldn't relax. I still had one more call to make, and I was afraid. I paced the house. I wasted time at my computer. I needed to call but I couldn't.

Five years before, I had received an e-mail from my brother. At the time, I had been out of work for several months. My life was very stressful. My brother's e-mail was nothing terrible but it made me angry.

I wrote back. As I typed, my anger grew. Months of frustration flowed into my nasty response. I said things that were not nice, but I hit send anyway. More thoughts occurred to me. I wrote a second nasty e-mail.

I basically told my brother to go to hell. I didn't care if I ever heard from him again.

The next day I received another e-mail from him. I didn't read it. I just deleted it, and then I blocked his e-mail address.

For five years, he tried to get through to me but I ignored him. I had lived with this terrible guilt. I thought about contacting him, but was ashamed of myself for what I'd said.

It was time to fix it. I picked up the phone and stepped outside. I wanted privacy. Ginny didn't know I was calling my brother. I took a deep breath, blew out a cloud of my breath into the cold December air, and dialed his number. Even after five years, I still knew it by heart. A phone rang 3,700 miles away in Nova Scotia.

There was no answer. I left a message. "Bob, it's Mike." I paused to take another breath. My hand holding the phone shook. "Bob, I guess I'll start by saying I'm sorry. I said some things I regret. I want to wish you and Delores a Merry Christmas and hope all is well with you. I realize you may not want to talk to me, but I thought I would try. I want to make it right again. If you want to talk…" I left my number.

I walked back into the house and looked at Ginny. "I did it."

She looked puzzled. "You did what?"

"I called Bob."

"Oh, honey!" She walked up to me and put her arms around my neck. "I'm glad. You needed to do it. It's family Mike and it's been too long." She kissed me. "You did right, hun."

Christmas came and went. I waited for the call that never came. I prayed for his forgiveness. The phone didn't ring. Then a week after I called, I received an e-mail. My brother left me a message on my Facebook page. He said he listened to my voice message over and over and knew I was sincere. In the weeks to follow, we e-mailed back and forth. The healing began.

Why had I let five years of my brother's life slip through my fingers? Why was I too proud to call and say I was sorry?

If I had the answers, it would never have happened in the first place, but I knew I don't want it to happen again. I had wrecked my relationship with my brother. Like a jigsaw puzzle that has been dropped, the pieces had scattered everywhere. It was time to gather them up and try to put them back together.

Since then, we have grown close again. Even though I haven't been able to afford the trip home, we are still family.

I swallowed my pride. I did it. Five years was too long. After all, he's my brother.

~Michael T. Smith

Chicken Soup for the Soul: The Power of Forgiveness

In the Nick of Time

Every traveler has a home of his own, and he learns to
appreciate it the more from his wandering.
~Charles Dickens

Unpredictable doesn't begin to describe our lifestyle when my husband was flying C-5s. By choice, we lived in a rural area of Dover, Delaware. We could have lived on base, but we always made it a priority to try to live out in the community so that our family could integrate and experience "regular" life as opposed to base life. So we were living on a small farm complete with sheep, chickens, the occasional pot-bellied pig and Amish neighbors.

I learned early on that life would be very different here. Four-day missions turned into month-long excursions with little or no direct contact with my husband. Well-meaning base personnel would call and give us updates that frequently led to tearful disappointments when missions would change, and children who were bouncing with anticipation would have to be told it would be another week... at least. Eventually, I asked them not to call unless they knew for a fact that his plane had crossed that golden line over the ocean that meant it couldn't turn back.

It was situation normal when my husband announced that he would be leaving the day after Thanksgiving for a four to six day mission. No big deal, status quo, so we got our Christmas tree early, enjoyed Thanksgiving with friends, and then said our goodbyes. By this time, the farewells barely left a ripple in our days, and we got on with whatever we were doing. Our children were young and homeschooled, so this meant diving into projects and keeping a fairly normal schedule.

This also meant I was on 24/7 duty, and it was getting critical after about two weeks. He wasn't back, and I hadn't had a second to do my Christmas shopping, let alone bake all the goodies my children were dreaming about. Three weeks in, it looked like we were going to be on our own for the holiday. This realization landed me on the front porch of our nearest Amish neighbor, tearfully asking if they would please watch my youngest while I ran out to get everything I needed for Christmas.

Mattie was a beautiful Amish woman, probably in her sixties then, and more than happy to take him in for a few hours. This is someone who helped me chase my sheep when they snuck out of their fence on more than one occasion, taught me about Rhode Island Reds, and shared eggs, canned fruits, baked goods and the occasional recipe. I thought she hung the moon. I tried my best to return these favors, but I was more the type who had to explain that I had baked them a beautiful pie, which had looked great until my youngest son accidentally sat on it.

Over the course of December, I received a couple of calls indicating that my husband might or might not be on his way — which I did not relay to the kids. I wanted to avoid any unnecessary heartbreak. We went ahead and made sugar cookies and a gingerbread house with full gumdrop trimmings, and planned our traditional Christmas Eve dinner of homemade bread and New England clam chowder. The gifts were wrapped and ready to be placed under the tree on Christmas Eve.

Christmas Eve morning, the phone rang. It was a ham radio operator letting me know he had a MARS (Military Auxiliary Radio System) patch call for me. It was my husband letting me know that they had crossed that golden line, and he would be home. I knew he wouldn't call unless he was positive, but I also knew better than to say anything because things change when you least expect it.

I proceeded with our normal Christmas Eve activities. Christmas music and sugar cookies fueled the day while the smell of baked bread filled the house. I put the finishing touches on the table and our soup as the kids played out the Christmas story in the living room. They couldn't wait to take their baths and get into their Christmas pajamas so we could have dinner and read *The Night Before Christmas*.

We sat around our carefully set farm table and said grace, prayed especially for Daddy, and dug into our favorite meal of the year. From where I was sitting at the table, I could see our front door clearly, and there framed in the window stood my husband — tired, scruffy-faced and still in his flight suit. My heart skipped a beat as he raised a finger to his lips to keep me from saying anything. I held my breath as he knocked on the door. Three heads snapped up from their bowls, and our home erupted with shouts of "Daddy's home! Daddy's home! He's really home!" They were at the door before he could get it fully open and were all over him in a second.

We laugh about our "Hallmark Card Christmas" now, but the feelings are still fresh — even twenty-five years later — and all that joy wells up in my heart all over again. Being a military family has its challenges and hardships, but it can have its sweetness, too. I won't pretend it was easy being the one left behind, to hold down the fort or whatever phrase we use to describe the day-to-day. It could be downright hard, but it made those homecomings all the more significant and memorable.

~Susan Mulder

Chicken Soup for the Soul: Military Families

A Fluffy, White Angel with Paws

Angels have no philosophy but love.
~Terri Guillemets

Two days after our first Thanksgiving as a married couple, my husband, Michael, and I welcomed a Great Pyrenees named Huck into our home. At just eight weeks old, he was charged with the prodigious job of helping unite two families into one. Yes, it was a big job, but there is nothing like puppy love. Long before we'd eaten all the turkey and stuffing leftovers, he'd won us over with his wobbly run and the steadfast devotion that shone through his dark eyes. We may have not shared the same blood, but we now shared a puppy, and that made us a family.

Now, here we were, just five years later, and Huck was gone.

"I'll never get another dog," I cried into my husband's shoulder as we sat on the couch.

It felt like heartbreak was stalking our family. Four months earlier, we'd lost our son, Ryan, my stepson, in a tragic accident. This new devastation further splintered our already broken hearts.

Michael and I opted to have Thanksgiving alone. Although it would be just us, I prepared the usual feast: turkey, dressing, broccoli casserole, the works. The tantalizing smells of Thanksgiving filled our huge old farmhouse, but instead of the usual joy-filled clatter, it echoed with silence. Grief stole our appetites for food and conversation. We spent the day staring at each other over a much-too-large turkey.

When the page on the calendar turned, instead of enjoying the hustle and bustle of the Christmas season, I wished we could skip December. I just wanted the holidays to be over.

Then my mom called. "Hey, Randy and I would like to come see you guys for Christmas."

I knew they didn't want us to spend Christmas alone, staring at an empty chair where Ryan should be. But we hadn't even bothered with holiday decorating. We didn't even have a tree.

"Oh, Mom, we'd love to see you, but holiday flights from Nebraska to Ohio are so expensive."

"That's right, they are, so we've decided to drive. It will be an adventure."

The next day, my phone pinged with an incoming text. I picked it up and saw it was from our college-aged daughter, Alexa. "Hey, found a cheap flight. I'll be there as soon as finals are over." Our younger daughter, Maddie, would be here, too. The only one who couldn't make it was our son, Ross.

Ready or not, we were going to have a full house to celebrate Christmas. We sprang into action. We found a small, living evergreen, perfect for replanting in honor of Ryan and Huck when the holiday was over. Then we faced the crowds to fill the space underneath it and to stock our barren refrigerator. Everything came together nicely, but it still didn't have that home-for-the-holidays feeling. Something was missing.

As Christmas and the arrival of our guests marched closer, I found myself sneaking in online searches for female Great Pyrenees puppies. I wasn't sure if I could take the next step, but it didn't matter; there were none to be found within 200 miles of us.

I looked at other breeds; there are so many choices out there to love. But I kept coming back to those little, white bundles of fluff with dark eyes, and pink and black feet. Finally, it hit me. I was no longer just thinking we "might" get a puppy; I wanted a puppy for our family — for Christmas.

On December 14th, I found a litter of Great Pyrenees puppies in our home state of Ohio. Immediately, I e-mailed the breeder. Of eight, three were left, and only one was female. I asked for a picture. Twenty minutes later, she texted me the picture, telling me that the one on the far right was the one that was available. She was all white, exactly what I had been imagining.

I was shocked when she texted her address. They were less than twenty-five miles from our house.

I called Michael. "Hey, honey, I was wondering if we might go look at something for Christmas after you get off work." I was worried about telling him we were going to look at puppies because we hadn't even discussed getting another dog. My fears were put to rest once we arrived at the farm, and he held the pink-bellied bundle. She curled right into the curve of his neck. He was ready to take her home that night, but we had to wait until she was old enough to leave her mama.

Less than two weeks later, real joy found its way into my heart for the first time that holiday season as our guests arrived and oohed and aahed over our new family member — Scarlett O'Hara — who was fast asleep in her red-and-white, polka-dotted bed under the Christmas tree.

About six months later, I looked up at a drawing done by Ryan that hangs on the wall above my desk. I started really missing him, and soon the tears were flowing. Through my sobs, I heard a low, nasal whine coming from Scarlett, who was lying on the floor next to me. I reached down to pat her, but she got up, walked over to me and laid her chin on my knee. As I rubbed her head, she just sat there looking up at me with eyes that seemed to say, "I understand everything you are going through. Here, pet me. Let me help you heal."

A couple of weeks before Scarlett's first birthday, we were walking her at our favorite park. Michael had brought along his camera and was snapping pictures of the garnet and brown leaves on the trees circling the pond. "Hey," I said, "get one of Scarlett. I'll put it on Facebook so everyone can see how much she's grown." Then I gave Scarlett the hand signal to sit.

Later that night, after I had posted the picture, my cousin, Charlotte, commented, "She's beautiful, and wow, look at her halo." I read the comment, and then looked at the picture again. I hadn't even noticed the white gauzy circle that appeared to be floating a few inches above Scarlett's head in the photo.

It really did look like a halo. Fitting, I thought, since I always call her my angel on earth. No, she isn't perfect. Occasionally, she still has an accident inside, and I've lost numerous shoes and the downstairs bathroom rug to puppy teething. Still, to us, she is so much more than a dog — she's family.

Although she's not a rescue, she rescued us. As Michael is fond of saying, "Huck came into our lives to unite our family, and Scarlett came into our lives to help our family heal."

~Amy Catlin Wozniak

Chicken Soup for the Soul: The Dog Really Did That?

58

Double Exposure

A mother's love runs deep and its
power knows no limit.
~Author Unknown

The last time my mother was at our house was Thanksgiving Day. She had been diagnosed with advanced stage cancer two months earlier, and she was already showing signs of weakness. So instead of the usual "Thanksgiving at Grandma's house," we decided to have it at ours.

By the time everyone arrived, the house smelled of turkey and stuffing, and the tables looked festive and inviting. It was a good day for my mom and dad, with a house full of children and grandchildren. We ate and laughed about times growing up. Then, while the kids played, we put the football game on TV and played pinochle with my dad.

It was nice for us to see my mom dressed up and out of their house for a change. She spent most of that day sitting in the comfortable rocker in the living room. We took lots of pictures that Thanksgiving.

After that day, Mom's condition worsened quickly. She died two weeks later, just before Christmas. It was the first of many holidays and special occasions without Mom there to celebrate with us.

Time lessened the grief, but we still missed her very much. She and my dad had always been there for their grandchildren's birthdays, school events and special times in their lives, and my dad still came. One of those special occasions arrived the following spring.

Our youngest daughter made her First Holy Communion, which

is a special celebration in our church. I got out the white dress and veil that my mother had bought for me when I made my First Communion. I washed it and hung it out to dry. The lace sparkled in the sun. I replaced the yellowed ribbon and sewed a new white slip. How sad, I thought, that Mom would not be here to see her granddaughter on this day. Sarah was especially close to her grandma and grandpa. She had spent a lot of time with them before she started school, since they babysat her when I returned to work. It would be the only First Communion of our six children that my mom would miss.

We had lots of family over that day and, as usual, we took lots of pictures with family and friends. I was anxious to see the pictures, and quickly took them in to be developed. This was back before digital cameras, when you had to load the film into the camera, and then take the film to the drugstore to have the pictures developed.

When I picked up the photos I opened the folder, and for a moment my heart almost stopped. Right on top was a picture of Sarah in her communion dress sitting on the arm of the rocker, and next to her, sitting in that comfortable rocker, was my mother! The picture was a little fuzzy, but there was no mistake — it was Sarah and her grandma, on the day that she made her First Communion.

When I got over my initial shock and looked through the rest of the pictures, I realized that the photos had been double-exposed — communion pictures taken on top of Thanksgiving pictures. In the time that had passed there were holidays and birthdays when I had taken other pictures. But somehow I had missed taking in this one roll of film from Thanksgiving. And I had re-used that roll of undeveloped film on that day, thinking it was a new roll of film.

What were the odds! But that day in May, my daughter's picture was taken sitting next to her grandma. It was as if my mother was sending a message from heaven saying, "See, I haven't missed anything! I've been right here beside you all the time."

~Peggy Archer

Chicken Soup for the Soul: Angels and Miracles

59

The First Christmas

Gifts of time and love are surely the basic
ingredients of a truly merry Christmas.
~Peg Bracken

This was my first Christmas alone. I had known it would be difficult, but I had no idea that it was going to be this hard. John had died in September, on the 25th in fact, so Christmas was three months to the day since his death. I tried hard not to feel sorry for myself but was only successful part of the time.

I learned to play bridge, bought tickets to the symphony, and enrolled in a weekly watercolor class. These things helped pass the time, it was true, but in many ways I felt like I was just going through the motions. I had dreaded the last day of November, knowing that when I tore off the calendar page on the thirtieth it would mean that Christmas was just around the corner, and it would be the first one in forty-six years without my beloved Johnny.

I heaved myself out of the La-Z-Boy with a deep sigh. No sense dwelling on it. I had to stop feeling sorry for myself. Thank the Lord, my daughter Wendy still lived in town, although she had been talking more and more about moving out east since her divorce from Dave. She felt there were more job opportunities in the advertising field out there. Wendy was a go-getter, all right. I could have predicted that she wouldn't stay in Swan River for long, even if her marriage to Dave had worked out. Well, she was here in town for the time being anyway, and at least we'd have each other's company for Christmas dinner.

With that thought in mind, I propelled myself toward the kitchen where the turkey lolled nakedly in the roaster, ready for stuffing. I'd make the stuffing, peel the potatoes, and start on the piecrust. Wendy was making candied yams and some new recipe for blood pudding, of all things! John would have hated it. Truth to tell, so would I.

But, sweet man that he was, John would have eaten it anyway, grinning all the while so as not to hurt Wendy's feelings. Such a kind heart. A prince among men. Oh, how I missed him!

A shrill ring startled me from my melancholy reverie. Quickly, I wiped my hands on my apron and reached for the phone. It was Wendy.

"Hi, Mom," my daughter said breathlessly. "I'm on the run here, so I won't keep you. I just want to know whether you'd mind it terribly if we had a couple of guests — some friends of mine. I know it's short notice, but you always cook enough for an army anyway, and I know you'll enjoy meeting them. So, how about it? Is it okay?"

I suddenly felt so tired. I really didn't want to entertain strangers. Just getting through the day was a monumental effort by itself. Reluctantly, I agreed, but Wendy, a sensitive girl from the time she was a child, knew that I didn't mean it. Despite that fact, Wendy rolled along enthusiastically.

"Great then, Mom. I'll pick them up on my way over. See you at six o'clock."

The line went dead before I could ask my daughter exactly who she was bringing, much less say goodbye. *Well, it didn't much matter, I supposed. I would put on a brave face and soldier through it.*

The rest of the day flew by, it seemed. There was so much for me to do, what with the cooking, the baking, arranging the centerpiece, and getting the table set. Then I still had myself to get ready — no small task these days. Wendy was always telling me that I was still an attractive woman, and that any man would be thrilled to be seen in my company. She was such a flatterer, that one. No wonder she was successful in advertising!

The doorbell chimed at precisely six o'clock. I could always count on Wendy's being on time. She had gotten that from her father. John hated being late for anything. Putting on a wide smile, I bustled to the door and opened it to my company. Wendy appeared to be alone. Puzzled, I peered out into the clear, wintry night but could not see anyone else on the porch. Suddenly, I heard giggling, and then in the next instant, I felt two sets of woolly arms around me, familiar and comforting.

"How are ya' doing, Clairey-Clairey-quite contrary?" one voice trilled. "Good to see ya, luv."

"Give us a kiss then, ey? Show us you're glad to see us," the other one boomed.

My throat tightened; I felt the tears well up, then spill hotly down my cheeks. I was speechless. Joy and disbelief flooded through me simultaneously. Teddy and Mary-Rose were throwing their suitcases into the front hall in a noisy jumble, both speaking to me at the same time and tugging on my sleeve as they vied for my attention, just as they had when they were children. In a boisterous hodgepodge, Wendy squeezed her aunt and uncle through the narrow entryway, picking up the suitcases, and setting them aside out of the way. Her beaming face, flushed from the cold, creased in a radiant smile.

"All the way from England, and not so much as a 'how d'ya do'!" Teddy teased. "What do you think we should do, Mary-Rose? Maybe we should just turn around and get the next plane for Manchester, ey?"

At last, I found my voice. I had last seen my brother and sister, fraternal twins four years my junior, when I'd gone back home to bury our dear mother. That was thirteen years ago. Of course, they had written, and there was the occasional long-distance phone call, but it was not the same as seeing them. Then, when John had died, they had sent a long, heartfelt telegram and apologized that they could not be with me. Despite my disappointment, I had understood. Manchester was far away; they had their jobs and their families, after all, and it would have cost the Earth to get to Swan River on time for the funeral. And now, incredibly, here they were. Thank the Lord, here they were! With my eyes brimming over, I untangled myself from my siblings' arms and moved over to Wendy, who was standing quietly near the staircase that led upstairs, watching the happy reunion unfolding in front of her.

"Wendy, dear girl of mine, did you orchestrate all of this?" I whispered.

"No big deal, Mom," Wendy replied.

"Oh, my sweet girl, it's a very, very big deal, and I thank you from the bottom of my heart. Now, did you bring along that delicious blood pudding you said you were going to prepare? I can't wait to try it. I'll bet your dad would have loved it!"

~Sharon Melnicer

A Chicken Soup for the Soul Christmas

60

The Best Christmas Ever

Whatever you do, they will love you; even if they don't
love you, they are connected to you till you die. You
can be boring and tedious with sisters, whereas you
have to put on a good face with friends.
~Deborah Moggach

Christmas was always my favorite time of year. I grew up
with family coming and going all day long.

But Christmas wasn't like that anymore. Now we lived
miles away from home and family. This Christmas, I was
particularly melancholy.

The year 1995 was not a banner year for me. I had been diagnosed
with breast cancer. As the holidays approached, I was nearing the end
of my radiation treatments and physically drained. My mood was
plummeting as Christmas neared.

I vowed that I would reclaim my love for Christmas and, despite
my illness, give my children a holiday they would remember.

I confronted my children. "This has been a tough year for the
whole family with Mom being sick. So, what do you say, let's celebrate?"

My children's eyes lit up. "What are we going to do?" fourteen-
year-old Robyn asked.

"I'll tell you exactly what we are going to do. We are going to
have our favorite foods. We will have a great big spread, just as if we
had a full house," I said.

I reached for a pad of paper from my desk. "Okay, you each get to pick one hors d'oeuvre and one dessert."

Lists in hand, the next day I set off for the grocery store. Exhausted from my last radiation treatment and the shopping, I dragged the last of the grocery bags into the house and set to work. The small kitchen heated up. I kicked off my sweatpants and continued working in a T-shirt.

Finished with four desserts, I focused on mine. For years, my mother had made me a custard pie. Even after I married and began having Christmas dinners at my home, she would arrive with her recipe on an index card and produce a custard pie. Mom finally left her index card in my recipe box.

I went to get it — no recipe. In a panic, I started to tear apart the kitchen.

The phone rang, and I was grateful for the distraction.

"Maureen, why are you calling today?" I usually speak to my sister on Christmas morning.

"I'm going to be too busy to talk to you tomorrow."

I was taken aback. *What was so important she couldn't find a minute to talk to her sister on Christmas?*

My sister and I were on patchy ground. We had a falling-out shortly after my mother's death three years ago, were estranged for a year, and were still trying to repair our relationship.

To distract us from the awkward moment, I launched into my lost recipe saga.

Maureen interrupted abruptly, "I don't have time for that."

I was stung. I thought she might understand the emotional impact of losing something of my mother's. Not only was she too busy to talk to her only sister on Christmas, but she didn't want to listen to my saga. It wasn't just about the recipe. The index card was in my mother's handwriting. With her deceased, it was irreplaceable.

"Have a nice Christmas," she said as she hung up.

I was hurt by my sister's abruptness. Already worn out by weeks of chemotherapy and radiation treatments, her attitude was the last thing I needed.

Late in the afternoon, the phone rang again.

"I got the impression from our earlier conversation that I hurt your feelings when I called earlier," Maureen said.

Out of the corner of my eye, I saw my husband entering the kitchen from behind me. I noted a dark shape lurking behind him. *Oh no, he brought someone home with him, and here I am in a T-shirt and underpants.*

I held up a finger to tell him to be quiet.

"I was a little hurt," I admitted. "What is so important that you won't have a minute to talk with your sister?" I had all I could do to be polite.

Paul was trying to catch my eye. I waved him off.

"I am going to be hugging you," Maureen was gloating. "I am in your living room." She screamed.

Confused, with the phone still to my ear, I pushed past my husband. There, standing in my living room, was my sister, whom I was cursing only a moment ago.

Paul took the phone from my ear and his cell phone from Maureen as I threw myself into my sister's arms. Standing slightly behind her were my young niece and nephew. I opened my arms to them as well.

I glanced over at my husband. He looked mighty pleased with himself.

The story unfolded. My husband saw a commercial on television offering airfares for $99 round-trip if you flew out Christmas Eve and returned on Christmas Day. He thought I had been through so much in the last year and was so down in the dumps the last few weeks that he was inspired to give Maureen a call on the off chance that she might be willing to fly down.

He said, "Your sister didn't even hesitate. She said she would come."

We spent the rest of the evening in a joyous reunion, and then went to the Christmas vigil. I was proud to introduce my sister and her children to my friends. Paul took us out to dinner, then we returned to our house and dug into "Robyn's dessert."

Later, I fell into bed beside my husband, who never ceases to amaze me, savoring the evening.

The next morning, a note from Santa was on our tree. He said he was surprised to find Jennifer and Nicholas in Tennessee. He apologized that he left their presents in Massachusetts, but left them each one small gift (all my sister could smuggle in her overnighter). Jennifer and Nicholas thus sat contentedly watching my children open their gifts.

After a hearty breakfast, Paul drove my sister to the airport. Christmas had barely dawned. Two sisters bid farewell amid a deluge of tears.

Maureen said, "We may have had our differences in the past, but we will always be sisters. Sisters are meant to be together at Christmas, aren't they? Your husband made it possible. How could I say no?"

My sister and her children were back home in time to have dinner. My niece and nephew told all their friends about finding Aunt Bonnie with her pants off. And I thanked God that my husband and sister gave me the best Christmas ever.

~Bonnie Davidson

Chicken Soup for the Sister's Soul 2

61

The Christmas Card

Forgiveness does not change the past,
but it does enlarge the future.
~Paul Boese

When I was nine years old, my uncle Frank was killed in an automobile accident. He was driving late at night on a backcountry road when a big ten-point buck ran out in front of him. Uncle Frank had no time to apply the brakes. His death was instantaneous, and to make things worse, Uncle Frank was killed early Christmas morning.

Uncle Frank was my mother's only brother and she was totally inconsolable when the sheriff brought us the news. Mom and Uncle Frank were as close as any siblings could ever be — that is, until their big argument. I was too young to really know what the argument was about, but I knew they had a big disagreement and very angry words had been exchanged. Uncle Frank had stomped out of our house and we had not seen him since; he was killed two weeks later, before the two of them had the chance to reconcile.

There was too much pain in our family that year to celebrate Christmas very much. I hurt for myself, for the first loss I had experienced, but I also hurt for my mother because she seemed so tortured, so guilt-ridden. "Frank knew you loved him with all of your heart, honey," my father consoled my mother.

"I will never be able to tell him again how very much I love him and how sorry I am for all of the terrible things I said to him," my mother sobbed.

My uncle's death changed our family forever. My mother cried for a long time after my uncle's death, but she finally dried her tears and announced as we finished dinner one early March evening, "No one in this family will ever leave each other angry again. We will never go to bed while angry at each other. We will make things right immediately. Do I make myself clear?" We all nodded our heads in agreement and I think we were relieved that a part of Mom's tough spirit was back.

Still, the ensuing Christmases were very difficult for us. The fact that Uncle Frank died on Christmas Day hung over our family like a fog that refused to dissipate, and we all knew Christmas was especially difficult for Mom. She tried to make Christmas enjoyable for us but she could not seem to get rid of her own personal guilt.

Then came that fateful Christmas Eve; I froze as I pulled the mail from the mailbox. Among several other Christmas cards was one from my Uncle Frank. *How could this be? Uncle Frank had been dead for five years*. The envelope was dull and faded, and did not display any postmarks, but sported a postage stamp that had been outdated for three years.

I thought my knees would buckle as I walked the Christmas card inside the house to my father. The look on my dad's face confirmed my disbelief. "What's this?" Dad said in a whisper. "Is this some kind of joke?"

"Where has it been all this time?" I asked. "And how did it make its way to our mailbox without being postmarked?" The look of disbelief in Dad's eyes told me that we would never get the answers to our questions.

When my mother saw the Christmas card from Uncle Frank, she almost fainted, but Dad caught her and was able to help her onto the sofa. Mom just held the card and cried for a long time before she got herself together, and with shaking hands, gently opened it. Tears welled up once again in Mom's eyes as she silently read the last note Uncle Frank had ever written. Mom was unable to speak so my father took the card from her hand and read it to the rest of us:

I'm so sorry, Maggie, for all the awful things I said to you. You were right and I was wrong. I was just too stubborn to admit it. I am coming to celebrate Christmas with you all. Phone lines are still down from the storm so I have not been able to reach you. I love you Maggie. Let's make this the best Christmas ever. Love to you all, Frank.

Uncle Frank was on his way to our home to celebrate Christmas with us and to renew his love and relationship with my mother. Knowing what had been in Uncle Frank's heart healed my mother and our family. I saw an almost instant relaxation in my mother's features; her face was once again soft and calm, her gait and stature displayed a life and energy that I had not seen in a very long time. My mother was finally at peace.

We never figured out exactly where that Christmas card had been for five years or how it finally made its way to our mailbox. In my heart I believe God had a hand in directing that long lost card to us so that my mother could finally have peace. If there was ever a Christmas miracle in our family, that Christmas card was it.

~LaVerne Otis

Chicken Soup for the Soul: Grieving and Recovery

62

Mysterious Visitors

Millions of spiritual creatures walk the earth unseen,
both when we sleep and when we wake.
~John Milton

For many years now we have hosted Christmas at our home. We invite close friends and family to take a chair at our table and share in the good cheer of the holidays. Before we eat, I am usually called upon to make a toast, and often raise a glass to absent friends and family. An old custom suggests you set one more place at the table with an extra chair in the event of an unexpected visitor at your door. It also serves to remind us of those who can only be with us in spirit.

For as long as I can remember, our front door opens by itself on Christmas Day. There is no set time, but I can usually count on it around the time of the opening of presents. You might think there is an explanation behind the mystery of this strange occurrence — a gust of wind, a guest not pushing the door closed. However, I believe it is a visitor. The door is not left ajar in order for this to happen. By the time we are aware of this presence the door is already beginning to open of its own accord. Our conversation stops and we all take a breath as we watch the door slowly open inward. There is no sound of footsteps and one of us usually gets up to close it. We have no clear explanation as to why this happens, but it does not seem menacing.

The first time we had one of these visits was not at Christmas, though.

It was an early summer's evening in the first few weeks following our daughter Christina's birth. She was in the crib in her room, asleep, and my wife and I were settled in for the evening in front of the TV. Suddenly, I saw a featureless, grey form move quickly in the periphery of my vision. It took a moment for it to fully register, but the figure was clearly headed toward the stairs to my daughter's bedroom.

"What was that?" Lydia asked. My heart skipped a beat when I realized we had both witnessed the same thing. I jumped up and ran quickly to the stairs. My first stop was the baby's room, but our daughter was sleeping soundly. There was no intruder there. I closed her door and tore through the rest of the rooms on that floor. I even raced into the bathroom and threw back the shower curtain. I looked inside every closet. The entire top floor was as it should be. There was no one there.

I was visibly shaken when I went back downstairs, where Lydia anxiously awaited my return. I told her I had found nothing. We sat together then, and thought about what had just happened. We were still emotionally raw from all the events that had led up to Christina's birth. You see, my father had died only a few days before she was born. I buried him in the middle of my wife's labour. I needed some time to say my final goodbye at the funeral, but Lydia's labour had begun earlier that day. We can't explain why, but her labour stopped and did not start up again until I returned to her. I was thankful for the time to say goodbye to my dad, but what happened with my wife's labour was strange.

During the birth we were on a roller coaster of emotion, overjoyed for the new life about to take a first breath, and at the same time saddened by my father's passing. I knew he tried to hang on in order to meet his new granddaughter, but his illness had run through his body like wildfire. This birth was a powerful reminder of the old wisdom that one life sometimes has to make way for a new life to begin. We were witnessing the great circle of life firsthand.

As Lydia and I discussed the shadow we both saw, we considered my father's passing and wondered aloud if something of his essence might have returned for a brief visit. I won't say it was a ghost, but similar stories have been told by others. We did not realize what a strange turn of events was in store for us until Christina's first Christmas.

The baby was resplendent in a beautiful, red Christmas outfit. A first Christmas Day in a new house is magical for so many reasons, but it is even more so when celebrated with your first child. Our daughter was mesmerized by all the twinkling lights on the tree as we began to place her presents around her day cradle.

Something wasn't quite right, though. I could not quite determine what was happening, but the atmosphere in the house changed. I looked up from the sunken living room and noticed the front door slowly opening as if a hand was gently pushing it from the outside. My wife was busy with opening Christina's presents and had yet to see what kept me from joining in. I walked over to the door, and Lydia looked up and asked if I had opened it. I told her it must have been a breeze, the only excuse I could think of at the moment. It took me a moment to close the door, but once I had the room began to feel normal again. The baby was looking in my direction, with just a hint of a radiant smile on her face. We have no clear explanation as to what this was, or why this happened.

Two years later our son Donny was born, and soon again it was Christmas Day. I was on the floor setting up a toy train set when, again, the door opened as quietly as before. This time, we were not as disturbed. In fact, it has happened now like this on this special day for so many years we would be more concerned if it didn't happen.

Now at Christmas when our front door seems to open of its own accord, my family stops for a moment to consider if it might be the essence of a loved one who has returned for a brief visit. We have come to believe it is a visitor from our past. I like to think it is my dad. This may be an unsettling prospect to some, but not to Lydia and me.

Unlike Scrooge's hasty denial of what he was witnessing and George Bailey's unwillingness to see the truth, my family has an open mind to our intimate connections to the universe, and beyond. And if, perchance, your door should open of its own accord on Christmas Day, you might say a silent prayer for a loved one you would give anything to see at Christmas again.

~Don Jackson

Chicken Soup for the Soul: Christmas in Canada

Chapter
7

A Book of
Christmas
Miracles

The Gift of Gratitude

63

A Spark

How beautiful a day can be when kindness touches it.
~George Elliston

Shortly after moving into a new Clovis, California neighborhood in 2002, I noticed my neighbors all had the same routine: drive into the driveway, use a remote control to open the garage door, and drive in with the door closing behind them. Everyone had a lawn service, which meant no one worked or puttered in their yards. Rarely did I see children playing outside. I didn't know even one of my neighbors. It seemed so impersonal and isolating to me. My neighborhood needed a spark.

The next Christmas season, it was time to be that spark. I sent invitations to each house on my street inviting the neighbors to my home for a Christmas cookie exchange. To my surprise, they all came bringing trays of freshly baked cookies.

It was a delightful evening getting to know one another. We discovered we all felt the same way—we needed to connect. Several began to talk about vandalism or other minor crimes they had experienced in our area. We agreed that the simple solution was to exchange phone numbers and alert each other to potential problems. By the end of the evening, someone offered to host the cookie exchange the following Christmas.

Two years later, in addition to what was now our annual Christmas cookie exchange, we decided to hold mid-year block parties, giving us another opportunity to connect. We received permission from the city to shut down our street for an afternoon. Neighbors brought out tables, chairs, barbecues, and lots of food. We rented a bounce house, hired a disc jockey and invited someone from the police department to speak to us. It became an annual event and included our official Community Watch meeting to discuss all issues concerning our neighborhood.

When the police department implemented the Clovis Community Watch program (CCW), I was voted to represent our neighborhood as the block captain. I met with other block captains and local police officers to help promote community safety, awareness, and connection.

In 2016, block captains were invited to work with the police on a more substantial community awareness program. We met in a local park monthly, but the cold months were coming. Someone asked, "Where can we meet during the winter?"

"My house is always open," I volunteered cheerfully.

An officer sitting behind me said jokingly, "Great! How about Thanksgiving? I am on patrol and won't get to have Thanksgiving dinner." Everyone laughed and agreed that I should open my house to everyone in attendance for Thanksgiving dinner.

"I am agreeing to host CCW meetings only," I said, dismissing that idea.

As I drove home, the words of the officer — "I am on patrol and won't get to have Thanksgiving dinner" — kept playing in my head. By the time I pulled into my garage, I made the decision that I would provide dinner for him and the other officers who kept my family safe during the holiday.

My surprised husband easily agreed when I told him, "I am preparing Thanksgiving dinner for all Clovis officers who will be on patrol Thanksgiving."

My intention was to buy, prepare, and serve the meal myself at the police station. I could not ask anyone else to give up their family time. But then my next-door neighbor asked, "What are you doing for Thanksgiving?"

"Preparing dinner for the Clovis Police who will be on patrol," I answered.

"I'll buy the turkey," he volunteered.

Another neighbor said she would cook it. Others called or came to my door to volunteer salads, side dishes, and desserts. Some offered money. So many asked to help.

Thanksgiving Day arrived. I could hardly wait to meet the other volunteers at the police station to set up for the feast that would be served later that day. Decorations in red, orange, brown and yellow gave a warm, welcoming feeling to the room. The buffet tables were over-filled with all the traditional and favorite foods associated with the holiday. By noon, everything was perfect and waiting for our special guests: Clovis police officers who could not be with their families.

The officers stepped into the break room, waiting to fill their plates from the bountiful offerings. "There are really people who would take time out from their family holiday to provide this incredible meal for us?" one asked.

"It is our honor to do this for you," I said.

The mood was light as the officers ate and shared conversation and laughs. When the last meal was served and the last officer left, it was time to clean up and go home, secure in the knowledge that these men and women were keeping our city safe. It made me happy to know that in some small way, my friends and I did something to make their holiday easier.

Just as with the cookie exchange and block parties, preparing and serving Thanksgiving dinner for police officers promises to become an annual tradition. It started with "a spark" years ago in the form of a simple idea and a simple invitation.

~Georgia A. Brackett

Chicken Soup for the Soul: My Kind (of) America

64

The Blessings Box

Life's challenges are not supposed to paralyze you,
they're supposed to help you discover who you are.
~Bernice Johnson Reagon

The house seemed huge and empty. There was no talking, laughing, crying, stomping, thumping, music playing, television blaring. It was all gone.

My children, who were now nineteen and twenty years old, had both left for college at the same time. They moved too far away for quick visits and I found myself alone, struggling with this depressing change in my life. I had devoted my life to raising my children and although I worked, it was either at their school or from home where I would see them every day.

As the days turned to weeks and weeks to months I found that my loneliness and anxiety was only getting worse. I found a part-time job that got me out of the house. My husband tried to be around more and we worked on our marriage, but still, I felt like I was in mourning, dealing with the loss of my children, the family we once had. I suddenly had no purpose, no reason to get out of bed in the morning, no motivation to do anything.

My son Eric lived hours away in Virginia now and was active in ROTC and school. My daughter Emma lived even farther away from our Maryland home, in Vermont, and kept busy with school, her church and a job. She also fell in love with a young man she met at church. My kids were doing what I always prayed they would do — grow up and become respectful, serving adults—but I missed them terribly.

Of course, Emma's time was preoccupied with school and her new love. We adored him as well and when he asked if he could surprise Emma at Christmas by driving down from Vermont we were all thrilled. Suddenly the entire family was going to be together to celebrate Christmas. As excited as I was, I could not help but dwell on the fact that this time would go by quickly and in a matter of a few weeks, I would be back again in my empty, cold house. As hard as I tried to enjoy life with all the holiday festivities and kids home, I dared not let myself get too happy because I knew that once they left and the holidays were over I would be more depressed than ever.

After Kyle surprised Emma we all gathered in the living room to exchange some gifts. I smiled at all the happy faces and the love that filled the room. The house echoed with Christmas music, laughter and talk; a fire crackled and popped and sent a warm glow throughout the room. Having my kids at home was the best Christmas present ever. And then Emma handed me a wrapped gift. I slowly unwrapped it and held in my hands. It was a wooden box.

"I made the box from old barn wood," Kyle said, smiling. And I knew immediately how special that was because Kyle was a carpenter and tore down old barns for the beams and timber.

"And I did the wood burning," Emma followed up.

I ran my fingers over the intricate scrolls and curves of the word "Blessings" and the flowers and vines Emma had burned into the wood. On the underside she had burned:

Merry Christmas, Love Emma and Kyle.

"It's a blessings box," Emma said. "You write down things you are thankful for and put them in the box. Then you can read them later when you're feeling down or sad and remind yourself of all the good things in your life."

That night, while the family was all there and the house seemed full of love and joy, I cleared a spot on my nightstand for the box. I wrote down the first thing I was thankful for and dated the paper:

"Blessed to remember that no matter how far away my kids are they will always be my kids." I folded it up and tucked it into the box.

The next night I did the same thing. "Thankful for my husband and all he does for me."

And the next night, before bed, I wrote: "Thankful for the big house that can accommodate the family when they come to visit."

And the nights after that: "Blessed that I have a job to go to each day." "Thankful that I'm in good health." "Thankful for my parents."

I wrote down my blessings and prayers and things I was thankful for, no matter how big or small, for each night until the kids left. The holiday decorations came down and the house was once again empty, cold and lonely. My husband worked each day and I did too, but when I came home I felt like I was being swallowed up in the cold and loneliness of the house. As I changed into my pajamas one day after work, I spied the blessing box sitting under a pile of books and I quickly pulled it out. I ran my fingers over the box and the dovetail woodworking that was so carefully and thoughtfully done. I ran my fingers over the words and flowers and smiled, remembering the two special people who had made this gift for me.

One by one I pulled out each piece of paper, unfolded it, and read. I read them out loud so I could hear clearly what I had written.

"Thankful for the big house that can accommodate the family when they come to visit!"

I breathed in deeply as if trying to suck in the chill in the air, and the silence. I remembered the holiday season when the kids were home and thought about future visits. I thought about how not even distance can take my kids away — they will always be my children, and our home will always be their home. With each note I tucked in that box, I was reminded of all the good things in my life, all that I had to be thankful for.

As each week passed, and I wrote a note for the box nearly every night, it helped me to stay focused on the positive. And when I needed a lift or a reminder, there was always a word of encouragement in the Blessings Box.

Now I write notes weekly and re-read my notes of thankfulness often. It has helped me cope with depression and anxiety and has given me a new outlook on life. I'm learning to embrace the quiet times and even the big, old, empty house that has blessed us with so many memories and promises of more to come.

I am blessed and forever thankful for a daughter who recognized a need in her mother and helped her to cope and adjust with a simple idea, a precious gift that has changed everything — a blessings box.

~Jennifer Reed

Chicken Soup for the Soul: The Power of Gratitude

A Side of Kindness, Please

Help one person at a time, and always
start with the person nearest you.
~Mother Teresa

I
t was Christmas Eve and we decided to have breakfast at Cracker Barrel. We got there early, shortly after eight. It was busy, but to our delight there was no wait.

As we looked at our menus, the conversation between the server and two Hispanic men at the table next to us caught our attention.

"We just want to pay," one of the men said. "Check, please?"

"There is no check. It's all taken care of."

"We don't understand."

"You don't owe anything."

"But we ate. We must pay."

"Not today. Merry Christmas!"

Apparently, someone had paid for their bill. The waiter was having trouble getting the men to understand that, though. He walked away to help another table, leaving them looking uncomfortably at each other.

They spoke in hushed tones in Spanish. They looked around at the other tables. Most of the ones directly around them, like ours, looked back, smiling.

They didn't smile back. They looked nervous. I wondered what they were thinking. Did they think it was a joke or a setup of some kind?

They had a right to be suspicious. It was a tense time in the world. Donald Trump had just been elected president. Hispanics and Muslims were the target of a lot of derision and hatred.

After several minutes, they got up to leave. They walked out slowly, cautiously. Were they hoping their kind benefactors would reveal themselves so they could thank them? Or were they expecting to get stopped and accused of dining and ditching?

I wiped tears from my eyes, which was the moment our server came to take our order.

"I'm sorry," I apologized. "I just witnessed a random act of kindness that melted my heart."

"I know. That was one of my tables that did it."

"Really? What a very cool thing to witness. Especially on Christmas Eve."

A short time after we placed our order and were waiting for our food to come, I noticed a man get up and walk in our direction. He'd been seated at a table with a large group of people next to where the Hispanic men had been sitting. He approached an older couple behind us. They were gathering their things to leave.

"Excuse me. Were you the ones who paid for those men?" he asked them.

The man had a thick Southern drawl, wore a trucker hat, and fit my stereotyped view of someone who was not in favor of immigration. The older couple was white and in their seventies.

I'm ashamed to admit it, but I judged them both. I doubted an older white couple would've noticed the Hispanic men and bothered to pay for their meal. But if they did, I feared this guy in the hat was going to say something nasty about it.

"Yes," the husband said humbly.

The redneck removed his hat and reached out to shake the man's hand.

"That was a mighty nice gesture, sir," he said. "Can I give you a little something toward it?"

"Oh, no, son. That's nice, but not necessary," the husband said.

"Save it for another time," the wife said. "If you ever see a chance and feel so compelled to do something, do it then."

The man nodded, replaced his cap and went back to his table.

"That was really awesome of you two," I said as they approached our table.

The wife smiled at me and put a hand on my shoulder.

"There's been a lot of ugliness in the world lately, hasn't there? Some people have seen it more than others. We saw a chance to let someone know not everyone is against them."

She gave my shoulder a little parting squeeze, and then she and her husband left.

Our food came, and a short time afterward a mom and dad and their two small children were seated at the table the Hispanic men had vacated. The family was also Hispanic.

I saw the man in the hat looking at them. I wondered if he was thinking the same thing I was. I knew he was when he stopped the server and motioned toward the family. The server looked, nodded and walked away.

I was pretty sure he'd just arranged to pay for the family's meal. I grabbed my napkin because the tears had started flowing again.

"Why are you crying now?" my husband asked.

"It's a Christmas miracle. Or maybe just the Christmas spirit made visible. I'm not sure which. Maybe both. Whatever it is, what a great breakfast this turned out to be."

Both my tummy and soul were nicely filled up.

~Courtney Lynn Mroch

Chicken Soup for the Soul: My Kind (of) America

66

Christmas Spirit

The only blind person at Christmastime is he
who has not Christmas in his heart.
~Helen Keller

The line of disgruntled customers snaked around the counter and disappeared somewhere in the menswear department. There were just two more shopping days before Christmas, and most of the shoppers in line were in panic mode, coiling to strike. One of those customers was my husband, Dale.

Dale is one of those people who shop better under pressure. They are the no-nonsense shoppers who depend on fast service because every minute counts as the countdown before Christmas continues. But the service here was anything but fast.

The problem was the elderly lady at the front of the line, who was twittering happily to the lone salesgirl manning the cash register.

"This sweater is for my granddaughter," the lady explained. "She's going to be a teacher, you know. And she's doing very well. She has a very nice boyfriend who is an architectural technician. He's just started a job with a good company, but you know, we haven't seen any sign of a ring yet. Young people seem to wait so long these days. They've been going out for quite a while now. Why, I was married with one child and another one on the way when I was her age."

On and on she rattled as she painstakingly counted out her change, oblivious to the writhing serpent of customers behind her. When she finally zipped her purse shut and picked up her parcel, the clerk motioned to the man next in line.

"Thank you, dearie," said the lady as she started to move slowly away, checking the contents of her shopping bag. She was almost to the end of the counter when suddenly she turned back. "Oops! Excuse me," she cried. A collective hiss went down the line. Several fangs were bared. An ominous rattle of keys began in someone's pocket.

"What's this for?" she asked, holding up a piece of paper.

"It's a discount coupon that will give you fifteen percent off your next purchase here at the store, from now until the end of January," replied the weary salesgirl.

"Well, thank you, my dear, but I won't be needing this," she beamed. "Here, you can use it right now!" she said, handing it to the man next in line. The man's eyes widened, and he mumbled a word of thanks as she shuffled to the door.

Then an amazing thing happened. The man stepped up to the counter and used the coupon that the elderly lady had given him. When the clerk handed him another coupon for his next visit to the store, he promptly turned around and gave it to the woman in line behind him. After she had used that coupon toward her purchase and the clerk gave her another one, the woman then passed it back to the shopper behind her. By the time it was Dale's turn, the salesclerk had a smile on her face, and so did Dale as he turned around to give his coupon to the lady behind him. And so it went, on down the line until there was nothing left of that disgruntled snake, not even a rattle. One small act of kindness had snowballed into a mountain of goodwill.

Dale says it was one of the best gifts he got that Christmas — when he discovered that the Christmas spirit is still alive and well in our world.

~Lisa Beringer

A Chicken Soup for the Soul Christmas

67

The Gratitude Book

*Somehow, by accident, I've realized I have lived
a rich, wonderful, rewarding life. Gratitude,
gratitude, gratitude for that.*
~Betty Sue O'Maley

I learned the power of gratitude from my mom. When she was diagnosed with terminal cancer, she began shouting from the rooftops how thankful she was for the amazing life she'd lived. She was given a horrible prognosis—an estimated fourteen months left to live. The easy response would have been for her to choose anger. Instead, she chose gratitude.

A week after she was diagnosed with her brain tumor, my mother wrote a surprisingly upbeat analysis of her situation:

This illness gives you plenty of time to prioritize and do all the things that you might want in order to feel you have lived a complete and fulfilled life.

So far, the first and predominant feeling I've had, rather than fear or resentment, is this rush of great, overwhelming gratitude for the life I've already lived and all the people, places, and experiences in it. Everyone should be so lucky as to feel this!

I had only just begun knowing my mom as a friend, after years of rebellion in which I pretended that I didn't need her. *She* may not have been angry, but *I* was. She wouldn't get to know her grandchildren and she wouldn't be able to continue the writing career that she had just begun after raising four kids.

If there was any blessing in my mother's illness, it's that it gave her fifteen months to truly live like she was dying — and for her family, the time to tell her how much she meant to us. She was clearly flooded with gratitude, often writing about how lucky she'd been for having the life she'd lived. Another of her early musings read:

> *I truly am in possession, still, of a tremendous sense of gratitude for my life and the wonder of everything in it. If only the feeling could be bottled, sold, and dispensed as needed!*

The more she told me how thankful she was for the life she'd been given, the more I began thinking about how very thankful I was for her. I knew it wasn't just me, though. She had a family, a large circle of friends, and a larger circle of acquaintances whose lives were better because of her.

My mother's influence extended far beyond the six of us in her immediate family. Everyone she met remarked on her kindness and wisdom. I had to make her understand that. I needed her to know just how incredible she was.

And that's how I got the idea for the Gratitude Book. I reached out to everyone I knew and asked them to spread the word. "If you've been touched by Betty Sue O'Maley in any way, please write a short note so she knows how she's brightened your life." It was a much larger undertaking than I'd originally thought. E-mails and letters came pouring in and I worked to put them all together as quickly as possible since there was no way of knowing when her last day might be.

I was able to put the gratitude notes together with beautiful photos of her life just in time for Christmas that year. It was the most important present I'd ever given, and the look on her face when she opened it was priceless. My mom would die five months after receiving the Gratitude Book, but she would die knowing how special her life had been to hundreds of her grateful admirers. My hope is that everyone who wrote a piece for the book was also given a gift — the gift of slowing down and thinking about just what they have to be thankful for — particularly all the people who have made life a little better for them.

My mom was taken from this life too soon, but she still managed to appreciate all that she'd been given. I try to remember how she lived and honor her by remembering my blessings every day.

~Carrie O'Maley Voliva

Chicken Soup for the Soul: The Power of Gratitude

68

The Christmas Tree

Christmas is not as much about opening
our presents as opening our hearts.
~Janice Maeditere

I t was late November, and I had been out of the military for less than a year. The holidays were quickly approaching, and money was tight. My wife and I had uprooted our life in the military to move back to my hometown in a quiet suburb of Chicago. We had not yet gotten fully into the civilian swing of things, but we wanted to make sure it was a festive holiday for our seven-year-old son.

When we looked at Christmas trees in our local Target, I sat on hold with my credit card company, determining whether we had enough spending power to buy a tree. My wife pointed at a tree that she and my son had selected. I was forced to shake my head sadly. Like the champ she is, my wife smiled and walked back to our son to begin swaying him toward a less expensive tree.

While watching them shop, I saw an older woman begin to walk toward them. I walked in their direction, too, wondering what possible reason this woman could have for approaching my wife. She walked up calmly to my wife and said something, and then my wife gave her a hug. I was now more confused than ever. After being freed from my wife's embrace, the woman walked away without a word.

My wife explained that the woman had heard us talking. She asked if I was a veteran. When my wife said yes, the lady had handed her five twenty-dollar bills and told her to have a merry Christmas. I didn't know what to do. "Should we give it back?" I asked my wife. I had never been in this position before and wasn't sure of the protocol for such an amazing act of kindness.

We ended up deciding that the best way to honor the woman's kind intentions was to do just as she had instructed and use the money to have a merry Christmas. We picked out the tree of our son's dreams and headed to the checkout.

As we were paying, still in shock, my wife motioned to a woman standing in line a few lines over. "That is the woman who gave us the money," she said. I walked over and told her how much her help meant to me. She said it was not a problem, and before I knew what I was doing, I was giving the woman a big hug, too. She laughed and hugged me back. Afterward, I returned to my family, who were laughing and waving at the lady. My son was yelling "Thank you!" and the kind stranger was quietly mouthing, "You're welcome."

We went home and set up our new Christmas tree. While decorating the bright green tree with the glassy red ornaments we had in storage, we spoke about how unbelievably kind that woman had been. With Christmas songs playing in the background, I couldn't help but think that this is what that kind stranger had intended. There was no buyer's remorse to be found. We were not stressed out or worried about the expense. We were just... happy. We were together and smiling and enjoying what would turn out to be an outstanding first Christmas in that new place. Every year since, while setting up our Christmas tree, we tell the story of that kind stranger and how much her generosity meant to us.

~Vincent Olson

Chicken Soup for the Soul: My Kind (of) America

69

Rich Beyond Measure

*The greatest good you can do for another is not just to
share your riches, but to reveal to him his own.*
~Benjamin Disraeli

Today I feel rich beyond measure. What began as a new idea for my department's celebration of the holiday season has become a very moving and enriching experience.

I was tired of the usual "draw names and buy a joke gift for under $15" way of holiday celebration, so I proposed that we try something different. "How about giving each other the gift of acknowledgment?" I asked. Everyone agreed; they were even enthusiastic. A few days before Christmas, six of us gathered in my office. To start, I asked that we all observe a few ground rules. The person whose turn it was to be acknowledged could only say "thank you." I also pointed out that it might be natural to feel uncomfortable giving and receiving acknowledgment, but if some people were truly uncomfortable, they could ask for their acknowledgment in private. Silence and pauses were deemed to be all right. They were probably just opportunities to let the good stuff sink in.

As we began our process, it struck me that the tribes and communities that pass their cultures along through story telling are very wise people. Invariably, whoever was speaking would tell a story that illustrated the acknowledgment he or she wanted to make.

Each of us started our communication by saying to our colleague, "(Name), the gift you give to me is…" As each group member spoke to the person being acknowledged, I began to see sides of my colleagues of which I wasn't aware. One male staffer acknowledged another male for his state of grace that shone through. Another said, "I rest easy knowing you are the one in your position." Other comments included: "You give me the gift of your patience," "You listen to me," "I knew the moment I met you that I belonged here," and so on. It was a privilege to be there.

The spirit and connectedness we shared for those sixty minutes became bigger than we were. When we finished, no one wanted to speak; we didn't want to break the spell. It had been woven with heartfelt, authentic, simple truths that we had shared with each other. We were all humbled and enriched by it.

I believe we will always treasure the gifts we gave each other that day. I know how priceless my own acknowledgments were for me. It cost each of us nothing but our willingness to see the gifts in others and to speak it out loud.

~Christine Barnes

Chicken Soup for the Soul at Work

70

Finding Christmas

*Because that's what kindness is. It's not doing
something for someone else because
they can't, but because you can.*
~Andrew Iskander

The sound of my infant daughter's crying burst through the baby monitor. *She can't be awake already,* I sighed, glancing at the clock. Only fifteen minutes had passed since I'd put her down for a nap. Caring for her and my six-year-old son, coupled with suffering from a bad case of the baby blues, had turned my days into blurs of diapers, bottles, crying, and whining. To make matters worse, Christmas was approaching. I had no idea how I would finish my shopping and gift-wrapping or bake the three dozen cookies I had promised my son's teacher for his class party.

I was lucky if I managed to take a shower each day. With my mom living only ten minutes away, I desperately wanted to turn to her for support. But she was in another state caring for my grandmother, who was recovering from a heart attack. I battled tears as I gently lifted my daughter, red-faced from crying, out of her crib. I dropped heavily into the rocking chair and cradled her. And as I rocked her back to sleep, I let my tears flow. Without my mom, I was unsure how to quiet the apprehension and worry I felt.

My mother's stay with my grandmother was lasting longer than expected. "I'm not going to get home in time to put up my Christmas tree," she had told me on the phone. "Your dad is still on a business trip so he won't be around to do it either."

"Don't worry about it, Mom," I told her, hoping I sounded reassuring. "You'll get done what you can and the rest won't matter this year."

But I knew better. Mom always made Christmas at her house magical. Every year, the scents of cinnamon, sugar, and chocolate would mingle as she baked her special cookies and fudge. The fresh balsam wreaths she would hang on every door brought a sweet, woodsy scent to each entrance of her home. She'd also make sure the aging, handmade felt Santas and Styrofoam snowmen blended perfectly with the newer ornaments that adorned her tree. She'd spend hours finding the perfect gift for each person on her list and planning the menu for Christmas dinner.

It looked like this year would be different. As I had hung up the phone, I thought, *I should put up her tree this year.* I quickly dismissed the idea. *Who was I kidding?* I could barely drag myself to the coffee pot each morning. I doubted I'd even finish decorating my own tree. But I couldn't get the idea out of my head. I couldn't stop thinking about the weariness I'd heard in my mother's voice. I became ashamed at my self-centeredness. I realized that I wasn't the only person who was tired and overwhelmed this year. My mother had always made Christmas special for me, and now it was time for me to make it special for her.

A few days before Christmas, my husband and I loaded the kids into the car and drove to my parents' home. Amazingly, my daughter fell asleep on the way there. When we arrived, I placed her — still strapped safely in her infant car seat — on the couch. We began to work. My husband brought the much-loved artificial Christmas tree up from the basement, along with box after box of tree ornaments and decorations. While he strung the lights on the tree, my son and I began looking through the boxes. It felt like Christmas morning had arrived early. Each decoration I found transported me to a wonderful childhood memory.

"I remember this! I made this in Girl Scouts," I exclaimed, as I pulled out a round ornament decked out in glitter and fabric scraps.

"And look at this one," I said, holding up a large, blue, hand-blown glass ball. "This was my grandma's ornament. I remember hanging it on her tree when I was a little girl."

"Mom, these are cool," my son said. His blue eyes sparkled as he studied several faded, red-and-white candy canes made of twisted pipe cleaners.

"I made those when I was about your age," I said.

"Can we make some for our tree?" he asked.

"Yes, that will be fun," I answered, smiling. My joy at watching his excitement canceled out any thoughts of my own exhaustion.

Miraculously, nothing went wrong. No knots were in the light strands, and each jewel-toned bulb shined brightly. No ornaments were dropped or broken, and my daughter enjoyed a rare and extended slumber while we worked. I forgot about my fatigue and depression because I was focused on how my mom would react when she saw our handiwork.

We worked for several hours hanging ornaments and arranging other holiday decorations around her house. Then it was time for the finishing touch. My son giggled as he was put on his dad's shoulders. My husband lifted him high above the tree's branches to put the star on the tree. I looked at my daughter, still sleeping, and smiled at her sweet, contented expression. I had to blink away the grateful tears that suddenly filled my eyes.

The next day, we made the three-hour trip to pick up my mother. I could see dark circles under her eyes and the worry lines etched in her forehead as she gazed out the car window.

"I can't believe Christmas is only a couple days away," she sighed. "I am never going to get my tree up. I still have shopping, wrapping and baking to do."

I simply nodded and smiled. My son bounced in his seat the entire way home, talking nonstop, but somehow managing to avoid blurting out our secret. When we arrived at my mom's home, he and I ran into the house ahead of everyone else and turned on the Christmas tree lights.

My mother walked in and he yelled, "Look, Grandma!"

Her gaze was drawn to the tree standing regally in the corner. Her eyes grew wide and she gasped, covering her mouth with her hand. She started to cry and then ran to me and held me tight. We laughed and cried at the same time.

"Thank you. I can't believe you did this," she whispered, choking back her tears.

It was one of the best moments of my life. What we did for my mother changed my whole attitude that Christmas. It shifted my focus from my troubles to my blessings and the feeling of pure joy I received by giving to another. I had truly found Christmas.

~Annette McDermott

Chicken Soup for the Soul: For Mom, with Love

71

A Christmas Memory

Christmas is doing a little something
extra for someone.
~Charles Schulz

The snow fell softly, its delicate lace-patterned snowflakes lingering on my woolen poncho. I half-carried, half-dragged my cumbersome load — a large garbage sack loaded with gifts — across the whitening street. It was almost midnight on Christmas Eve, but I was in no hurry to get home. Tears blurred the kaleidoscope of multicolored lights that blinked cheerily from our neighbor's houses. More subdued candles dimly lit every window at our house in their halfhearted attempt to feign cheer. Suddenly I stopped and stared. A white-bearded, red-clad, overstuffed figure was tapping gently at our front door and muttering "Ho! Ho! Ho!"

What is he doing here? I thought bitterly.

Christmas wasn't coming to No. 5 Jodi Lane this year. I feared it might never come again. My mind raced back to that day in November, the day our joy seemed to disappear forever.

The fall weather was just turning crisp, and my husband Jack and I and our three children squeezed into the car to head out for the Junior Midgets Sunday afternoon football game. Our two older children, Tara, four, and Sean, eighteen months, ran up and down the bleachers while I tended the baby, Christopher, who was three months old. He was snuggled up warmly in his carriage, napping on his stomach, oblivious to the noise and chill in the air.

"I haven't seen your newest addition yet," one of our friends, Tony, called, coming to my side. He smiled and peeked into the buggy. Always eager to show off the baby, I lifted him out, his face turned toward Tony. The smile faded from Tony's face, and horror filled his eyes. *What was wrong?* I turned Christopher to me. His beautiful, perfect little face was a contorted, grayish-blue. I screamed.

Another parent — a New York City policeman — leapt from the bleachers, grabbed Christopher from my arms and began applying CPR before the screams had died from my lips. An ambulance was on standby for the football game, and the policeman ran toward it with our lifeless baby cradled in his arms. Jack ran behind them. By the time they pulled away, I had collapsed, and a second ambulance was called to take me to the hospital.

When I arrived minutes later, the policeman who had carried Christopher away opened the door of my ambulance. His name was John, and his brown eyes were kind as he jumped up and sat by me in the ambulance. I didn't like what I saw in his eyes. He reached out one of his massive hands — hands that had tried to save my baby — and held mine.

"Let's pray for a moment before we go inside," he said gently.

"Is he alive?" I pleaded.

I didn't want to pray — not then, not for a long time afterwards. John led me into the hospital to Jack, and we stood together as we heard the medical explanation: SIDS (sudden infant death syndrome). Our son was another infant who had simply died in his sleep. No one knew why or how. There had been little anyone could do at the hospital. Christopher was dead when I lifted him from the carriage. He had died sometime during his warm, safe naptime.

We had set out that morning — a family with three happy, healthy children. Jack and I returned that evening huddled and bewildered in the backseat of John's car. Tara and Sean were at a friend's house. And Christopher, our baby, was dead.

John and his family lived about three blocks from us. A twenty-year veteran of the NYPD, John was experienced in dealing with death, but he was neither hardened nor immune to it. It was his patience and compassion that carried us through the worst hours of our lives.

The weeks that followed encompassed the two most joyous family holidays of the year — Thanksgiving and Christmas — but for us, they were a pain-filled blur. Jack and I were so overwhelmed with grief, we cut ourselves off from everyone and each other.

By the beginning of December, if I could have stopped Christmas from coming for the entire world, I would have done it. *Christmas has no right coming this year,* I thought angrily.

But now, close to midnight on Christmas Eve, Santa Claus was intruding at my front door. If ever I had entertained a belief in the existence of Santa Claus, this was certainly the moment of stark reality — the time I knew he didn't, never did and never would exist.

Angry and exhausted, I set down the load of packages I'd bought for the children weeks ago. I had donated Christopher's presents to Birth Right shortly after his death. Tara's and Sean's gifts had been hidden safely from their spying eyes at a neighbor's house until this evening. I felt a pang of guilt. Jack and I probably hadn't done a very good job of preparing for Christmas this year; we had numbly gone through the motions of selecting and decorating a tree with Tara and Sean.

By the time I reached the front steps, Jack had opened the door and was looking blankly at the bulky figure. His eyes landed on me, behind the Santa; he probably thought I had dragged the guy home in a feeble attempt to revive some Christmas spirit. I shrugged my shoulders, indicating I was just as bewildered as he, and entered the house behind the red-suited man.

Santa ignored us. He merrily bounced up the stairs and made a beeline to the children's bedrooms. He woke Tara first, gently calling her by name. She sat straight up and smiled. Of course Santa was standing by her bed! What else could you expect on Christmas Eve, her four-year-old mind reasoned, and she immediately launched into a recital of her wish list. "A Barbie doll with lots of clothes, a tea set, *Candyland* and a doll that really wets," she finished happily. Santa hugged her and made her promise she would go right back to sleep. "Don't forget, I've been a very good girl," she called after him.

Santa walked into Sean's room. Sean wasn't so enthusiastic about waking up (he never was), and he was a bit skeptical, but he remembered getting a reindeer lollipop at the mall from some guy who looked like this and decided to let him stay. Santa lifted him out of his crib. Sean smiled sleepily and gave Santa a hug.

I looked at the big strong hands that gently held my son and, lifting my eyes to Santa's face, saw kindly brown eyes gazing at me over the folds of his fluffy white beard. I remembered those strong hands and the warmth of those eyes.

"Oh, John!" I cried and burst into tears. Santa reached out to Jack and me and held us close. "Thought you might all need a little Christmas tonight," he said softly.

Soon Santa left, and we watched him walk out into the snow-covered street toward the warmth of his own home and family. Jack and I wordlessly placed our packages under the tree and stepped back to see their bright paper glow under the Christmas tree lights. Santa had come to No. 5 Jodi Lane. And so had Christmas.

~Lenore Gavigan

Chicken Soup for the Mother's Soul II

72

Giving Thanks with a Broken Heart

Gratitude is an art of painting an
adversity into a lovely picture.
~Kak Sri

My Methodist church has always co-sponsored a community Thanksgiving Eve service with the local Baptist church. For many years, I sang in the choir during the services when my church was the host, and I had simply thought of the service as part of the holiday routine. We sang the traditional hymns, "We Gather Together" and "Come, Ye Thankful People, Come," and heard a sermon, and the choir sang a Thanksgiving anthem.

After the death of my nineteen-year-old daughter in a car wreck, nothing about church seemed routine. For a while, I continued to accompany my husband to services as usual, but in a few months, I shut down. Everywhere I looked in that church, I envisioned my daughter. The memories were not soothing; they were painful.

I turned to the Crystal Cathedral on TV for my Sunday morning worship time, and my husband went to church alone. This went on for a year or two. One time I tried going to church but the hymn was "Majesty," which my daughter used to accompany with her friends in a praise dance. I broke down in the pew and quickly left. I tried again in a few months but the opening hymn was "It Is Well with My

Soul." Well, it wasn't well with my soul, and I didn't feel like being a hypocrite. I left again. My husband got a ride home with his sister.

The second year after the car wreck, I found myself sitting in church on Thanksgiving Eve, next to my sister-in-law. The church was almost empty. I looked around at the bare pews; there were almost more people in the choir than in the congregation. *Why were my sister-in-law and I, of all people, sitting in this church on Thanksgiving Eve?*

My sister-in-law and her husband had also lost a child. Their thirty-two-year-old son had died two years before my daughter. He had been diagnosed with skin cancer on his neck a few years earlier. He went to the doctor and had it removed, but never went for additional follow-ups. Their son had led a tortured existence for several years, unable to shake his addiction to drugs and alcohol. His friends had mistaken his bizarre behavior for alcoholic rage, and when someone notified my sister-in-law, he was beyond help. His skin cancer had metastasized to his brain, and the brain tumor was inoperable.

The only help that could be given to my nephew was medication to relieve his pain. My husband and I helped take turns sitting by his side in the hospital. He was coherent enough to talk about his childhood, and my husband and he would talk of Little League baseball, hunting, and fishing — all of the pastimes my nephew had loved. He died just a few weeks after the diagnosis, leaving behind two young sons.

During that Thanksgiving Eve service, I wondered why these pews weren't filled with the people whose families were whole. I thought, rather meanly, of the number of people in my church who could have filled the pews with their children, their sisters, brothers, aunts, and uncles. They should have been the thankful ones. *What in the world were my sister-in-law and I doing at this service?*

As the service continued, it dawned on me. Perhaps it was because we were so painfully aware of just how precious life is. Is it possible I am more thankful than those people who have never suffered a tragedy? Certainly, many of them thank God for their families and their many blessings. No, I just think we are more aware. Perhaps we live a little closer to the eternal, knowing that our children are already there. Perhaps, having known great grief, we are more eager to seek out joy.

I have heard others say that you cannot be healed unless you have been broken. This broken heart of mine will never be fully healed; there will always be an empty place there that I fill daily with memories of my lovely daughter. But such a loss has made me more eager to experience joy, to embrace the blessings of this day, and to seek the good things life has to offer with as thankful a heart as I can muster. "Come, Ye Thankful People, Come." I am coming, and I am trying. Create in me a thankful heart. Amen.

~Kim Seeley

Chicken Soup for the Soul: Finding My Faith

Chapter
8

A Book of
Christmas
Miracles

Answered Prayers

73

Lost and Found

*And I tell you, ask and you will receive; seek and you
will find; knock and the door will be opened to you.
For everyone who asks, receives; and the one who
seeks, finds; and to the one who knocks,
the door will be opened.*
~Luke 11:9-10

We had waited nearly two years to get a Chesapeake
Bay Retriever puppy. I daydreamed of names, felt the
brown puppy fur between my fingers, and smelled
a young warm-bellied pup. The breeder called with
a possible dog for us; he was four months old, had no training, and
could not be AKC registered. I explained he would be our family dog
and accompany my husband and son hunting. I assured her that his
age and lack of early attention was okay with us. For some reason
unbeknownst to me, I was determined to have this dog, no matter
what. Thus, on a windy day, in late December, we met him. He was
shy and afraid of us, of everything really, but I just knew he was my
dog. We named him Kenai after our favorite river in Alaska, where
my parents lived.

Less than one month later, our only child, our sixteen-year-old
son, Justin, died. As I grieved, whimpering and crying in my pain,
Kenai sat at attention at his fence, listening for my movements in the
house. He watched and waited, 24/7. I spent more than an hour each
day sitting cross-legged on a railroad tie in the yard, Kenai lying across

my lap. His fur became a prayer blanket to me, his eyes a healing solace. I sometimes wondered if he was an angel, sent to companion me in my grief.

On April 1st, a little more than two months after Justin died, I made a business trip to California. It was a mistake for me to travel so soon. I didn't realize how exhausted I was and how little energy I had to expend. I couldn't wait to get home. On a Sunday evening, I called to check in with Jim, my husband. He sounded awful and told me he had some very bad news. While at the fire station on Interstate 80 in Wyoming where he volunteers, a train passed, blowing its whistle. Kenai, standing next to him, had bolted in fear, simply disappearing into the stark barren landscape. Jim searched for hours and finally drove the forty-five minutes home, bereft. He knew how much Kenai mattered to me, and couldn't believe this loss.

When I got home, we drove to Wyoming and searched and searched. No one had seen him. On Holy Thursday, a friend and I drove to every house, every ranch, and posted lost dog signs. I berated myself for seeking a lost dog, while there were places in the world with people searching for missing family and friends. Yet I knew the loss of our son had left us hopeless. We could do nothing to change it. I had to do something now to try to find Kenai, to ease our loss. I had to believe again.

Kenai was only seven months old — a shy, frightened dog. But I had to try, to hope for a miracle. I posted a missing dog report on dogdetective.com.

The summer passed. Whenever we went to our cabin, ten miles south of where we lost Kenai, I scoured the landscape. I knew that perhaps someone had found him and kept him, or he had been eaten by a predator, or killed by a car. But I still looked. Something inside me believed in hope. I stopped telling my husband what I was doing. He felt bad enough.

Nearly nine months passed. Christmas was coming and we planned to visit my parents in Alaska. It had been the worst year of our lives, and we needed a respite. On December 23rd, we left Colorado in a snowstorm. Two feet of snow had fallen; cattle were dying on the plains.

Arriving in Alaska, the serenity and beauty welcomed us. My parent's cozy lodge was a comforting place to spend Christmas.

The morning of December 24th, my husband was on the telephone. I heard snippets of the conversation. "In a dead cow carcass? Brown dog? Skinny? Can't get near him?" He hung up, shaken, and explained. A rancher out with her cows had spotted a small animal on a distant ridge. She determined it was a dog. She could see it had a collar and flash of silver around its neck. When she approached the animal, it ran. Searching the Internet for lost dogs, Brenda found my notice I'd long given up on but never deleted. She promised to leave food near the cow carcass the dog used for shelter, and warned there was another big storm coming.

At Christmas Mass, I couldn't concentrate. Images of shepherds, ranchers, sheep, dogs, mangers, cradles, and cow carcasses traversed my mind. Was it possible that Kenai had survived all this time, alone? Did I dare I believe he was alive?

I asked myself, as I do every Christmas, "How is the Christ-child birthed within me this year?" Might the birthing be hope in a dog that was lost and found? That what seemed to be dead could live? Dare I believe and hope for a miracle?

Brenda promised to keep feeding him until we returned on December 31st and could meet her at the ranch. She was certain the skittish dog was Kenai. Though he wouldn't let her within twenty-five yards of him, the kibble she left on the snowy ground was wolfed down each morning.

January 1st dawned clear and sunny and we drove to Wyoming. Entering the ranch, we stopped to scan the landscape with binoculars. On a distant ridge we saw him. There was no doubt now. My stomach started to churn. Within a few minutes, we met Brenda. I could barely breathe. There was only room for one of us in her tractor cab. Jim stared at me and whispered, "Go."

Maneuvering to the ridge top seemed longer than ten minutes. Cows followed as we lurched through icy snow drifts. The sun radiated brilliance against snow and rock. We stopped where Brenda had left food for Kenai. Heart pounding, I stepped from the cab.

Brenda backed the tractor away. I walked forward. Suddenly I saw a flash of brown on the other ridge. Clapping my hands, I called, "Kenai, Kenai, Kenaiii," over and over and over. Could he hear me, would he remember?

Kenai stopped and sniffed the air. Instantly wiggling with recognition from nose to tail, he raced through snowdrifts toward me. Whimpers and cries erupted from both of us. I fell to my knees in the snow, arms wide open, calling him. I could see his puppy collar! A solid, furry hay-smelling body launched into my embrace. He was undersized, but unharmed. We jumped up, tumbled around each other, playing, touching, petting, tears pouring forth. I can't believe he remembers! He's safe!

When Jim was within one hundred yards of us, I knelt, presenting to him Kenai. Kenai looked to me, then rushed to Jim as I watched, sobbing with joy.

Oh yes, I hope. I believe.

~Pegge Bernecker

Chicken Soup for the Soul: Living Catholic Faith

74

Heavenly Possible

"For I will restore health to you and heal you
of your wounds," says the LORD...
~Jeremiah 30:17

I sat numbly with the occasional tear slipping down my cheek. I kept replaying the doctor's words: "I believe it is cancerous, although it seems to be a strain I have not seen before."

The tumors were on my tongue, and part of it would have to be removed. I was told it would severely impede my speaking ability and there would be little to no chance of singing again. This was devastating to a pastor and a singer.

I couldn't remember a time in my life when I had not been singing. My first solo was at age three. I never had any training, but I let my heart guide my voice and they seemed to make a good team.

I had joined the church to sing in the local Christian choir as a young girl. After that, I joined worship teams, Christian bands, appeared in musicals and even went on mission trips which focused on spreading the news via song. Now my songs would be silenced forever. How could God use me if I was silenced?

I had the surgery and went through two painful months of recovery. And then tumors returned. I went to another doctor, and had more surgery and lost more of my tongue. Now there was no chance of singing and even speaking would be difficult.

I remember speaking to a dear friend before the surgery, asking her what I should do. Deb, in all her wisdom, said, "Be the first."

"What?"

She reminded me of the struggles I had overcome my entire life. I had already survived two other kinds of cancer. She told me I was strong and that I needed to be the first to do what the doctors said couldn't be done. Be the first to speak well. Be the first to sing. Just trust God, believe in myself and do it!

Upon waking after surgery, I had a nurse approach me, laughing. She said that before I went completely under the anesthesia someone had commented on the size of my breathing tube. They were worried about it scarring my throat. Apparently I sat straight up and pointed to the doctor and said, "Look here, buddy, I am a preacher and I am a singer. DO NOT harm my throat; I have work to do."

I should have known then that God had a plan.

Unlike the first surgery, my recovery from this one seemed to be on fast forward. I was forming words again after days instead of weeks and months. Within a week I found myself trying to sing again.

Shortly after that was Christmas. I found myself in the back pew of a church where I didn't know anyone. The music to "O Holy Night" began to play. Remember my first solo at age three? It was to that song. This had to be a sign. I closed my eyes and at the same time opened my heart.

I asked God to allow my spirit to sing even if my mouth couldn't. Then the words spilled out. When the song was over, I opened my eyes and discovered that people were staring at me. So much for hiding.

I apologized profusely for singing too loudly. But the people were crying. They said they had never heard singing like that — that it was like angels were backing me up. I explained that they were and then gave my testimony.

The lady in front of me was dealing with cancer and had asked God for a sign. She got it through me.

When I returned to my surgeon for a follow-up, he and his intern began asking my husband questions. Finally I smiled and began answering them. The intern looked quickly at his chart, thinking he had the wrong one. He then asked, "Didn't you just have some of your tongue removed?"

I smiled and said yes. Then he looked at the doctor and said, "Should she be able to speak?"

The doctor replied "No," and smiled.

I looked at the intern and said, "What is medically impossible, is Heavenly possible."

~Pastor Wanda Christy-Shaner

Chicken Soup for the Soul: Angels and Miracles

75

Our Blowtorch Christmas

*There is no ideal Christmas; only the one Christmas
you decide to make as a reflection of your values,
desires, affections, traditions.*
~Bill McKibben

Christmas dinner was in the oven and our electricity was about to fail. We stared out the window. In front of our house was a power pole with a black box near the top, and the black box was sending out a shower of sparks — pretty, like a small fireworks display.

"Better phone the power company," someone said.

"It's Christmas," someone else said.

"Will they even answer their phone?"

My husband made the call. "They'll send someone when they can," he reported, "but they have no idea when that might be."

I sighed. Dinner was supposed to be early for the sake of the kids. On the bright side, they had new toys to occupy them. There was Christmas music on the stereo. The lovely smell of roasting turkey was starting to fill the air. We adults drank our wine and ate our appetizers and watched the sparking black box in fascination.

Eventually, as we knew it would, the display of sparks fizzled. Then the lights and the music went out. That meant the furnace and the stove were out too. I felt panic. New at this Christmas-dinner giving game, I had prepared carefully, hoping not to appear too clumsy to my very competent mother-in-law.

Thank goodness we had a fireplace. We put more wood on the fire and made sure everybody had a sweater. We dug out lots of candles and set them up ready to light when darkness fell.

My vegetables and potatoes were scrubbed, peeled, cut up, sitting in a water bath, all ready, except that they were raw. Earlier I'd taken my homemade buns out of the freezer and put them in a brown paper bag ready to warm in the oven at the last minute. My cookbook said the turkey needed fifteen minutes roasting time to the pound, and that meant it needed at least another hour in the oven. Relishes and cranberries were lined up in their little dishes under plastic wrap; right now they seemed to be the only part of dinner we could eat. For one gloomy minute I contemplated ordering pizza.

My mother-in-law favoured improvisation. She had spotted the green salad and the tomato aspic, a tradition of my family, in the fridge. "Why not," she suggested, "dine on these, some cheese, and the buns? It would be everything we really needed."

So we had a plan. Just to check, I inserted the thermometer into the turkey and found it was actually already fully cooked! It seems that modern turkeys need far less roasting time than the old cookbook suggested. Things were really looking up.

Darkness was falling so we lit the candles all round the room. My husband carved the bird and we loaded our plates with the turkey and cranberries, the salad and aspic and pickles and buns. We barely missed the rest of the menu. Laughter and jokes replaced the music missing from the silent stereo.

In the slightly chilly air, nobody, even the kids, seemed very interested in the ice cream bombe I'd made. But thank heavens for seasonal excess. There were tins of Christmas cake and cookies and other good things ready to fill the dessert gap.

"Those look delicious," somebody said. "All that's missing is a good cup of coffee." There was, of course, no pot of coffee, no hot water, no prospects at all. An awkward silence followed the ill-timed comment.

Then my husband disappeared into the basement and returned with a shiny tool.

"What's that for, Uncle Don?" one of the kids asked, as he filled a pot with tap water.

"Watch and see," he told them.

He struck a match near the tool. We heard a whoosh sound, and blue flame poured out of the blowtorch. He trained it on the pot until eventually the water began to boil! He then poured the precious boiling water through a coffee filter, and waited while it dripped into a carafe. And we had rich, fresh coffee to finish our improvised Christmas feast.

It was around that time that two men from the power company knocked on the door. "This shouldn't take us too long," one of them said cheerfully. He breathed out a smell as he spoke. *Mincemeat? Plum pudding?* I realized then he'd been called away from his own Christmas celebration — to help us with ours. As we watched, these two heroes climbed the pole and started working on the black box.

While they worked, my husband's sister sat down at the piano. It was now getting dark and in the room lit only by candlelight we gathered around her and sang all the wonderful Christmas songs we'd lost when the stereo went silent.

And then the lights came on: the lights on the house, the lights on the plantings in the back yard, and most important of all, the lights on the Christmas tree. At the moment they came on, all of us, child and adult, gasped. This is what we had been missing. We felt, I think, the same wonder at the sudden and brilliant appearance of those lights as our ancestors who lived before electricity must have felt when, for a few shining minutes once a Christmas, they cautiously touched a match to the candles on their hand-cut spruce tree.

~Gail Neff Bell

Chicken Soup for the Soul: O Canada The Wonders of Winter

Bringing It to Pass,
Football and All

*At the point where hope would otherwise
become hopelessness, it becomes faith.*
~Robert Brault

It was a crisp fall day in Madison, Wisconsin, when our University of Wisconsin football team defeated the University of Illinois in the final Big Ten Conference home game of the season. Now Wisconsin was headed to the Hall of Fame Bowl in Tampa, Florida, over the Christmas holidays. My twenty-two-year-old son, Michael, a senior at University of Wisconsin at Madison, was a four-year member of their marching band, famous for their wildly entertaining high-stepping antics that dazzled crowds.

I'd desperately wanted to go to the Rose Bowl game the year before to watch him perform, but the trip was too expensive. I didn't know anyone in Pasadena to stay with, and airfare was out of the question. On New Year's Day 1994, my house was full of relatives as we all watched Michael on TV. He played his drums with such precision during the Rose Bowl parade and game that my heart nearly burst with excitement and pride.

When the Wisconsin Badgers won the right to play in the Hall of Fame Bowl the very next season, I realized that that game would be Michael's last time ever to march with the band before he graduated.

I had to be there. Right! — a single parent with a small income and bigger-than-life dreams; that's me.

In late November, I mentioned my dream to my airline pilot friends who use the extra bedrooms in our home as their Milwaukee-area home away from home. One said he had a couple of low-cost "friend" passes that my fifteen-year-old son Andrew and I could use to get to Tampa and back.

"The passes are only about ninety dollars each, round-trip," he said. "But you'll have to fly standby."

I jumped at the chance as he set things in motion. Next, I had to find housing. I looked on the map and saw that our retired friends, Wally and Shirley, lived just forty-five minutes from Tampa. I was sure they'd put us up for the week in their Florida condo.

Everything seemed to be working smoothly until I called my dad in Illinois to tell him the good news. Dad planted my feet back on the ground when he said, "You're going to Florida between Christmas and New Year's? That's the busiest tourist week of the year down there! And you're flying standby? What do you think your chances are of getting on a plane that week?"

My bubble of optimism burst again when I heard on the radio that nearly thirty thousand Wisconsinites had already bought tickets to the Hall of Fame Bowl. Our chances of getting down there flying standby certainly didn't look good. In fact, they looked impossible.

Besides, there was another glitch in the plans. The airline we'd be flying on had only one flight a day to Tampa. How could I even think there'd be empty seats on that plane during the week between Christmas and New Year's?

I told myself disgustedly, "How could you be so stupid? This will never work!"

In addition to decorating for Christmas, buying gifts, cleaning house and planning meals for the holidays, I now had an additional stressor in my life.

I commiserated with my friend Heather, who told me, "Pat, stop worrying. Do something for me. Look through the book of Psalms.

Read it until you find a verse that seems to be speaking to you."

"Psalms? What am I going to find in there?" I asked Heather.

"Just do it. You'll find what you're looking for."

That afternoon I opened my Bible and read the first two psalms. Nothing hit me. The third verse said something about a tree yielding "its fruit in season," which only depressed me more. It made me think of ruby-red grapefruit and large, juicy oranges hanging on trees all over Florida—fruit that I certainly wouldn't be enjoying.

This can't be the verse that's supposed to make me feel better, I thought. I closed the book and opened it again at random. This time, my eyes went directly to Psalms 37:5: "Commit thy way unto the Lord; trust also in Him; and He shall bring it to pass."

Two things about that verse threw me for a loop. The part about committing my way to the Lord—my way to see my son perform in his last game, perhaps? The other was the notion that the Lord would "do this." If I did my part, then God would do His. In other words, if I really, truly trusted in the Lord, then He would bring all things to pass. That was the clincher, since Andrew and I would be flying standby on a "pass."

I thought, "Okay, Patricia, this is it. If Heather can be so dead-bolt certain of her faith, why can't you? You have to put it on the line. Do you truly believe that this is in the hands of the Lord and that He will bring it to pass?"

I only had to ask myself that question once. I sat down that moment and memorized verse 37:5. It was the first Bible verse I'd ever memorized in my life. I've been a longtime Bible reader and student, but memorizing is very difficult for me. I chanted the verse at least a hundred times a day during those weeks before Christmas: "Commit thy way unto the Lord; trust also in Him; and He shall bring it to pass."

The minute I turned the problem over to the Lord, I relaxed completely and virtually sailed through the preparations for Christmas.

Never again did I worry about whether or not we'd get on the plane, not even when I learned every flight had been greatly oversold with the exception of Christmas morning. And even for that flight, eighty of the eighty-four seats had been sold, with three weeks still to go before Christmas.

For the next three weeks, I repeated my newly memorized verse a thousand times: before I got out of bed in the morning, before each meal, during the day, in the car, in my home office, walking down the hall, in bed at night. I repeated it to all my friends and family and assured them that Andrew and I would be in Tampa for the Hall of Fame Bowl on January 2nd, and that we'd be flying down there on Christmas morning.

Christmas Eve day dawned holy and cold in Milwaukee. Andrew, my grown children, son-in-law, granddaughter, and friends Rusty and Heather and their two little daughters, all celebrated Christ's birth amidst my giggling excitement as I packed our bags for Florida. I shared my memorized Bible verse from Psalms with them as part of the grace before our Christmas Eve dinner.

"So Mom, are you just going to keep going back to the airport every day all week until you get on a plane?" my daughter Julia asked during dessert.

"No, honey, we'll be getting on the plane tomorrow morning. I'll send you postcards and bring you seashells!"

Never before in my life had I been so sure of something — something that to all the sensible people around me seemed to be the folly of the century.

Bags packed, car loaded, Michael drove us to the airport at 7:30 A.M. Christmas Day. The gate agent said there'd been four people with emergencies in Florida, and they'd been given priority standby status.

It didn't matter. I knew that when that gate closed we'd be on the plane.

That afternoon, Andrew and I picked grapefruit from the tree next to the hot tub in the backyard of our friends' house in Florida. Nine days later, after sunning ourselves on Gulf beaches, exploring exotic wonders and following the Wisconsin marching band as they performed all over Tampa, we watched as the University of Wisconsin defeated Duke in the Hall of Fame Bowl on a beautiful, sunny, eighty-degree day.

Michael's last performance with the band was stellar.

But not quite as stellar as my faith in the Lord — who brings all things to pass.

~Patricia Lorenz

Chicken Soup for the Christian Woman's Soul

77

The Tablecloth

Let God's promises shine on your problems.
~Corrie Ten Boom

A young minister had been called to serve at an old church that at one time had been a magnificent edifice in a wealthy part of town. Now the area was in a state of decline and the church was in bad shape. Nevertheless, the pastor and his wife were thrilled with the church and believed they could restore it to its former magnificence.

When the minister took charge of the church early in October 1948, he and his wife immediately went to work painting, repairing and attempting to restore it. Their goal was to have the old edifice looking its best for Christmas Eve services.

Just two days before Christmas, however, a storm swept through the area, dumping more than an inch of rain. The roof of the old church sprung a leak just behind the altar. The plaster soaked up the water as if it were a sponge and then crumbled, leaving a gaping hole in the wall.

Dejected, the pastor and his wife looked at the defaced wall. There was obviously no chance to repair the damage before Christmas. Nearly three months of hard work had been washed away. Yet the young couple accepted the damage as God's will and set about cleaning up the damp debris.

It was a depressed minister and his wife who attended a benefit auction for the church youth group that afternoon. One of the items put up for bid was an old gold-and-ivory-colored lace tablecloth, nearly fifteen feet long.

Seized with an inspiration, the pastor was the high bidder at $6.50. His idea was to hang the ornate cloth behind the altar to cover the ragged hole in the wall.

On the day before Christmas, snowflakes mingled with the howling wind. As the pastor unlocked the church doors, he noticed an older woman standing at the nearby bus stop. He knew the bus wouldn't be there for at least half an hour, so he invited her inside to keep warm.

She wasn't from the neighborhood, she explained. She had been in the area to be interviewed for a job as a governess to the children of a well-known wealthy family. She had been a war refugee, her English was poor and she didn't get the job.

Head bowed in prayer, she sat in a pew near the back of the church. She paid no attention to the pastor, who was hanging the tablecloth across the unsightly hole. When the woman looked up and saw the cloth, she rushed to the altar.

"It's mine!" she exclaimed. "It's my banquet cloth!"

Excitedly she told the surprised minister its history and even showed him her initials embroidered in one corner.

She and her husband had lived in Vienna, Austria, and had opposed the Nazis before the Second World War. They decided to flee to Switzerland, but her husband said they must go separately. She left first. Later she heard that he had died in a concentration camp.

Touched by her story, the minister insisted she take the cloth. She thought about it for a moment but said no, she didn't need it any longer, and it did look pretty hanging behind the altar. Then she said goodbye and left.

In the candlelight of the Christmas Eve services, the tablecloth looked even more magnificent. The white lace seemed dazzling in the flickering light of the candles, and the golden threads woven through it were like the brilliant rays of a new dawn.

As members of the congregation left the church, they complimented the pastor on the services and on how beautiful the church looked.

One older gentleman lingered, admiring the tablecloth, and as he was leaving he said to the minister:

"It's strange. Many years ago my wife — God rest her — and I owned such a tablecloth. She used it only on very special occasions. But we lived in Vienna then."

The night air was freezing, but the goosebumps on the pastor's skin weren't caused by the weather. As calmly as he could, he told the man about the woman who had been to the church that very afternoon.

"Can it be," gasped the old man, tears streaming down his cheeks, "that she is alive? How can I find her?"

The pastor remembered the name of the family who had interviewed the woman. With the trembling old man at his side, he telephoned the family and learned her name and address.

In the pastor's old car they drove to her home on the other side of town. Together they knocked on her apartment door. When she opened it, the pastor witnessed the tearful, joyful and thrilling reunion of husband and wife.

Some people would call it an extremely lucky chance happening, the result of a hole in the church wall, an old tablecloth, a pastor's ingenuity in solving a problem and so on. But the combination of events was far too complex for it to have been merely "coincidence."

If one link in the fragile chain of events had been broken, the husband and wife might never have found each other. If the rain hadn't come, if the church roof hadn't leaked, if the pastor had decided not to go to the auction, if the woman hadn't been looking for a job or standing on that corner at just the right time.... The list of ifs is virtually endless.

It was simply God's will. And, as it has been said many times, He works in mysterious ways.

~Richard Bauman

Chicken Soup for the Christian Family Soul

78

Disappearing Dave

None are as fiercely loyal as dog people. In return, no
doubt, for the never-ending loyalty of dogs.
~Linda Shrieves

He was named "David Letterman" by the teenage son of the first family that owned him. And like David Letterman, he was a rogue through-and-through, a rogue in a tuxedo — all black with a white beard and a white ruff at his neck. When he ate spaghetti, his beard would turn orange. I was told there were ten puppies in his litter, and they all looked alike, except Dave.

We lived down the street from his original family. The children were away at college and returned only sporadically, so the mother had given her blessing for Dave to come and live with us. My brother and I were in elementary school, and we couldn't wait to get home every day to play with Dave. But Dave always knew when his first family's son was home on a break from school, and he would run away from our house and drop by for a weekend visit with them. We speculated on how he knew the son was home. Could he distinguish among the sounds of different car engines?

Dave was well known for other small disappearances, as well. He would go from house to house, gathering up any other dogs who could get loose, and together they would go marauding — knocking over trashcans and gobbling up chicken bones and other food.

There were woods behind our house, and Dave often chased after a deer, raccoon, or opossum. Sometimes, he came home skunked, and we would give him a bath with tomato juice. On the other side of the woods, there was an ice cream stand that also sold pizza and sandwiches. Dave often emerged triumphantly from the woods with a stale bun locked in his jaws. How he got the buns out of the tall Dumpster, I can't imagine, since he was a medium-sized dog, fifty-five pounds at most.

His other trick at the ice cream stand was to walk up to the front, just as a regular customer would, and place his order. He would stand up with his paws on the countertop and howl until someone bought him a cone, or the owner, fed up with the noise, thrust one through the little window.

Once, when I went to look for him, a blond girl with chocolate ice cream on her face said to me, "That's the dog that ate my brother's ham sandwich!" I could picture it — the boy standing there dumbfounded while Dave happily scarfed down the goods. "Come on, Dave," I said, grabbing him by the collar and beating a hasty retreat.

When our friends and neighbors saw Dave loitering at the ice cream stand, they would stop and pick him up. He would happily get into anyone's car, sitting in the back seat with his ears perked up, confident they would chauffeur him home. Once in a while, someone we didn't know would pick him up and call the number on his tag, and we'd work out arrangements to have him dropped off or picked up.

And then he disappeared for good. After several months, we had to accept that he was not coming home. He never was very smart about crossing the road. He could have tangled with another opossum or one of the big beavers back in the pond.

An entire year went by, and nothing.

And then, on New Year's Eve, we heard a scratching at the screened door. It was Dave, with his tail wagging and his tongue hanging out. He was well fed, brushed, and had a red collar we had never seen before. It was a miracle.

We began making up stories about where Dave had been during his gap year. He sailed to Italy, the birthplace of spaghetti. He enjoyed the pizza, too, with pepperoni, sausage, and extra cheese. Then he hopped the train to Paris and took up sidewalk painting. He wore a beret and had a palette slung around his neck. He wintered in the Swiss Alps, catching snowballs thrown by blond ski bums, munching marshmallows and sleeping in a heap by the fire.

Although we never found out the truth, it was probably something like this: A little old lady picked him up at the ice cream stand and brought him to her house, kept him confined to a neatly fenced back yard, loved him, and fed him biscuits. He could not escape until New Year's Eve, when she had company who were careless about keeping the door closed.

After that, I always looked over my shoulder, afraid another family would come running up and say, "That's Blackie! That's our dog!" But I shouldn't have worried. After all of his adventures, Dave had come home to stay.

In his later years, Dave would sit under the maple tree as if he were on an invisible chain. We joked that he was retired. His hearing and eyesight went. When you threw him a ball, he would come back with a stick, or not come back at all, hiding around the corner of the house to take a break.

My brother and I grew up, too. When I came home after my first semester in college, Dave couldn't see or hear me. I knelt down and put my arms around him, and he shoved his snout into my sweater. When he smelled me, he began to shake all over with excitement. I realized then that he had had no idea where I had been for all those months, or if I was ever coming home again. That was his own little holiday miracle.

~Gwen Hart

Chicken Soup for the Soul: The Dog Really Did That?

79

The Christmas Dance

You may be only one person in this world, but to one
person at one time, you are the world.
~Author Unknown

I have a particular fondness for grumpy old men. Perhaps because of this, they tend to be less grumpy around me.

In my work as a speech pathologist in a hospital, I cross paths with many such elderly gents. The one I remember the most is Harry. Harry was a fiercely independent soul and landed in the hospital after a stroke (thus, my involvement — he had speech deficits). Feisty and "difficult," Harry alienated many staff, yet he and I formed a close bond. Though he never said so, I think he found comfort in having someone try to communicate with him despite his poor speech.

Harry had a double whammy with his speech; he had grown up in Eastern Europe and never lost his thick accent, nor become fully fluent in English. He muddled along in speech therapy, using writing to communicate when the words just couldn't be understood. I never knew if it was the stroke or his age that gave him his stooped posture and shuffling gait.

He came into the hospital in November and was anxious to return home as soon as possible. As the end of December neared, he became more and more "crotchety" as his agitation and impatience grew. After numerous frustrating sessions, I finally found out why. Though he'd kept it private before, Harry admitted he was married. His wife, Delores, now lived in a nursing home, and suffered from severe dementia.

They met later in life; he said he fell in love with her spirit and with her long white hair. She had been sick for more of their marriage than she had been well. Yet prior to coming into the hospital, Harry had visited his wife every day. Every single day, no matter what.

Naturally, Harry wanted to see Delores at Christmas. The medical team resisted — Harry continued to have cognitive deficits that would make it impossible for him to be discharged safely to live alone just then. I wondered what could be done. So, after much internal deliberation (and consultation with colleagues), I offered to take Harry to see his wife the week before Christmas. He was delighted, and the doctors agreed to allow him a two-hour pass for the visit.

The change was magical. I had never seen Harry look as happy as he did that day. He combed his wispy hair and pestered the nurses to help him shave. Though our two-hour time limit for the visit was brief, he insisted on stopping on the way to buy his wife a poinsettia. He told me she had always loved to have them around during the holidays, and he wanted her to see it and know she was loved.

Despite staff attempts at warmness, nursing homes during the holidays have a heavy air of loss and sadness. Delores's was no exception. We found her in the dining room sleeping in her chair with her white hair draped like a curtain across her face. She barely looked up at her husband as he tenderly woke her. Cafeteria noises tinkled in the background as he led her back to her room.

Once there, Harry fussed around and placed the poinsettia on his wife's bedside table. The air in the room was warm, yet the bare white walls and plain hospital style décor made it feel cold. An uneaten dinner sat on a tray on the small bedside table. Harry cut up the cold turkey and coaxed his wife to eat. While her face remained blank, she allowed him to feed her.

Then, he turned on the radio. The signal was weak but a CBC Christmas special drifted out, with Bing Crosby's "White Christmas" playing softly. When Delores heard the music she looked up and seemed to really see Harry for the first time since our arrival. She reached out to him shakily and touched his clean-shaven face. Harry closed his eyes for a brief moment as she traced her finger along his cheek.

Then he took her hand and pulled her gently from the armchair, his unsteadiness magically quelled as he focused on his wife. They stood facing each other, not speaking. And then they danced. Her hands stayed gently on his face; his hands moved to her hips. A slow tender swaying dance. Delores's green eyes never left Harry's face, and she would occasionally hum through smiling lips. Harry glowed with love. I had never seen anyone, "crotchety" or not, express as pure a love.

It is a moment I will never forget, because that day I learned what it means "to love and cherish until death do us part." Most of us avoid thinking about what these words mean if our partner continues to live, but lives between the lines. Harry simply and generously lived this truth far past what many would consider necessary.

Though Delores spent the majority of her days lost within herself, Harry brought her out of herself in that Christmas dance. He loved her enough to invite those moments, savour them with her, and let the memory sustain him until the next time. I had often heard the term "unconditional love," but the day I watched Harry dancing with his wife, I finally knew what it meant.

~Crystal Johnson

Chicken Soup for the Soul: O Canada The Wonders of Winter

80

Life, What a Beautiful Gift

Perfect love sometimes does not come
till the first grandchild.
~Welsh Proverb

I t was the first week in December. My daughter Julie and I had decided to go Christmas shopping. We have always been extra close, and I always looked forward to this special time together. We would do some "serious" shopping, go out for lunch, and catch up on what was happening in each other's lives.

Over lunch, we discussed what gifts we would buy our relatives and friends. I always felt this was a real chore, as I was always worried about treating all five of my children equally, finding something they didn't already have. Julie, on the other hand, is a person who always seems to find the perfect gift for everyone. Everything has to be the perfect color, the perfect size, the perfect scent! She goes back and forth, from store to store, to get the best bargain.

That day, while eating, our conversation somehow switched from Christmas gifts to life's blessings. This made both of us think of my illness. Although I had been extremely sick several times, for the most part, I still considered myself truly blessed. In fact there had been several times when my M.S. or lupus were out of remission, and my doctor said it was indeed a miracle that I was still alive. Maybe it was a miracle, or maybe God just had other plans for me.

Realizing how lucky I was, when Julie asked me what I wanted for Christmas, I tried to tell her without ruining her Christmas spirit, that I didn't expect or even want a present. I explained just getting together with my beautiful family was all I could hope for.

Julie looked disappointed in my reply. "Oh, Mom," she said, "you are always so darn practical! There has to be something little you want."

I repeated what I had said, "I have a fantastic husband, beautiful children, and now two beautiful granddaughters. I have it all! What more could anyone want in one life?" I was speaking with my entire heart. I truly felt that way. I loved my family so much that little else was important. Each day I thanked God for giving me yet one more twenty-four hours to share with them.

Suddenly, without even thinking, I added, "I know this is selfish, but you know, I really would love to have a grandson before I die! Now that would be neat!"

Julie just shook her head, and said, "I give up!"

"Well, you asked what I would like, didn't you? I have always wanted a grandson! I love little boys! I'll never forget how happy I was to have your brother after all you girls! Oh, I love all of you equally, that is for certain, but there is something very special about little boys! Now if you can find a way to get me a grandson before Christmas, I will take him and love him without complaining!"

"You're impossible!" Julie added. "Let's finish our shopping. You won't accept a little gift, yet you ask for the world! Mothers!"

Hours later, Julie dropped me off at my house. Exhausted from shopping, I hugged her and promised to let her know if I thought of anything "easier" for her to get for me.

When I went in the house, the first thing I did was check our new answering machine for messages. The blinking red light indicated there were several.

The first message was another daughter whose voice assured me that she was concerned because I had gone away for that long without first obtaining permission! I thought it was ironic remembering the times my children had forgotten to call me when they were going to be late. Funny how time changes roles. The second message was to remind me of an upcoming craft auction at church, and the third to confirm a dental appointment. Who needed to be reminded of such things? I started to walk out of the room, when I heard the last voice, that of my husband. He sounded more than a little confused.

"Barb! Are you home? If you are home, then pick this thing up! Can't you hear me? I need to talk to you... Q-U-I-C-K!" Frustrated, when at last he realized he was talking to an electronic piece of equipment, he lowered his voice and said, "Please, Honey, when you get home... CALL ME!"

Wow! This was so unlike the cool man I was used to! What could be wrong? I knew I had to call him back at once.

Call I did. It was not only a shocking call, but also an unplanned answer to a prayer, and that something little I had wanted for my Christmas gift. About the same time I was telling Julie that I would like a grandson before my life was finished, a young girl in a nearby town had called my husband at work to tell him that she was the mother of a little grandson we had never met! We were both in shock. This woman explained she had a brief relationship with our son, had gotten pregnant, and had a little boy who was now seven months old! She said she had pleaded with our son to tell us about the baby. However, he was afraid we would be disappointed in him if we knew, so he had made her promise not to tell.

For some unknown reason that day, she had decided that it was unfair to us to keep this grandchild a secret any longer. Since our home number was unlisted, she had called the place my husband worked and told him the story.

My husband gave me the woman's number, and said she had told him I was free to make arrangements to meet our little grandson if I liked. Grandson! Liked? I was a doubting Thomas. I had to see for myself. I called the woman, and within an hour, I was on the way to see this baby. If she was telling the truth I had a grandson! No matter how complicated the details of his conception were, I knew I would love him. I was happy, sad, excited and tearful all at the same time.

When I arrived at the given address, I was met at the door by the woman and her other children. I sensed all of them were trying to evaluate me, and this made me feel terribly uncomfortable. My first impulse was to turn and run. Something within me told me I had to stay. I offered her my hand; she took it. She invited me inside. Walking ahead of me to a nearby table, she picked up an envelope and handed it to me. "Here are the paternity papers," she said. "Here's proof that Toby is your grandson!"

I had just learned something else: Her baby's name was Toby. I questioned the baby's last name, and I was told he had received my son's last name the previous day in court.

Nearly collapsing, I lowered myself to the nearest chair. I didn't realize the girl had left the room until I saw her return, carrying a little boy. She walked up to me, placed the most beautiful little baby into my arms, and said, "Son, I think it is time you meet your grandma!" Toby looked right up at me and gave me the biggest smile... I cried.

At that moment, little Toby became a very important part of my life. My son and the baby's mother had made a big mistake. However, God himself had created little Toby, and God doesn't make mistakes. I had a grandson! A beautiful bundle of joy! What a precious Christmas gift!

Later that evening, my husband and I had a long talk with our son. We told him we knew about Toby, and I was hurt that he could even think for a moment that his father and I could have loved him less for having made a mistake. I told him if we only love our children when they live their lives the way we feel they should, then that isn't really love. He told me that when Toby's mother first discovered she was pregnant, she had considered an abortion, and we cried together, thanking God she hadn't. Later, we even laughed a little over the speedy way in which God seemed to answer my Christmas gift request!

Since then many Christmases have passed. Toby spends a lot of time with his father and with us, as well. Every day, but especially on Christmas, I am so thankful for this very special gift I received eight years ago.

~Barbara Jeanne Fisher

Chicken Soup for the Grandparent's Soul

81

The Day Time Stopped

I believe in prayer. It's the best way we
have to draw strength from heaven.
~Josephine Baker

The mantel clock on the brick fireplace did not chime at mid-morning on July 21st. Coincidentally, the battery-operated clock hanging on the pantry wall stopped a little before noon. Even the cuckoo clock stopped its perpetual tick-tock.

I put water on for tea and forgot it. The metallic stench of the kettle burning filtered through the house. I raised the kitchen windows and let the humid heat intrude through the screens. Shortly afterward, a fireman came, but not because of the burning kettle. He checked the water temperature from all of the faucets and peeked into my dishwasher. He checked the locks on the doors. With a grand smile, he left a scribbled report on the dining room table. And before the navy uniform slipped into the haze of the summer day, he said, "This is for the social worker from the Division of Children and Youth Services. Her name is Shaunna, and she will be here with the baby in a couple of hours."

I floated to the doorway of the spare bedroom, empty for three long years. It loomed with an echo for more than thirty-six menstrual cycles and more than 12,040 days of prayers. Empty tan walls, cleanly painted, looked back at me. No pictures brightened the room, no clothes hung in its closet, and no lamps invited anyone to visit. The room waited, longing for a baby to bring life to its bleakness and cure the vast solitude. The room twirled in time; I dozed and daydreamed back to the past three Christmases.

* * *

Snow clung to the windows. I draped festive holly across the fireplace mantel and fastened a red velvet bow to the brass fixture on the mantel clock. It chimed, the classic centerpiece illuminated by white twinkles of light. I placed my hands across my belly and smiled. Surely there would be a baby next Christmas. God was good and wonderful, I knew. The thought of a newborn by the tree or growing in my womb filled me with joy. I sat in the bentwood rocker and felt the beauty of the Christmas season. I prayed, "Lord, a baby next Christmas, please?"

The following year was fraught with visits to the infertility clinic. Marital vocabulary and conversations included words like hystersalpingograms, sperm counts and motility, Clomid, AIH, artificial insemination, and fertility calendar. I found excuses for skipping friends' baby showers. I hurried by the diaper and baby food aisles, and left the room during Pampers commercials.

The next Christmas season arrived with fragrant boughs and the red velvet bow adorning the clock's crown again. With each quarter-hour chime, I prayed, "Maybe a baby next year, Lord, maybe a baby next year." I rocked and let my tears make a white haze of the Christmas tree.

Another year passed with no hint of a pregnancy. Christmas vacation began with a blizzard. Driving through the snow, I felt like I was breaking inside. A huge lump formed in my throat, and I became angry with God. "No baby again?" I cried. "Why are you so good to others and not to me!"

"Relax!" my husband said. "There's no rush. We're fine! It'll happen when it happens."

He didn't understand. Something was wrong inside my head and my body. I could feel no pain, but neither could I feel joy. I immersed myself in a master's degree program and in music at church. I taught, wrote, developed curriculum, and kept a basal thermometer by my bed to remind my husband of when it was time for "baby-making days."

Another Christmas — no baby. The fireplace mantel and candlelit windows were storybook. I rocked and rocked and felt nothing. Nothing. Nothing. I thought the tree stared awkwardly at me. At times, I fancied it mocked me. I shivered in front of the fire and sweat in the snowy night. I felt large in my slender body. Doubtful and sad, I wanted to pray, "Maybe a baby next year, Lord, maybe a baby next year," but I felt God had abandoned me.

* * *

The telephone rang, jolting me from my nap. Christmases past flew into the blank tan walls of the spare room, and I jumped. Dazed, I answered the phone.

"It's me," said my husband. "I'm picking up a crib at the house. Ma said it's in good shape. It will be a while. Dad and I have to dig it out in the attic."

"The social worker called," I said with a bit of fear. "She said they can't leave the baby unless we have a crib."

"Don't worry," he assured me.

Miriam, a home-finder for foster care who knew of us, had called earlier that morning. "A failure-to-thrive eight-week-old boy needs bonding immediately. He's been neglected and abandoned. He was removed on Friday when a relative called and said, 'The baby's life is in danger.' He needs to be in a foster home until the parental rights are terminated. The process may take up to a year, perhaps more, but then you'd be able to adopt."

Everything became a beautiful blur. We were becoming emergency licensed foster parents with the intent to adopt. I was going to be a mother!

I went back to the empty room. Suddenly, I saw where the crib would be. I became a whirlwind of creation. I lifted a blue braided rug from the dining room and pulled the rocker into the spare room. *The baby's room*, I thought with imaginative awe.

An eight-week-old baby boy was to be delivered in two hours!

The doorbell rang before my husband was home with the crib. Shaunna, a sweet woman in her twenties, stood cradling an infant the size of a newborn! Time stopped. With a full smile, Shaunna shifted the sleeping baby boy into my arms.

I really didn't know how to hold a baby. As we walked inside, she gently showed me how to hold his weak, tiny head. I couldn't take my eyes off him. Sleeping, his eyelashes drifted down to his cheeks. Only a thin layer of skin covered his malnourished body. His full lips were pursed into a pout. But when he opened his eyes... Lord, when he opened his eyes... his soul saw mine. With adoption, he would be Joseph Patrick, the son of my soul.

* * *

"You sent me my baby this Christmas, Lord. You sent me a baby this year!" Not yet adopted, he was a thriving seven-month-old struggling to sit up by himself. However, the following Christmas would be a sacred celebration of answered prayers. We signed adoption papers three days before Christmas, and he was baptized the following evening.

That Christmas the tree stood like a regal king. I fancied it honored me. White lights were diamond gems, stars of the Christmastide. I rocked and rocked and glowed like the velvet bow on the clock as it chimed. My prayers had been answered. I became a mother in three hours, the day three clocks stopped... the day time stopped to answer prayers.

~Patricia Barrett

Chicken Soup for the Soul: New Moms

82

The Hanukkah Parade

May love and light fill your home
and heart at Hanukkah.
~Author Unknown

Originally from Austria, my sweet grandmother was a small woman, barely five feet tall. Her two-foot-tall candelabrum was more than just a candleholder. It was a family symbol, a magnet that brought us all together. On Shabbat evenings, Baba (Jewish for grandmother) would don a special Shabbat kerchief, a white linen square with a border of delicate lace. With great fanfare she would light each candle. Once she had finished lighting the last candle she would stand in front of the candelabrum and close her eyes. Tears ran down her cheeks. She prayed for her husband, her married children and for us, her grandchildren. She spoke in Yiddish, *"Her mein tier tata, hiet oif mein man, kinder un di eyniklach."* (My Dear Father, watch over my husband, my children and my grandchildren.)

We all stood by the Shabbat table in awe. Baba looked like a queen speaking to the King of Kings, to Almighty God himself. When she finished her prayer, we began our Shabbat.

As our family grew, my grandmother spent more time with her candles. By the time she reached her ninetieth birthday she had many married grandchildren with children of their own. There were now five generations in my baba's family. Before every Shabbat, Baba would shine her silver candelabrum and pray, "May my *mazel* (luck) always shine!" When lighting the candles, she prayed for each family member, never omitting any of us.

Her candelabrum was made of solid silver with a heavy silver base. All year it had three branches, each with two candlesticks. In the middle was a stem for another candle. The traditional custom for Shabbat is to light one candle each for the father, mother and children. As each child is born, another candle is added to the Shabbat lighting. For most of the year Baba's candelabrum was fitted for six candles.

But during the week of Hanukkah, she would add another branch of two candlesticks each, making a total of ten candles. Her candelabrum was built in such a way that the candleholders could be removed so that oil cups could be inserted for the special lighting on Hanukkah. Our Shabbat candelabrum was thus transformed into a beautiful Hanukkah menorah.

During the eight days of Hanukkah, she turned over her prized menorah to my Zaida (Jewish for grandfather) to light the candles for the holiday. Hanukkah was our happiest time. All of us children, grandchildren and great-grandchildren came to Baba and Zaida to receive Hanukkah *gelt* (a small gift of money, usually a fifty-cent-piece or two) and join in the lighting of the menorah.

Imagine the two-foot menorah with ten candles shining in all its glory. Zaida stood proudly like a *Kohain*, the high priest in the temple, when he lit the candles.

When my Zaida died, Baba sold their two-story house in Winnipeg's north end to move to a tiny, one-bedroom apartment not far away. Although she couldn't take all of her cherished things, of course she packed her precious candelabrum. First she wrapped it in a large piece of worn, cotton flannel and then again in tissue paper. Then she placed it gently into the box she had made a special trip to get from California Fruit on Main Street.

But when the van drove away from her new apartment that day, after the movers had piled all the cardboard boxes containing her possessions in the middle of the living-room floor she was horrified to discover her treasured menorah was not there. Her first thought was it had accidentally been left in the back of the truck, or perhaps it was still at the old house. But after a call to the moving company and a visit back to the old house, it was clear that someone had stolen her menorah.

My baba was livid. Her small body shook like a willow in a storm as she spoke about her most prized possession. How could anyone take it? How would she light her candles?

But Baba believed her menorah would return. "I have prayed that the menorah would protect us, and I'm sure the menorah has done just that. Now I pray that the menorah protect itself and be returned to me." With silent determination she prayed and prayed. The family did not know what to do. The weather was growing colder and Hanukkah was fast approaching.

Then, one day in November, a childhood friend from Austria unexpectedly came to visit her. They had been friends for years, both here in Winnipeg after they married, and before that, as young girls in the old country. Upon arrival Mrs. Stern announced, "I never saw another menorah like yours until today. My mouth fell wide open when I saw a menorah exactly the same, in the window of the pawn shop I passed on Main Street, while walking here."

Baba immediately called my mother and her siblings. We were dumbfounded. Could it be that Baba's friend had actually seen the stolen menorah? Baba was now geared up and ready for action. "Let's get my menorah!" she declared. "It soon will be Hanukkah — and I need it back!"

Then she hastily pulled on her winter coat. Once we were all gathered, Baba, my parents and I, Aunty Tzeril and Uncle Simcha, Mrs. Stern, and our friendly neighbourhood policeman from the North-central Precinct made our way to the pawn shop. Baba was so excited she forgot to put on her headscarf, her gloves and her overshoes.

Her eyes sparkling, and with a shout of confirmation and sheer joy, when we arrived at the shop Baba pointed to her beloved menorah standing in the window just as Mrs. Stern had reported. With a quick movement, she bent her head toward it and spoke softly to it like an old and trusted friend. In Yiddish she whispered, "Yes, you have done well. You have protected us and now you have protected yourself. *Kim a haim mit mere.*" (Come home with me.)

Before anyone could say anything, Baba grabbed the menorah off the shelf and held it close to her heart. Nobody could stop her.

"Baba," I protested, "you can't just take it. That's stealing! It's against the law!" Much to my confusion, my mother clamped her hand over my mouth and imperiously marched me out of the store. Meanwhile, Aunty Tzeril stayed behind with the policeman and pawn shop owner "to do the paperwork."

By this time, the commotion had attracted quite a crowd. Neighbours, both Jewish and non-Jewish, joined my grandmother in her triumphant walk home. Along the way, the closer we got to her apartment building, more and more people joined us. My diminutive baba, still wearing her apron and house-slippers, marched proudly home, the menorah she was carrying almost as big as she was. She was followed by our ragtag procession of excited family, neighbours and friends. What a sight to see! It truly was a grand Hanukkah parade!

Today my baba's cherished menorah sits on my own mantel, right in the center, holding the position of honour. I polish it daily, making sure that it gleams, like she so lovingly did all those years ago.

~Sharon Melnicer

Chicken Soup for the Soul: Christmas in Canada

Chapter
9

A Book of
Christmas
Miracles

The Best of All Gifts

83

The Miracle

What greater gift than the love of a cat?
~Charles Dickens

"Alex! Don't move," I whisper to our gray and silver Manx. She sits still on the deck railing, her ears lying back against her head, hair standing on end, a most violent sound emanating from her throat. Ten feet past Alex is a black bear. The bear looks merely curious, but Alex, in her usual feisty mood, is certain she is going to attack anything that comes into the yard. She has already been known to break up a three-way dogfight and teach the neighbor's dog a lesson. And here I am standing in the line of fire between a black bear and her.

I know I should probably go inside, but I'm terrified to leave Alex. I continue to soothe her. "Shhh, it's okay he's just curious. He means no harm. And if he did I'm pretty sure you wouldn't win." I pet the top of her head. The bear cocks his head and slowly saunters back into the woods. My legs turn to Jelly with relief. "Goodness cat, I don't know where you get your attitude from but it sure is something."

"Are you talking to the cat again?" My husband ventures outside.

"Yep. Just talking her down from scrapping it out with a black bear. You know — everyday conversation." I grin. "Speaking of animals, when is Gunnar bringing Walker over?"

"He said he would bring him over tomorrow and they will pick him up again in December."

"I sure hope he and Alex get along. Even though he's a Doberman and looks intimidating, I'm still worried she is going to beat him up. I would hate to let your brother down."

"No kidding. Let's just see how it goes tomorrow."

The day is upon us and Walker has been left in our care for a few months. "Hey Walker, buddy, how are you?" I scratch our temporary resident's ears. Alex is sitting close by. She eyes him but surprisingly hasn't made her usual fuss. Walker doesn't seem to mind her either. He hasn't barked, growled or even tried to chase her. He is such a good dog. I'm at ease the rest of the day. Yes, this will work out well.

"Todd, have you seen Alex? I've been calling for her since I got up this morning." I peer into the woods, wondering where she could be. The early morning fall frost is still fresh on the step. "It's so unlike her. She is usually right at my heels looking for her ears to be scratched."

"No, I haven't seen her. Did Walker chase her off?" He looks puzzled.

"I don't think so. He hasn't even gone near her. I'm going to go ask the neighbors if anyone has seen her." I head off to ask around.

Hours later I'm home with no good news. I plunk down on the deck steps next to my husband. "Nothing. No one has seen her." I lay my head on his shoulder, weary with worry about my cat. "I guess we'll just keep looking. I won't give up on her."

"I know you won't. Maybe Walker told her where to go," he jokes, trying to lighten the mood. "Or maybe she thinks we replaced her," he wonders seriously.

I jump up. "Here kitty kitty." I walk off into the woods looking for her.

The snow is gently falling. It's been three months since we have seen Alex. I put her food out. It doesn't seem like it ever disappears but I refresh it daily. Hoping beyond hope that she is out there somewhere. I pause at Walker's dish. I don't need to fill his dish today; he went home with Gunnar. It sure is lonely without the furry babies around. I look up at the snowflakes gently falling. I wonder if God would hear my prayer.

"God, wherever Alex is, please take care of her. I know she might be with you, or maybe just living with someone a few roads over, but wherever she is, please keep her safe. Especially tonight on Christmas Eve. I wish I could see her again. Amen."

I head indoors for the typical Christmas Eve festivities. The cookies are laid out for Santa with his milk. I write a quick note.

Dear Santa,
All I want for Christmas is my cat.
xoxoxo

Todd and I hit the bed exhausted. It's a restless, dreamless sleep. I clamber out of bed during the wee morning hours. The bathroom window is illuminated with bright moonlight. Beautiful sparkling snow shining in the moonlight. It's magical. I notice right where the moonbeams come down onto the yard sits a little animal, quiet, not moving. It's very small, like a cat. It doesn't move a muscle. I squint. *Oh my goodness, it looks just like Alex. But no, it can't be. She's been gone for over three months. I blink and the yard is empty. I rub my eyes. I must have been dreaming or hallucinating.* I hurry and go back to bed. Again I fall into a restless sleep but I dream of a gray and silver Manx curled up next to me.

"Mom! Mom! Mom and Dad get up! Santa came!" The kids are hopping up and down on the bed.

We stumble out to our recliners and watch the gift opening through squinty, sleepy eyes, inserting oooh's and ahhh's in the right places. All the gifts have been opened. The kids are playing quietly with their new toys. I am enjoying the quiet when I hear a knocking at the door. *Who in the world could that be at this hour?* I hop up from my chair and answer the door. When I open it I see no one looking at me, but I hear the sound again coming from the lower part of the screen door. I glance down and there sits my beautiful baby. Gray and silver, fluffy and fit. I stand awestruck for several seconds, sure that she must be an illusion.

"Meow." And she paws the door again.

"Honey, who is it?" Todd is asking.

"It's Alex... It's ALEX!" I gently open the door and scoop her into my arms. I squeeze her, hug her, kiss her, tears stream down my face.

Todd comes to inspect the miracle.

The kids come running. "Alex! Alex! Alex!"

I'm crying as I hold my beautiful gray and silver cat, my husband's arms around me. Our kids are jumping up and down around us, cheering. Hugs and kisses, and "oh we missed you" all around. It's the most beautiful sight. It's the most beautiful moment.

The moment is ours. Our family's most special moment. A miracle witnessed and the best Christmas ever.

~Denise Taylor

Chicken Soup for the Soul: The Cat Did What?

A True Christmas

You don't choose your family. They are
God's gift to you, as you are to them.
~Desmond Tutu

I plopped the last of the ready-made cookie dough onto the cookie sheet and shoved it into the oven. These standard-issue chocolate chip cookies would be a far cry from the bejeweled affairs I'd baked for twenty-six years, but the only reason I'd even summoned the effort was because my youngest son, Ross, had opened and re-opened the cookie jar four times the previous night, saying with fourteen-year-old tact, "What? No Christmas cookies this year?"

Since today was the twenty-third, and his older siblings, Patrick and Molly, would be arriving Christmas Eve, Ross informed me that they would be "big-time disappointed" if there wasn't "cool stuff" to eat. This from the same kid who had never watched a Christmas TV special in his life and who had to be dragged into the family photo for the annual Christmas card.

I never considered a family picture this year. A big piece of the family was now missing — or hadn't anybody noticed?

All my friends had been telling me the same thing since the day of the funeral:

"Pam, the first year after you lose your husband is the hardest. You have to go through the first Valentine's Day without him, the first birthday, the first anniversary..."

The Best of All Gifts | 315

They hadn't been kidding. What they hadn't told me was that Christmas was going to top them all in hard-to-take. It wasn't that Tom had loved Christmas that much. He'd always complained that the whole thing was too commercial and that when you really thought about it, Easter seemed to be a much more important Christ-centered celebration in the church.

The phone rang. Molly was calling collect from the road. She and two dorm buddies were driving home after finals.

"Do you know what I'm looking forward to?" she said.

"Sleeping for seventy-two straight hours?" I asked.

"No." She sounded a little deflated. "Coming home from Christmas Eve services and seeing all those presents piled up under the tree. It's been years since I've cared what was in them or how many were for me — I just like seeing them there. How weird is that?"

Not weird at all, my love, I thought. I sighed, took a piece of paper and penciled in a few gift ideas for Ross, Molly, Patrick, his wife Amy and my grandson, Shane.

And then I snapped the pencil down on the counter. A part of me understood that the kids were in denial. Tom's sudden death eleven months earlier had left them bewildered and scared. And now at Christmas, their shock was translated into exaggerated enthusiasm. The Cobb family Christmas traditions provided a sense of normalcy for them. Patrick had even asked me last week if I still had the old John Denver Christmas album.

But as far as I was concerned, there just wasn't that much to deck the halls about. Tom was gone. I was empty and unmotivated. At worst, I wished they'd all just open the presents and carve the turkey without me.

When the oven dinged, I piled two dozen brown circles on a plate and left a note for Ross: "I don't want to hear any more complaining! Gone shopping. I love you, Mom."

The complaining, however, went on in my head as I elbowed my way through the mob at the mall.

Tom was right, I thought. This is all a joke.

It really was everything he hated: canned music droning its false merriment, garish signs luring me to buy, tired-looking families dragging themselves around, worrying about their credit card limits as they snapped at their children.

Funny, I thought while gazing at a display of earrings I knew Molly wouldn't wear. All the time Tom was here pointing this out to me, it never bothered me. Now it's all I can see.

I abandoned the earring idea and took to wandering the mall, hoping for inspiration so Molly would have something to look at under the tree. It wasn't going to be like years past — I should have told her that. She wasn't going to see a knee-deep collection of exquisitely wrapped treasures that Tom always shook his head over.

"You've gone hog-wild again," he would always tell me — before adding one more contribution. Instead of buying me a gift, he'd write a check in my name to Compassion International or a local food pantry, place it in a red envelope, and tuck it onto a branch of our Christmas tree.

"This is a true Christmas gift," he'd tell me. "It's a small demonstration that Christ is real in our lives."

I stopped mid-mall, letting the crowds swirl past me.

Tom wasn't there, a fact that the rest of the family didn't want to face or discuss. But he could still be with us, maybe just a little.

I left the mall and quickly found a Christmas tree lot. The man looked happy to unload one very dry tree for half price. He even tied it to my roof rack.

Then it was off to Safeway, where I bought a twenty-four-pound Butterball turkey and all the trimmings. Back home, the decoration boxes weren't buried too deeply in the garage. I'd barely gotten them put away last year when Tom had his heart attack.

I was still sorting boxes when Ross emerged from the kitchen, munching the last of the two dozen cookies.

"Oh, I thought we weren't going to have a tree this year," he said between mouthfuls.

"Well, we are. Can you give me a hand getting it up?"

Two hours later, Ross and I stood back and admired our Christmas tree. The lights winked softly as I straightened a misshapen glittery angel

Molly had made in second grade and Ross's first birthday Christmas ball.

I wanted to cry.

The house sprang to life when everyone arrived Christmas Eve. In the middle of our church service, however, my spirits sagged. There was no lonelier feeling than standing in the midst of one's family singing "Silent Night" — surrounded by a vivacious college daughter; a sweet, gentle daughter-in-law; a handsome, successful twenty-five-year-old son; a wide-eyed, mile-a-minute three-year-old grandson; and an awkward teenager whose hugs were like wet shoelaces — and being keenly aware that someone was missing.

Back at home everyone continued to avoid the subject.

"The tree is gorgeous, Mom," Molly said. She knelt down and began hauling gifts out of a shopping bag to add to my pile.

"I love what you did with the wrappings, Pam," Amy said. "You're always so creative."

"I forgot to buy wrapping paper," I told her. "I had to use newspaper."

It was Christmas as usual — easier to pretend everything was normal than to deal with harsh reality. Ross and Patrick sparred over whose stocking was whose, and Shane parked himself in front of a bowl of M&Ms. They all got to open the customary one present on Christmas Eve, and after doing so, they schlepped off to bed.

But there was one more thing that had to be done. I went over to Tom's desk, found a red envelope in the top drawer, and stuck into it a check made out to the American Heart Association. It seemed appropriate.

"I know the kids — and even I — have to go on with our lives, Tom," I whispered. "But I wish you were here."

It occurred to me as I tucked the red envelope midway up the tree that one of the kids would say, "Oh, yeah — I remember, he always did that," and then there would be an awkward silence and perhaps sheepish looks.

I hoped so.

Morning, or at least dawn — came way too soon. Shane was up before the paper carrier. I dragged myself into the kitchen and found it already smelling like a Seattle coffeehouse.

"This is what we drink at school," Molly told me and handed me a cup.

"Is anyone else awake?" I asked.

She nodded her head, and for the first time I noticed a twinkle in her eye that was unprecedented for this hour of the morning. "What are you up to?" I asked.

"Mom!" Patrick yelled from the living room. "You've got to see this!"

"At this hour of the..."

What I saw was my family perched on the couch like a row of deliciously guilty canaries. What I saw next was our Christmas tree, dotted with bright red envelopes.

"Man, it got crowded in here last night," Ross said. "I came down here about one o'clock and freaked Amy out."

"I almost called 911 when I came down," Patrick said, "until I saw it was Molly and not some burglar."

I had never heard a thing. I walked over to the tree and touched each one of the five envelopes I hadn't put there.

"Open them, Mom," Molly said. "This was always the best part of Christmas."

From Patrick, there was a check to Youth for Christ, to help kids go on mission trips like the one Dad supported him on to Haiti five years earlier. From Amy, a check to our church for sheet music, because some of her best memories of her father-in-law were of him helping the children's choir. From Molly, several twenty-dollar bills for the local crisis pregnancy center, "because many of the women who go there have probably never experienced the love of a husband like Daddy," she said. From Ross, a twenty-dollar bill for a local drug program for kids, "since Dad was all freaked out about me staying clean."

The last envelope was lumpy. When I opened it, a handful of change spilled out.

"Mine, Gamma," Shane said, his little bow-mouth pursed importantly. Amy finished his thought. "He wants this to go to the animal shelter — you know, for lost dogs. Like the one he visited with Dad just before he died."

I pulled all the envelopes against my chest and hugged them.

"You know what's weird?" Molly said. "I feel like Daddy's right here with us."

"Yeah, that's pretty weird," Ross said.

"But true," Patrick said. "I feel like he's been here this whole time. I thought I'd be all bummed out this Christmas—but I don't need to be."

"No, you don't, my love," I said. To myself, I added, Neither do I. I have my family, and I have my faith.

~Nancy Rue

Chicken Soup for the Soul: Christmas Treasury

Gifts to Keep

Grandma's heart is a Patchwork of Love.
~Author Unknown

O nly three Christmas gifts were under the artificial fir tree. All the other presents had been opened. These three big packages were wrapped identically, green ribbon tied around red-and-white striped foil. Inside were gifts that my mom had planned to give her three grandchildren — my son, daughter, and niece. Gifts she had begun making, but didn't finish. A heart attack had ended her life in April.

Six months later, Dad sold the family home and moved into a one-bedroom apartment. The first Christmas without Mom was made even sadder as our family sat cramped in a small living room — so different from Mom and Dad's home where we'd always celebrated past Christmases.

Dad looked at his three teenage grandchildren. "Those presents are for you from your grannie," he said as my brother and I and our spouses sat nearby. Alicia and Sarah, age seventeen, and Eric, age fifteen, all frowned. "She was making something special for you to have this Christmas," Dad said. He looked at me as tears flooded his eyes and then he lowered his head.

Taking a deep breath, I said, "It's three almost identical gifts."

"Is it something we asked for?" Alicia asked.

"No," Dad said. "It's something you can use now. Your grannie

hoped you'd each keep it and maybe even pass it on to your kids."
The teenagers sat up straight, pulled their shoulders back, raised their
eyebrows, and looked at each other.

"Is it something that we've seen her working on?" Sarah asked.

"No, she kept it a secret from all of you. But your parents and I
knew," Dad said.

"So, how do we know which box is ours?" asked Eric.

"By numbers. The same way Grannie always let you choose. Take
one of those folded papers in the basket. They're numbered 1, 2, 3, and
the presents have numbers on the bottom of them," Dad explained.

As Alicia, Sarah, and Eric held the unopened gifts, silence filled
the small living room. They had quickly ripped into the other packages,
but now they sat cross-legged on the floor beside Dad's chair. Silent
and still. "Go ahead, open them," Dad said.

The teenagers paced themselves so that they saw their gifts at
the same time. "A quilt!" Sarah and Alicia said, almost in unison. Eric
stood and wrapped his quilt around his shoulders. It fell to the floor.
The girls did the same, holding their quilts close around their bodies.

"I love it!" Sarah said, "But Grannie always said that she'd never
make a quilt." She pulled her white and navy blue patchwork quilt
tighter around herself.

"This is beautiful! My quilt is just like yours. Same colors. Same
everything," Alicia said to Sarah. Then she turned to her brother.
"Yours is the same, except it's dark red. Almost maroon." They held
their quilts up and compared. The quilt pattern, with triangles and
rectangles, was exactly the same. All three quilts had solid white pieces
and some calico printed fabric; only the solid blue and maroon pieces
were different.

"Grannie made so many things but this is the best." Eric lifted his
quilt over his head and sat down on the floor. None of us adults said
anything. We wiped tears, coughed, and took deep breaths.

"Yeah, this is the best. But don't forget all the matching outfits
she made when we were little," said Alicia.

"Remember the stuffed Raggedy Ann and Andy dolls?" Eric said.

"Wonder why she decided to make us quilts now?" Alicia and Sarah held their quilts in their laps as they, too, sat on the floor.

Dad blew his nose, wiped his eyes with his wet handkerchief and said, "Your grannie wanted you to have something that you'd keep. You girls will be going off to college next year; maybe you can take your quilts with you. She began cutting and putting the pieces together about two years ago. She was determined to finish them for this Christmas, but…" Dad's voice faltered and he looked at me.

I continue the story. "She'd finished one, was quilting the second, and had pieced the third, but hadn't started quilting it."

"So who finished the quilts that Grannie didn't?" Sarah asked.

"Dad and I found a lady named Mrs. Horst who finished the last two. We really wanted you to all have your quilts for Christmas. Mrs. Horst is an excellent quilter and normally makes tiny stitches. When Grannie quilted, her stitches were much longer. Mrs. Horst wanted her quilting stitches to be exactly like Grannie's so the quilts would be the same," I said.

"She even wanted to do the binding exactly like the one your grannie did," Dad added. "She said quilters did bindings and corners differently and she did them the same way as the one that was finished." Alicia, Eric, and Sarah held the corners of their quilts close together.

"They look the same to me, " Eric said. All of us were silent —each in our own thoughts, as the lights on the tree twinkled in Dad's tiny apartment.

"Aunt Susan, do you know which one Grannie really made?" asked my niece Sarah. I shook my head and smiled.

"I'll answer that," said Dad. He blew his nose one more time. "She made them all. That wonderful lady stitched for your grannie. When we picked up the finished quilts, she told me that she'd said prayers of blessings as she quilted and she hoped that someday she could make such beautiful quilts for each of her five children."

The three quilts have been used and loved. They covered twin beds in college dormitory rooms and were moved to apartments when each of Mom's grandchildren married. And now, more than twenty years later, those quilts cover Mom's great-grandsons' beds. Mom's quilts were gifts to keep.

~Susan R. Ray

Chicken Soup for the Soul: For Mom, with Love

86

The Christmas Doll

Blessed is the season which engages the
whole world in a conspiracy of love!
~Hamilton Wright Mabie

It was the afternoon before Christmas Eve as I stared blearily at my youngest daughter's list. Major dental surgery two days earlier had left me swollen, in pain, and most definitely *not* in the holiday spirit.

To make matters worse, a certain creative young lady had provided me with the world's least helpful list:

"Something red. Something old. Something you can put things in. Something weird…"

Well, you get the idea.

After completing the massive grocery shopping necessary for an extended family gathering the next day, I was just plain tired and cranky.

But no matter how hard it was to please my daughter, I could not let her down. Then her older sister came up with the solution. The local antique emporium was sure to have something that fit the list of criteria.

Owned by an extremely nice couple, the place was a dusty maze packed with treasures and, well, not-so-valuable items.

And it was absolutely the *last* place I wanted to go.

Three years previously, I had left the place in tears after selling them my grandmother's silver flatware and my treasured composition ballerina doll. That year had been difficult, and though I told myself that things are only things, it hurt to trade my remaining cherished possessions for mundane items such as electricity and food. The shame of crying in public over it only made matters worse.

Still, after this period of time and with a grossly swollen face as a disguise, it was unlikely the owners would recognize me.

And, sure enough, the place offered gifts for every possible taste.

A one-eyed, stuffed baby alligator certainly qualified as "weird" in my book, while the antique red lacquered box earned points in at least two of the desired categories.

We took our treasures to the counter. As one owner tallied and wrapped, the other studied my face. "Dental surgery," I muttered, wondering where his usually impeccable manners had gone.

He disappeared into the back room while I paid. But as we turned to leave, he reappeared with my old doll cradled in his arms. "We knew you didn't want to lose her. I figured eventually you'd come back," he said.

Maybe it was the painkillers because I didn't understand him at first. He held out the doll. "It's our Christmas present to you." Needless to say, there were hugs and tears all around, more than enough to embarrass my daughter.

The rest of the holiday went by in a blur. Dinner was prepared, gifts opened and most forgotten. I stopped looking like a chipmunk. The holiday season was officially over.

But that doll remains in my room, a reminder of the great and quiet kindness that lives around us every day of the year.

~Lizanne Southgate

A Chicken Soup for the Soul Christmas

87

My Special Angel

*Perhaps they are not the stars, but rather openings
in heaven where the love of our lost ones pours
through and shines down upon us to let
us know they are happy.*
~Inspired by an Eskimo Legend

The day I married my childhood sweetheart was the happiest day of my life. We had been friends since the third grade and had always assumed that one day we would marry and raise a family. Our dreams had come true.

Over the course of the next three years, we lived in a dream world. We loved one another from the very depths of our souls and treated each other with respect, kindness, and compassion. We never thought of ourselves and always put the other first. There was nothing we would not do for each other.

We were seldom apart. We had common interests that ensured that we enjoyed each other's company. We would walk to the store together, holding hands, just to buy a loaf of bread. As well as being husband and wife, we were lovers and best friends.

After three years of marriage, I discovered I was pregnant. We were both delighted. We spent hours in the stores, picking out clothes, furniture, and accessories for the newest addition to our family.

Our daughter was born on a bright, sunny day in February. Our area had been hit by a heavy snowfall the week before and the world was white and beautiful. It seemed that this was an omen. Our family would have a bright future.

For the next ten months we nourished our daughter, watched her grow, learn to walk, and say her first words. My husband's heart soared the first time she looked at him with her big brown eyes and uttered the word, "Daddy." The world had never been so perfect.

Christmas was a great joy. We dressed Michelle in a red Santa suit and hat, played Santa and watched with joy as her eyes lit up at the sight of her first Christmas tree. We lay together later that night and reminisced about the joys of the day. We were ecstatic and talked of Christmases to come.

In the wee hours of New Year's Eve, my world came crashing down. I awoke to find my husband sitting on the edge of the bed, clutching his chest and crying out in pain. Before I could throw back the covers and get to him, he began screaming. He stood, pushed me to one side and staggered into the living room. I followed, fear gripping me as I asked over and over what was wrong. He never answered. His screams rebounded off the walls of the small room and almost deafened me. Suddenly, he fell face first onto the hardwood floor. Then... silence.

The deadly sound of silence seemed to fill the room even more than the screams of a moment before. I scrambled for the telephone and called an ambulance. It seemed an eternity before it arrived. I later learned it was actually a little over four minutes.

After I made the call, I dropped to my knees beside my husband. I shook his shoulder, rolled him onto his back and called out his name as tears ran down my face and fell onto his. There was no response. As the ambulance pulled into the driveway, siren wailing, I already knew that he was dead.

The next few days were a nightmare. I picked out his casket, made funeral arrangements, and stood by his coffin shaking hands and accepting the sympathy of family and friends. I felt no emotion whatsoever at this time. It was as if I had turned to stone.

At the cemetery, my father stood beside me, his hand on my shoulder in a gesture of comfort. I knew his heart ached. He and my husband had gotten along splendidly. I couldn't bring myself to comfort him. When they began to lower my husband's casket into the ground, I began to sob, deep wracking sobs that seemed to tear away my soul. As far as I was concerned, my life was over. Not only had I lost a husband, but also my lover and best friend. It had all happened in the blink of an eye. I leaned against my father's chest while he smoothed my hair with his work-worn hand and crooned words of comfort. I remember wondering at the time how the world could be so cruel.

Over the next few weeks, I went through the normal grieving process. I was angry with my husband for leaving me, angry with God for taking him, and angry at the world in general. I didn't have the opportunity to go through the denial process. My husband had died right before my eyes and the reality of it was not to be denied.

For three weeks, I barely slept a wink. Each time I drifted off, my husband's screams revisited. Then, I would awaken, hoping it was all a bad dream and trembling uncontrollably. I couldn't eat, lost weight and wished that I had died with him.

During this period, I stayed at my parents' house, refusing to set foot in my own home. I couldn't bear the thought of entering the living room where my husband had died, and was afraid the bedroom would echo his screams of pain. I ignored my infant daughter, locked myself in the bedroom of my childhood where I remained for hours, and turned a deaf ear to my mother's pleas to come out and join the family. Though I continued to wish I had died with my husband on that fateful night, I never once contemplated suicide. I didn't realize it at the time, but this was a good indication that I was going to make it.

After a month, my father told me that I either had to go back to the house to live or give the landlord notice that I was moving. I understood the logic of this but wanted nothing more to do with that house. I wrote a notice to terminate my tenancy, asked Dad to deliver it and begged him to sell everything in the house with the exception of our personal belongings and a few mementos. At first Dad protested but finally he relented. He thought I should face my fears—my ghosts—so there'd be closure. Again, I refused.

Dad made arrangements to meet a used furniture dealer at the house and one day, just after my daughter's first birthday, went to take care of things. It seemed like he was gone for hours and my imagination ran wild. *Had something happened to him?* In my sorry state of mind, I felt the house was cursed.

When I heard Dad's truck pull into the driveway, I breathed a sigh of relief. All of the reminders of that terrible night would now be gone. I would never have to step into that house again.

Dad entered the house looking haggard and drawn. He took off his coat and hat, hung them up, took a small package out of his pocket and handed it to me. He told me he had found it in the mailbox at the house.

The return address on the envelope was that of the jewelry store where my husband and I had purchased our wedding bands. I tore it open, curious to see what was inside. When I dumped the contents, I found an angel pendant about a half-inch high on the finest gold chain I had ever seen. Embedded in one of the angel's wings were three birthstones. An amethyst represented my daughter, a blue sapphire for me, and an emerald for my husband. I looked at Dad. He shrugged. Apparently he knew nothing about it.

It was then that I realized there was something left in the envelope. The letter inside was addressed to my late husband. It was a letter of apology, indicating that though they had promised Christmas delivery, there had been a delay and they were giving him a partial refund. A check was enclosed along with a handwritten note from my husband. The note read: *When you wear this beautiful angel, always know that I am near.*

As I read, I could feel my husband's presence and almost see the smile on his face. I fastened the chain around my neck, knowing that he would be beside me always to guide me through the trials and tribulations of being a single parent. Peace enveloped me and in that moment, I knew that for his sake and that of my infant daughter, I must get on with my life.

Luckily for me, Dad had ignored all of my requests. The furniture was still in the small house where my husband and I had lived, loved, and laughed since the day we were married. The notice that I had told Dad to give to the landlord was still in his pocket. Michelle and I were going home.

The very next day, I bundled Michelle into her snowsuit and took her back to that house. I made a decision to pursue my lifelong dream of being a published writer. That fall, I enrolled in a writing class. Over the course of many years, my writing began to sell. How proud my late husband would have been.

The grief didn't leave overnight. Sometimes, I would awaken in a cold sweat, frightened and lonely. When this happened, I would hold my special angel between my fingers and rub her gently. Always, peace would envelop me and I would fall into a relaxed sleep.

I lost my special angel some years ago. At first, I was heartbroken. Then, I realized that I no longer needed to depend on her for peace and comfort. My only hope is that she brings peace and comfort into the life of the person who found her. She will always be my special angel and I will never forget the gift that my first husband sent me from beyond the grave. It truly was a gift of love.

~Mary M. Alward

Chicken Soup for the Soul: True Love

88

The Last Tamale

Unable are the loved to die. For love is immortality.
~Emily Dickinson

During the holidays there were always wonderful treats to snack on, but my favorite of all foods was my grandmother's tamales. Every year my grandmother would start early and shop in the specialty Mexican food store in the old downtown area. My grandmother had very little money. She was a widow who was too old to work. But she was also a giver. She always wanted to take care of others. It filled her with such pride and joy when she could help someone else out. During the Christmas season, Granny would work tirelessly around the clock making those tamales. After the presents were opened and our bellies were full, she would send us home with a batch of tamales to enjoy later.

Two years ago, my grandmother became very ill. We knew our time with her was short — we just didn't know how short. Her wish was to make it through one more Christmas. Not only did she get her wish, but she also lived one more year past what the doctors had predicted. Early in December the next year, she was weak and fragile. Yet, she went to her favorite Mexican specialty shop and purchased the ingredients for her homemade tamales. She worked hard for over a week to make a large batch of tamales. She finished up and froze them as always. Then on December 23rd, my dear sweet grandmother went to heaven in her sleep. I flew in for the funeral. We all talked and reminisced about her and about how much she will be missed.

But my grandmother had one more wish that came true. She left us all with her special batch of Christmas tamales. And in a strange way it was like she was still with us. Although it was bittersweet — eating the tamales without her — we knew she was smiling from up above as we enjoyed her special gift to us.

~Celeste M. Barnard

Chicken Soup for the Soul: Food and Love

89

The Gift of the Magi

Wherever there is a human being, there is
an opportunity for a kindness.
~Seneca

My head was pounding. I willed myself to focus on my reading: *The Fall of the House of Habsburg*. I didn't think my mind could actually expand enough to hold all the information I was expected to spew forth in the coming days. Finals loomed like a dark thunderhead ready to break. I tried to rub the fatigue from my eyes and my temples, but to no avail. So I stood and stretched and looked through my blinds to watch the first snow of the season.

As I stared out the window, images of my freshman fall semester seemed to twirl earthward with the falling snow. Memories of the maps I had drawn on sticky notes and then attached to my notebooks to help me navigate my way between classes — in the vain attempt to hide my freshman ignorance. (I'm sure I hadn't succeeded.) My astonishment at finding out that I had enrolled in an upper division class: 300-level Honors Austrian History. (No one had informed me that the numbers in front of a class actually meant something.) The date my friends had set up for me with the guy I was head-over-heels in love with. The too many 7:00 a.m. classes that I had slept through. (I swore never to take a class at that time again.) Indeed, going off to college was more than just taking more challenging courses. It was learning a whole new way of living.

I sat back down at my desk and tried to focus on my studies. In just seven more days, finals would be over and all the students in my freshman college dorm would be leaving to go home — except for me. I would be moving temporarily to another dorm for the Christmas break. Instead of feasting on homemade pies and chewy cookies, roasted turkey and buttery rolls, I would be choking down cafeteria food. Not a prospect I looked forward to.

I had no choice. I was a student from Pennsylvania attending college in Utah and my family of ten couldn't afford to pay for my ticket home. The only reason I was even able to attend college at all was because of the several scholarships I had received.

I stared back at the white fluff dancing through the air. This would be my first Christmas away from home. I was already so homesick I could weep. I tried to block out the Christmas music that filled my dorm floor with its merriness. I tried not to watch my neighbors as they trimmed their doorways with silvery garland and lush red holly berries. I tried instead to think about Austrian history. No luck. My heart and head were filled with too many other things — happy things turned sad. Stockings hung in a long row down our wooden banister. My younger brothers and sisters waking me up much too early with their giggles and excitement. Mountains of wrapping paper Dad would carefully sift through to be sure no gift was accidentally thrown away. Only there would be less wrapping paper in that mountain this year. I swallowed down the ache that was rising in my throat.

My wallowing in pity was interrupted by the ringing of the phone. I reached over and picked it up.

"Hello?"

"Hi, Teddi. This is Elsie." *What was my boss from my high school grocery job calling me for?* "All the full-time workers here heard that you weren't able to make it home this year, so we all pitched in and bought you a ticket. You're coming home!"

I screamed.

Fifteen minutes later I was off the phone and jumping up and down for joy. Neighbors came over to see what the ruckus was all about.

"I'm going home for Christmas! I'm going home for Christmas!

My friends at my high school job chipped in and bought me a ticket! I'm going home!"

My friend Ruth started belting out, "I'll Be Home for Christmas." The rest of those who had gathered and I joined in, "You can count on me!"

Christmas morning, I was awoken too early by giggles and shrieks of joy. But the smell of roasting turkey and buttery rolls baking while the mounds of wrapping paper grew higher and higher filled me with gratitude and love. The kindness of some special friends helped me, a lonely freshman, to have the best Christmas ever.

~Teddi Eberly Martin

Chicken Soup for the Soul: Campus Chronicles

A Passage Through Time

The most incredible thing about
miracles is that they happen.
~G.K. Chesteron

Approximately thirty-five years ago, my mother entrusted me with a family heirloom, a pine blanket-box. Due to its original grey milk-paint, chipped worn corners and lack of décor, I suspect it would not impress many. Yet, even as a small child, I was drawn to it and I suppose, its history.

Opening the lid time and time again I ran my small fingers over the names inscribed in pencil, the swirls of ornate lettering created by my ancestors who had traveled from England. I imagined them making their way as United Empire Loyalists into Upper Canada where they eventually settled at Stratford, which subsequently became my mother's hometown. From them, the box was passed down into her care and I'm certain it was my incessant interest that made her decision to pass this prize along to me instead of my brothers or sisters, an easy one.

As a married woman, I proudly presented the pine box, holding it amongst our most valued possessions. However it was not until the approach of my son's birthday that for me, its true purpose was revealed.

Jacob was born on Christmas Day... the best Christmas gift a mother could ever receive! As we approached his first birthday and of course Christmas, his natural inquisitiveness became evident as never before, as he was fascinated by the lights and glitter. Breaking with the past convention of an almost-to-the-ceiling tree, we decided to cut one down to a size that would fit on top of the pine box. After placing the tree in the stand we wrapped a tartan blanket around its base. Joyfully I hung the ornaments we had collected over the years and then methodically placed various bells around the bottom branches to serve as a warning jingle should Jacob's curiosity get the better of him.

Several years later, with his brother Bruce in the mix, our previous innovation had become a tradition. The trunk also served an additional duty. It harboured many of the treasures that were most dear to me: my wedding dress, the sleepers the boys came home from the hospital in, their baby shoes, special photos, and many of the other significant riches of our lives.

One year, while removing the ornaments after the holidays, I was shocked to discover that the tartan blanket at the base of the tree was damp. When I slowly peeled away the fabric it revealed that the tree stand had leaked. The top of the wooden box was discoloured and a large crack had formed on the lid.

I felt the beautiful trunk my mother had long ago so confidently placed in my care was now damaged and if that was not upsetting enough I still had to find out what treasures were ruined inside. My heart ached.

Earlier that same year I had experienced a different ache when I lost my mother-in-law. This very kind, gentle soul had finally succumbed to a weakened heart and quietly passed away.

When the extended family was packing up and removing articles from her home, my only request was for two of her china teacups and saucers. I wanted something, someday, far in the future, to pass along to my sons' brides… a gift of love from their nana.

I knelt in front of the damaged heirloom, took a deep breath and gently opened the lid. What I saw made me gasp. Sitting perilously, directly below the line of the crack were the two teacups and saucers now filled with yellowed water and pine needles. Miraculously, not one other item was wet; not one item was even remotely soiled, let alone ruined. All the water had dripped into those cups.

Stunned, I slumped back on my heels, my eyes filled with tears. I whispered a heartfelt thank you to my mother-in-law.

She was the one who protected our fortune, reinforcing in my heart that those who love us, whether physically with us or not, always surround us. This was her last Christmas gift to us.

As for the top of the box, oddly the crack, once dry, sealed as if never there. All that remains now is a slight blemish where some of the paint appears to have melted away, or as I choose to see it, a lovely reminder of this story. And as my mother and her mother and generations before her passed along this magnificent pine blanket box, so shall I, with the story of the tea cups added to its history, lovingly tucked inside.

~Nancy Koruna McIntosh

Chicken Soup for the Soul: O Canada The Wonders of Winter

91

Christmas Providence

Ask and you shall receive, seek and you shall find,
knock and the door shall be open unto you.
~Matthew 7:7

After exhausting other avenues, we turned to adoption. Soon, by word of mouth, we had located a birth mother due to deliver in the fall. We excitedly made plans for our new little baby. All was well until the day of the baby's birth. We'd had warning signs from the family, but the birth mother assured us that she would hold firm to her commitment to us. Then the day we were to take the baby home from the hospital, the family decided to keep the baby and "try" to raise it on their own. I cannot find the words to describe the loss, disappointment, and anger that consumed us.

After the agony we had endured throughout the year, we decided to spend Christmas alone together. A rented cabin in the mountains of Tennessee seemed to be the ideal getaway. The day before we were to leave, I awoke before Jennifer and began to recall what we had been through the previous twelve months. My heart ached as I thought of the pain she had endured and how much she deserved to have a baby of her own. I started to pray, reminding God of the kind, loving, motherly heart he had given Jennifer. I had asked God to bring a baby into our lives many times before, but this time I begged, "Please, God, give us a baby for Christmas." It would be a fitting end to an otherwise dismal year.

We really enjoyed our time away at the cabin in a beautiful part of the country. Our Christmas was very nice, and as we lay down for an afternoon nap, I was a bit saddened as I recalled my prayer. The day was half over, and nothing had happened, so I went upstairs to pray. I reminded God of my prayer for a Christmas baby. I didn't care how; I was ready to turn it over to God. I prayed that he would blow us away when his plan was revealed to us. Little did I know that his plan was already a gale-force wind.

The rest of our Christmas day was spent with the usual calls to and from family. Then I did something for the first time ever on Christmas... I called my brother Willard in Houston. During our conversation of "what did you get," he received another call.

When he resumed our conversation, he said, "Eric, you're not going to believe this but that call was from a friend saying her niece had a baby this morning. She was placing the baby for adoption, but the adoptive parents backed out because the baby is unexpectedly biracial." Willard went on to explain that their friend remembered we were trying to adopt. "She wants to know, are you interested?"

My mind immediately raced to my prayer. "Of course!"

After several calls to family, our attorney, and the birth mother, it appeared that this was going to happen. Knowing we would not sleep, we loaded up at midnight and headed back home to Alabama. The following morning, we flew to Houston and picked up our precious Christmas baby at the hospital.

I always believed that God had a plan, a big plan, to bring a baby into our lives, but I never expected a Christmas miracle!

~Eric Myers

Chicken Soup for the Soul: The Joy of Adoption

Chapter
10

A Book of
Christmas
Miracles

Through the
Eyes of a Child

92

Gifts for Jace

The giving of love is an education in itself.
~Eleanor Roosevelt

I'll never forget the day that one of my students shyly raised his hand and said that he had never received a gift. My shocked fifth-graders were discussing a reading story about a boy who was not going to be getting anything for his birthday because money was tight that year. Even though this class was very open during reading discussions, Jace's honesty surprised even me. What was even more eye-opening was the fact that this sweet, fifth-grade boy had gone ten years and never experienced the joy and surprise of receiving a present.

I searched my internal data bank for a reason that he might be saying this. Did he want attention from his peers? No, that was definitely not his style. Was he exaggerating? Again, he was not the type. Then I remembered his story. His mother was out of the picture and he lived alone with his dad. His father had a hard time holding down a job, and come to think of it, I didn't see his father at enrollment or parent-teacher conferences. Even though on the outside Jace was a bit disheveled, he always came to school with a smile and sincere enthusiasm for learning.

A couple of weeks after Jace's comment, he was absent from school. This happened to be the day I was sending home the annual note about the classroom Christmas gift exchange. Traditionally, each boy was to bring a gift for a boy in the three-dollar range and the same was true for each girl.

As we were discussing the specifics, a girl raised her hand and matter-of-factly suggested that we do away with our traditional policy, and each buy a gift for Jace instead. The enthusiasm grew as the students discussed the kinds of things they knew Jace would like, such as art supplies and Star Wars figurines. We took a quick vote and unanimously agreed to go ahead with this wonderful idea.

With great excitement, the gifts began to come in. Students with bright eyes would eagerly tell me how they found the "perfect gift" and how their parents spent more than three dollars on Jace's gift! One student bought a complete art set, knowing that Jace loved to draw. Another student found toy aliens for him, remembering a paper Jace had recently written about aliens where he surprised us all with a paper plate spaceship prop he had made. As the gifts poured in, I remember being so proud of my thoughtful, selfless students who were truly demonstrating the spirit of Christmas.

After several days of absences, you can imagine our disappointment when we learned that Jace's absences were due to the fact that he had moved away! I was sure of one thing. I couldn't let my students or Jace down.

I found my information sheet and called every number listed. Apparently, Jace's father had lost his job, causing them to relocate. No one knew where they were, and the cell phone number I had would ring with no response despite my continuous efforts. Even into our Christmas vacation, I constantly gave the phone number a shot. Finally, at 9:30 p.m. on Christmas Eve, I decided to try one last time. By then, I really didn't worry about calling at a late hour. I was so used to no answer that I was startled to hear a response. Amazingly, Jace answered the phone!

I explained the story to Jace and told him how his classmates really wanted to do this for him. I spoke with his father and the next thing I knew, I was driving to Jace's home.

As I drove down his road, I saw the porch light of his trailer flicking on and off signaling which home was his. I was thrilled to see Jace. It took several trips back and forth to my car to get all of the gifts inside. We filled the room with all of the carefully wrapped gifts that were especially for him. He was so surprised and grateful. I was glad that I had an unopened box of chocolates that I could give to his dad. Jace's joyful smile that evening lit up the sky like a strand of twinkle lights.

I went to sleep that night thinking about Jace and all of the fun he was going to have playing with all of his new presents during Christmas break. I thought about my thoughtful students and how excited I was to tell them all about finding Jace. With a smile of my own, I was thankful to be a part of one of the most important "lessons" of their lives.

~Angela N. Abbott

Chicken Soup for the Soul: Teacher Tales

93

My Renewed Joy

Kindness is a language which the deaf
can hear and the blind can read.
~Mark Twain

There was a knock at the door on that cold St. Louis winter day. My three-year-old hugged my leg as I turned the knob to open it. It was my neighbor from across the street. "I'm heading to the mall, want to come?"

I smiled hesitantly. I was still getting used to accepting help — people reading for me, or taking me places and guiding me as I walked. It was a constant reminder that I was now dependent on the kindness of others.

I was in the happiest period of my life, caring for my three-, five-, and seven-year-old sons. And without warning, my vision closed in, leaving me in total darkness. The retinal deterioration robbed me of my sight in only eighteen months. No cure. No surgery. No hope.

I spent nights awake, wondering what my life would be like. *How would I care for my sons? How deprived would they feel by having a blind mom?*

I tossed and turned, but no answers came — only a wave of anxiety as I faced a monster I could not defeat.

"You have to wait, sweet thing," I said to my three-year-old when he wanted cereal. I first had to find the correct box and make sure I poured the milk carefully and slowly to avoid overflowing the bowl, to avoid making yet another mess.

"Where is Daddy?" he asked.

Their father worked long hours to keep the family fed. And help from family was scarce as my mom was busy with her own trauma, because my dad, coincidentally, was also losing his sight. I inherited the gene from him, but his took much longer to manifest. He was fifty-five and I was only thirty.

"Can I come over and help?" my mom would often ask.

I did need her, but I couldn't put more burdens on her. "I'm okay. Don't worry. The boys and I are fine," I said.

I wasn't fine. Yet while I fought fear and worry, I managed to cook and clean. My memory sharpened and I memorized phone numbers to call for rides to my boys' soccer practices and Cub Scout meetings.

But in that cold December season, when Christmas carols echoed everywhere and most families around the neighborhood prepared to celebrate, I sunk deeper into my sorrow. Decorating the house, shopping for gifts, and baking cookies were tasks that seemed to mock my inability to get them done.

Christmas morning came, my first as a blind person. Three pairs of little feet bounced around our bed. "I want to open presents!" one of the boys shouted. "Me too!" his brothers echoed.

I felt around at the foot of the bed to find my robe, slipped it on, and followed their cheerful voices into the family room, where a pine scent filled the air. For a brief moment, the joy of my little boys made me forget I couldn't see.

Then my new reality set in. "Okay, we have to do this in order," I instructed. "Daddy will give one present to each of you and you will open it when we tell you to do so."

"Me first!" our youngest shouted as he ripped the wrapping off. "Wow! This is *cool!*" he screamed. Everything in me longed to see the expression on his little face. *What had he opened? What made him so excited?* I blinked back tears and chided myself — why couldn't I just enjoy what I was hearing? But the more they oohed and aahed, the more I was overwhelmed by my desire to see.

I rose from the couch. "I'll be right back." I felt my way along the wall back to our bedroom. My eyes burned as I fought back tears. I sat on our bed and said to myself, "Lord, why is this affecting me so? Please help me to understand. Show me how to cope... I don't know how."

As I silently cried, my husband came in. He put his arms around me. "What can I do for you, honey?"

"I'm okay." I brushed the tears off my face with the back of my hand.

"Mommy, Daddy, can we open some more?" the boys called out.

"I'll be there in a minute," I whispered to my husband. I yanked a tissue from the box on our dresser, and tried to swallow my pain with a deep sigh.

"This is the best present of all!" my oldest shouted! "How did you know, Mom?"

His words struck me. I froze. *How did I know? Of course I knew. I knew what each of them wanted, what they wished, what they loved and exactly what made them excited.*

I didn't need eyesight to know all about my sons. Without being able to see, I could still love them, care for them, please them and even discipline them.

A dark veil lifted from my heart. I didn't need eyesight to relish the moment with them, to delight in their shouts of surprise when they opened another present. I savored their silly comments. And I found a fresh new joy in their "I love you, Mom."

"Thank you," I whispered. But I was thanking God for opening the eyes of my heart. That day I learned to appreciate the richness I had in my three happy little boys.

And because of them, eventually I became a happy mom, a secure wife, and a fun friend again!

The day after Christmas I called my neighbor. "Want to head to the mall? Lots of bargains out there."

She helped me to the passenger seat and we took off.

Sometime prior, she had asked me if, after losing my sight, another sense had developed.

"Yes," I said, "my sense of humor did."

We joked and laughed while we rode to the mall. Holding on to her arm, we visited stores. With minute detail, she described items on the rack and we came home with bargains. Those shopping trips became our yearly routine.

I quickly learned to dare to expect great things, because each day without eyesight gave me the insight to see what makes life worth living, what brings significance to my days, and how I see each season shine with renewed joy.

~Janet Perez Eckles

Chicken Soup for the Soul: The Power of Gratitude

94

Christmas Lights

*Christmas is sights, especially the sights of Christmas
reflected in the eyes of a child.*
~William Saroyan

Before my dad died, Christmas was a bright, enchanted time in the long, dark winters of Bathurst, New Brunswick. The cold, blizzardy days would sometimes start as early as late September. Finally, the lights of Christmas would start to go up, and the anticipation would build. By Christmas Eve the ordinary evergreen tree that my father dragged in the door ten days earlier took on a magical, sparkling life of its own. With its marvellous brilliance, it single-handedly pushed back the darkness of winter.

Late on Christmas Eve, we would bundle up and go to midnight mass. The sound of the choir sent chills through my body, and when my older sister, a soloist, sang "Silent Night," my cheeks flushed with pride.

On Christmas morning I was always the first one up. I'd stumble out of bed and walk down the hall toward the glow from the living room. My eyes filled with sleep, I'd softly bounce off the walls a couple of times trying to keep a straight line. I'd round the corner and come face-to-face with the brilliance of Christmas. My unfocused, sleep-filled eyes created a halo around each light, amplifying and warming it. After a moment or two I'd rub my eyes and an endless expanse of ribbons and bows and a free-for-all of bright presents would come into focus.

I'll never forget the feeling of that first glimpse on Christmas morning. After a few minutes alone with the magic, I'd get my younger brother and sister, and we'd wake my parents.

One November night, about a month before Christmas, I was sitting at the dining room table playing solitaire. My mother was busy in the kitchen, but was drawn from time to time into the living room by one of her favourite radio shows. It was dark and cold outside, but warm inside. My father had promised that tonight we would play crazy eight's, but he had not yet returned from work and it was getting near my bedtime.

When I heard him at the kitchen door, I jumped up and brushed past my mother to meet him. He looked oddly preoccupied, staring past me at my mother. Still, when I ran up to him, he enfolded me in his arms. Hugging my father on a winter night was great. His cold winter coat pressed against my cheek and the smell of frost mingled with the smell of wool.

But this time was different. After the first few seconds of the familiar hug, his grip tightened. One arm pressed my shoulder while the hand on my head gripped my hair so tightly it was starting to hurt. I was a little frightened at the strangeness of this and relieved when my mother pried me out of his arms. I didn't know it at the time, but my dad was suffering a fatal heart attack.

Someone told me to take my younger brother and sister to play down in the recreation room. From the foot of the stairs, I saw the doctor and the priest arrive. I saw an ambulance crew enter and then leave with someone on a stretcher, covered in a red blanket. I didn't cry the night my father died, or even at his funeral. I wasn't holding back the tears; they just weren't there.

On Christmas morning, as usual, I was the first one up. But this year, something was different. Already, there was a hint of dawn in the sky. More rested and awake than usual, I walked down the hall toward the living room. There was definitely something wrong, but I didn't know what until I rounded the corner. Then, instead of being blinded by the warm lights, I could see everything in the dull room. Without my dad to make sure the lights on the tree were glowing, I could see the tree. I could see the presents. I could even see a little bit of the outside world through the window. The magic of my childhood Christmas dream was shattered.

The years passed. As a young man, I always volunteered to work the Christmas shifts. Christmas Day wasn't good, it wasn't bad; it was just another grey day in winter, and I could always get great overtime pay for working.

Eventually, I fell in love and married, and our son's first Christmas was the best one I'd had in twenty years. As he got older, Christmas got even better. By the time his sister arrived, we had a few family traditions of our own. With two kids, Christmas became a great time of year. It was fun getting ready for it, fun watching the children's excitement and most especially, fun spending Christmas day with my family.

On Christmas Eve I continued the tradition started by my dad and left the tree lights on for that one night, so that in the morning, my kids could have that wonderful experience.

When my son was nine years old, the same age I was when my father died, I fell asleep Christmas Eve in the recliner watching midnight mass on TV. The choir was singing beautifully, and the last thing I remember was wishing to hear my sister sing "Silent Night" again. I awoke in the early morning to the sound of my son bouncing off the walls as he came down the hallway toward the living room. He stopped and stared at the tree, his jaw slack.

Seeing him like that reminded me of myself so many years ago, and I knew. I knew how much my father must have loved me in exactly the same complete way I loved my son. I knew he had felt the same mixture of pride, joy and limitless love for me. And in that moment, I knew how angry I had been with my father for dying, and I knew how much love I had withheld throughout my life because of that anger.

In every way I felt like a little boy. Tears threatened to spill out and no words could express my immense sorrow and irrepressible joy. I rubbed my eyes with the back of my hands to clear them. Eyes moist and vision blurred, I looked at my son, who was now standing by the tree. Oh my, the glorious tree! It was the Christmas tree of my childhood!

Through my tears the tree lights radiated a brilliant, warm glow. Soft, shimmering yellows, greens, reds and blues enveloped my son and me. My father's death had stolen the lights and life out of Christmas. By loving my own son as much as my father had loved me, I could once more see the lights of Christmas. From that day forward, all the magic and joy of Christmas was mine again.

~Michael Hogan

Chicken Soup for the Canadian Soul

95

Grandkids for Christmas

The deepest wishes of the heart find
expression in secret prayer.
~George E. Rees

I was ten and my little sister was seven, the babies of a family of fourteen. Seven of my siblings had flown the coop, but my brother Wayne was the only one with kids. He and his wife had just been transferred across the country to California. Mama was looking at her first Christmas without little ones in the house. We all prayed she wouldn't be too sad, yet we suspected she was a bit depressed, though she didn't let it show.

On Christmas Eve we sat talking about my little nieces, wondering what they were doing. We imagined how empty the next day would be without them ripping open presents from Santa. When we couldn't stand it any longer, we called and passed the phone around, asked them if they'd been good girls and what they hoped Santa would leave under their tree. Mama busied herself in the kitchen, no doubt praying, as usual.

That's when our Christmas miracle began. We lived on a busy state highway in south Louisiana, on a section of road called Dead Man's Curve. The sound of screeching tires and smashing steel was not unusual to us. Many strangers found refuge on our living room couch while waiting for an ambulance, a tow truck or a family member to rescue them. Once a man died in my dad's arms on our front lawn, after being hit by a car as he walked along that treacherous road. My father, an ordained minister, baptized him there.

As we hung up from talking to our nieces, we heard the familiar sound of tires screeching. We held our breath, then heard an earsplitting crash. We bolted for the front door and rushed to the road. An eighteen-wheeler had plowed into a station wagon holding a young couple and their two little daughters. The truck was on its side in the ditch. The station wagon had crossed the road and a ditch, then landed inches from a row of trees. The truck driver and the young family crawled from the wreckage. Amazingly, no one appeared hurt, but the truck and car were going nowhere except the junkyard.

Someone stopped the traffic. Mom and Dad hustled everyone into the house, called the police and Mama started warming dinner. Next thing I knew the truck driver was gone. I guess someone picked him up. But the family was stranded. They were on their way to Mississippi to spend Christmas with elderly grandparents who were too old to drive and pick them up this late at night.

Within five seconds we all fell in love with the precious girls. The older girl was three just like my older niece, and the baby a few months younger than our little one. Mama rocked the baby to sleep and Daddy read Christmas stories to the girl until she dozed off in his lap. My sister and I offered to sleep on the den floor and give them our beds.

Mama scrounged around in her closet, found some toys, wrapped them and stashed them under the tree. Long after we drifted off to sleep ourselves, Mama's sewing machine whirred away making a painting smock, a dress and a pinafore for the older girl, a Christmas apron for the mother, and a bonnet for the baby. She wrapped up a handyman how-to book for the daddy and some of her popular homemade cheese straws.

When we woke up, Dad read the Christmas story from the Bible, then the three-year-old placed the figures in the manger, just like we did when we were that age. Everyone was amazed at the presents. The young couple was shocked to find something for them too.

About midday on Christmas, someone came from Mississippi to pick up the little family. We hugged goodbye and thanked each other for the wonderful Christmas we shared.

For many years after that, the family visited regularly every Christmas Eve. When their grandparents died and they no longer traveled to Mississippi, they stayed in touch, sent Christmas cards and even visited every few years. We marveled at how the girls, and later their little brother, grew.

There have been plenty of Christmases since then. Now I spend them with my own four kids. There've been other miracles too. But I'll never forget the year God sent my mama grandkids for Christmas.

~Mimi Greenwood Knight

Chicken Soup for the Soul: Answered Prayers

96

Just One Gift

Gratitude is the memory of the heart.
~Jean Baptiste Massieur

I t was the only Christmas gift I had ever received, and I remember it still. I was six years old, and my mother handed me the brightly wrapped box, explaining it was from her boss at the office where she worked. I nervously held the package in my lap, almost too afraid to open it. Why had a complete stranger given me a present?

My mother was a single parent and often worked several jobs to make ends meet. There usually wasn't much money left for extras. But that wasn't the reason why we never owned a Christmas tree or any gifts beneath it. I'd never received a Christmas gift because we are *Jewish*.

"He couldn't believe you didn't have anything to open on Christmas morning," my mother told me. "He wanted me to give this to you."

Although she explained to him that we celebrated Hanukkah and I'd received presents then, he insisted that all children should have a gift to open on Christmas. I could tell she felt uncomfortable, and I did, too. Still, I was only six and couldn't wait to see what was inside.

I carefully unwrapped the box and found a Raggedy Ann doll. Her red yarn hair was soft, and her black button eyes shone. I held her close, and she soon became my favorite toy. I may not have been able to describe the feeling then, but now I know what I felt — it was the Christmas spirit.

Growing up Jewish in a world that celebrates Christmas wasn't always easy. No colorful lights, decorated trees, or trips to see Santa Claus. Our Hanukkah celebrations were fun — lighting the menorah, spinning the dreidel, and having the benefit of eight nights on which to open gifts. Still, each December we were reminded of our differences.

But to my mother's boss, our differences didn't matter. What did matter were the magic of the season and the sharing of joy, and those don't differentiate between Christian and Jewish children. He just wanted to share his joy with me.

So, even though I don't celebrate the holiday, I understand what the Christmas spirit is all about. It doesn't matter what religion you follow, or even what you call it.

It's the spirit that prompts people to buy a toy for a child who may not receive any others. It's the spirit that brings Jews into soup kitchens to serve Christmas dinners, or drop coins in a *tzedakah* box for the needy. It's about sharing your own joy with others, no matter who they are.

I don't remember if I wrote the giver a thank-you note, but I hope I did. More than thirty years later, while I don't know what happened to that doll, I still have the most important gift he gave me — the gift of Christmas spirit.

~Ruth Spiro

A Chicken Soup for the Soul Christmas

97

Owed to Joy

Man is the merriest, the most joyous
of all the species of creation.
~Joseph Addison

The year my youngest daughter, Shelly, was four, she received an unusual Christmas present from "Santa."

She was the perfect age for Christmas, able to understand the true meaning of the season, but still completely enchanted by the magic of it. Her innocent joyfulness was compelling and contagious and a great gift to parents, reminding us of what Christmas should represent no matter how old we are.

The most highly prized gift Shelly received on that Christmas Eve was a giant bubble-maker, a simple device of plastic and cloth the inventor promised would create huge billowing bubbles, larger than a wide-eyed four-year-old girl. Both Shelly and I were excited about trying it out, but it was dark outside so we'd have to wait until the next day.

That night, after all the gifts had been opened, I read the instruction booklet while Shelly played with some of her other new toys. The inventor of the bubble-maker had tried all types of soaps for formulating bubbles and found Joy dishwashing detergent created the best giant bubbles. I'd have to get some.

The next morning I was awakened very early by small stirrings in the house. Shelly was up. I knew in my sleepy mind that Christmas Day would be held back no longer, so I arose and made my way toward the kitchen to start the coffee. In the hallway I met my daughter, already wide awake, the bubble-maker clutched in her chubby little hand, the magic of Christmas morning embraced in her four-year-old heart. Her eyes were shining with excitement. She asked, "Daddy, can we make bubbles now?"

I sighed heavily. I rubbed my eyes. I looked toward the window, where the sky was only beginning to lighten with the dawn. I looked toward the kitchen, where the coffeepot had yet to start dripping its aromatic reward for early-rising Christmas dads.

"Shelly," I said, my voice almost pleading and perhaps a little annoyed, "it's too early. I haven't even had my coffee yet."

Her smile fell away. Immediately, I felt a father's remorse for bursting her bright Christmas bubble with what she must have seen as my own selfish problem, and my heart broke a little.

But I was a grown-up. I could fix this. In a flash of adult inspiration, I shifted the responsibility. Recalling the inventor's recommendation of a particular brand of bubble-making detergent — which I knew we did not have in the house — I laid the blame squarely on him, pointing out gently, "Besides, you have to have Joy."

I watched her eyes light back up. "Oh, Daddy," she beamed. "Oh, Daddy, *I do.*"

I broke records getting to the store, and in no time at all we were out on the front lawn creating gigantic, billowing, gossamer orbs — each one conjured of purest Joy and sent forth shimmering in the Christmas sun.

~Ted A. Thompson

Chicken Soup for the Father & Daughter Soul

98

A Snowy Hospital Holiday

And the child grew and became strong in spirit, filled
with wisdom; and the grace of God was on Him.
~Luke 2:40

C hristmas Eve 1955, I sat on the wide marble windowsill of
my third floor hospital room in the Essex County Isolation
Hospital. I looked longingly at the circular driveway leading up to the front entrance and let my tears flow freely.
Not because the predicted snowfall turned into a major blizzard, but
for me, a twelve-year-old girl diagnosed with tuberculosis, confined
to six months of isolation and forced to swallow handfuls of pills.

And because it was Christmastime and I wasn't home.

A white blanket of snow covered the hospital's grounds and shiny
ice coated the trees... a scene any photographer would describe as
a perfect postcard picture. Who wouldn't appreciate this wonderful
winter Christmas gift from God? Me, that's who.

"God," I prayed, "I'm really mad at You and not sure I like You
much." That was true. I wanted to be with my family, not in a hospital.
I also had a slew of questions, which I didn't hesitate to ask: "Why did
you let my daddy die? Why did I have to get sick? Why am I stuck in
this room? Nobody can come in but the nurses, and then they have
to put on those ugly green gowns and gloves before they even touch
me. Why does a glass wall separate me and the rest of the world?" In

between my angry tears I told Him, "It's not fair that I can't celebrate Christmas with my mom and brother."

I soon realized that nothing I said made a difference and I had to accept what was. Besides, He was probably not even listening.

I'd have to spend the day alone in my room, on my ugly brown metal bed, reading another chapter of my favorite *Nancy Drew* mystery. Alone.

There'd be no going to church to celebrate Jesus's birthday, no caroling, no presents, no gathering of the relatives around the table, no sharing the stuffed turkey with all the trimmings, no playing games, no listening to family stories late into the night. This would all have to wait until next year when I returned home… if I got better.

I said "if" because my father died of TB just three months after he found out he had it. And I believed I would die too. I knew about God and heaven and eternal happiness but I was young and wanted to go to college, get married, have kids, and live to be a grandma. I prayed about that too, but got no sign that He even heard me.

I sat alone on the hospital room windowsill on Christmas morning. The nurses on duty bubbled with holiday spirit as they carried out their morning routines. They brought in the breakfast tray with a candy cane stuck in my bowl of oatmeal. They gave me my medication in a small red cup. "A splash of Christmas spirit," said one.

Later in the day they strolled up and down the hallway, sang Christmas carols and took requests for favorites. They passed out gifts, wrapped with jolly-faced Santa Claus paper.

Regular visiting hours weren't until two o'clock in the afternoon. I knew not to expect any visitors, especially after Father Francis, a priest from the nearby church, didn't show up with Holy Communion. His absence only proved how bad the blizzard was, because if he could have come, he would have. Just like my mother and brother. If they could have come, they would have.

Just after lunch, a loud "Ho! Ho! Ho! Merry Christmas!" and the jingling of sleigh bells echoed down the hallway. From my isolation room I observed through the glass wall. Most kids stood at their doors smiling with delight. A few of the younger patients made a speedy dash to the nurses' station shouting, "It's Santa!"

Yes, Santa Claus, dressed in his best red Christmas outfit and shiny black boots, had found his way to the hospital. Over his shoulder he toted an oversized black bag, bulging at the seams. He made his way to every room with gifts. For me, he handed gifts to a nurse who dressed in a green isolation gown to bring them into my room. I ripped open a Paint-by-Numbers kit, a new Nancy Drew mystery and a jar of multicolored hard candies. This surprise brought joy to my dreary room and heart.

The day went on and I still felt sad without my family there to enjoy the festivities with me. I looked out the window and noticed the driveway had been cleared and cars were inching their way toward the front door. A few people walked up the sidewalk after getting off a public bus. Traffic along the main road showed signs of things getting back to normal in the world outside.

Then out of nowhere, people bundled in winter clothing; carrying Christmas wrapped bags and boxes, filled our hallway. Families arrived, one by one in small groups. I heard squeals of happiness and hoped against hope that my mother and brother would show up too. But they didn't even have a car; there was no way they could come.

I wanted to pray, again, but so far, God had ignored every prayer I whispered. There was no use. I decided to take a bubble bath to pass the time.

From the bathroom, I heard a knock on the glass wall and I peeked out. There they stood, my mom and brother with rosy cheeks, wrapped presents and great big smiles. "Merry Christmas!" they shouted.

I rushed to the window and cried with happiness. "I didn't think I'd see you today!" They must have ridden the bus two hours to get there.

I wanted to burst out into the hallway, hug them and never let go. But instead, we put our open hands on the glass wall, palm to palm, pretending we were touching. I could feel their love through the glass.

That night my prayer included an apology. "I'm sorry God for doubting that You were listening. I really knew better. Thank you for getting my family to the hospital. This was the best Christmas ever. I'll never forget it as long as I live."

And I haven't.

~Helen Colella

Chicken Soup for the Soul: Answered Prayers

99

The Returning Light

If we shall take the good we find, asking no
questions, we shall have heaping measures.
~Ralph Waldo Emerson

Every year, as soon as Halloween is over, our son Matthew waits for the lights. He's been doing it for more than a dozen years. As the days grow shorter and the nights longer, as the temperatures drop and the leaves fall, he waits for the lights. He knows that they will come.

The neighbors across the street always put up a beautiful and brilliant (and tasteful) light display for the holidays and Matthew loves to wait for them to be turned on, which usually happens right after Thanksgiving. But he begins his vigil a month before their arrival. And then, each day between Thanksgiving and until the lights are turned off after the new year, he waits, excitedly, from mid-afternoon on. Each day he'll stand by the front windows or walk back and forth between the windows and the front door, in energetic and coiled anticipation, laser-focused, undeterred, intent on the moment of their nightly illumination.

And when each evening's moment comes, you don't have to be right with him when that moment occurs. You know it no matter where you are in the house. The effervescent squealing. The rhythmic clapping. The dancing around the house, the steps staccato, loud, repeated. It's pure joy. Pure delight on his face! And it happens every single night.

He waits for the lights. During the darkest days of the year. He stands and he waits. Transfixed by those lights brightening the dim, winter sky.

For all his limitations, in the world's view — his severe mental disabilities, his autism, his two-year-old mind in a twenty-three-year-old body, his inability to speak — Matthew knows something very profound, that light will shine in the darkness, that no matter how dark, how long the wait, eventually, and without fail, those lights will shine again. No matter how many seasons of the year without them, there will come a season when those lights will shine again. They always do.

Life brings its own seasons of darkness. Desperate, at times. Lonely. Painful. Full of fear. But despite those seasons, a new season can come and the light can be seen again. Whatever darkness I find within and around me, I look to my son, and remember that a light can pierce that darkness and can begin to bring beauty and joy again.

In that I find my hope and my happiness.

~Michael D. Gingerich

Chicken Soup for the Soul: Find Your Happiness

100

The Secret of the Cedar Chest

Good as it is to inherit a library,
it is better to collect one.
~Augustine Birrell

For many years I've kept my guilt regarding the cedar chest a secret. I felt deeply ashamed of the lack of self-control that led to my infamous behaviour. However, this Christmas I've decided enough time has elapsed (the statute of limitations on such crimes must have expired) that I can now confess.

To begin, I must admit to being an incurable bookaholic. I always have been. In fact, one of my earliest memories is of standing behind my mother as she washed the lunch dishes at the kitchen sink, a book in one hand, pulling on her apron strings with the other as I begged her to read, "just one chapter, please, just one chapter."

My mother contributed to my addiction. I cannot recall her ever refusing to leave the sudsy pan, dry her hands, and follow me to the living room. There, we'd curl up together and while away the afternoon, deep in our love for the printed word. A devoted amateur actress, she read with passionate expression. Carried away on the wings of her words, I would listen mesmerized.

The books I remember best from those days were the works of Thornton W. Burgess. My favourite among his bevy of loquacious animals was Reddy Fox. Reddy frequently outfoxed himself through some small flaw in one of his nefarious schemes.

When I finally learned to read on my own, I experienced one of the greatest epiphanies of my life. There was magic to be found on a printed page. It had the power to sweep me away into another time, another place, another spirit. Words flowed over, around and through me, enthralling me to the core. I read everything from the corn flakes box on our breakfast table to the set of University Encyclopaedias published in 1902 that I discovered in my grandmother's attic. (It wasn't until I looked for the word "airplane" and couldn't find it that I realized the venerable age of this fascinating reading matter.)

While other children hounded their parents for toys, I begged for books, books, and more books. The Christmas season presented the paramount opportunity for my supplications. Each autumn, I began to prepare a long list of titles I'd be delighted to find beneath the festive tree. Since we had no bookstore in our town, the Eaton's catalogue was the only place to purchase these desirable items. Consequently one special Sunday afternoon each November my mother and I would sit at the kitchen table with that lovely, plump book while I selected the books I most desired from the limited selection on the two pages that offered reading materials.

My mother, knowing how I devoured the contents of books the moment they arrived in our home, never let me know when she was picking up the parcel at the post office. And definitely, never where she hid the precious package.

Overwhelmed by my reading affliction, however, I'd become sly and unscrupulous. No book could remain unread anywhere within my ability to ferret it out. Thus, one day the year I was ten and desperate for a good read, I began my quest for her hiding place in earnest.

I dug through closets, into their darkest, most remote corners and topmost shelves. I burrowed under sheets and towels in the linen cupboard, and even checked beneath the mattress in the guest room. Nothing.

Stymied, I followed my mother into my parents' bedroom and sat down on the edge of the bed. I watched as she opened the cedar chest beneath the window. My father had handcrafted it for her on their engagement. She kept her most treasured possessions in it; things like her wedding gown, my christening dress, her collection of hand-embroidered linens and, anathemas to a Reddy Fox fan, a couple of fox fur capes. Their presence had always made me shy away from the cedar chest.

I watched as she folded a pillow slip she'd finished decorating with moss roses. When she bent over the cedar chest to store her handiwork, I started to turn away. I had no desire to see the pelts of those poor, unfortunate foxes.

Then something caught my eyes. Peeking out from beneath a lace tablecloth, the top corner of a shiny, new BOOK!

My mother hastily lowered the lid and glanced in my direction. Had I seen it? Struggling to appear nonchalant, I began to hum "We Wish You a Merry Christmas" as I swung my legs against the chenille bedspread, and gazed up at the ceiling. She hesitated, then drew a deep breath and headed out of the room.

"Come along, Gail," she called as she started down the stairs. "We have cookies to bake."

My heart dancing with joy, I skipped along after her. Visions of how I'd invade the cedar chest later when I was alone upstairs waltzed through my head.

That evening after I'd been tucked in bed and my parents were safely settled in the living room listening to Charlie McCarthy and Edgar Bergen on the radio, I slipped my bare feet onto the cold linoleum that covered my bedroom floor and tiptoed across the hall. I carried a small flashlight. My father had given it to me the previous Christmas, in case of power outages, he'd said. He'd never intended it to be used in a book burglary in his own home.

Trembling with the thrill of the forbidden, I eased open the cedar chest, slipped my hand beneath the folded linens, (being careful to avoid those fox furs) and felt them… not the usual two but four, count them four, slick new books, their dust jackets as smooth as silk.

I slid out the topmost volume. My breath caught in my throat as

I read its title. *The Secret of Shadow Ranch!* The Nancy Drew mystery for which I'd longed for the past two years and for which Eaton's had always sent a substitution!

Resting my back against the cedar chest, I squatted on the floor, opened the Carolyn Keene classic to page one, adjusted my torch and began to read. Although I wasn't then familiar with the term multitasking, I quickly became adept at it. While I read I had to stay alert for the slightest indication that either of my parents was about to come upstairs.

Oh, the bliss of those stolen moments. My heart hammering, I read Nancy's adventures for over an hour. My bare feet felt like blocks of ice on the cold floor. I shivered in my pyjamas but I continued.

Then I heard my father suggesting a cup of tea before bed. Trembling from the enormity of my crime, I eased open the cedar chest, slid the book gently beneath the table cloths and pillow slips and scuttled back into my own room.

Snuggled beneath the covers, the flashlight still warm in my hand, my overwhelming need for a book satisfied, I drifted off to sleep. Visions of Nancy Drew, Bess, and George riding the range at Shadow Ranch replaced the sugarplums that were supposed to dance through children's heads just before Christmas.

In the hard light of the next morning, I admit I had a few qualms. As I sat at the breakfast table and glanced over at my mother, I knew I was destroying her joy in the big surprise she must be hoping to produce on Christmas morning with that long-sought-after Nancy Drew title. But I was incorrigible. That night, as my parents listened to a Christmas concert broadcast from Halifax on the living room radio, I cautiously opened *The Secret of Shadow Ranch* to Chapter Five and read on.

By the time Christmas Eve arrived, I'd devoured all four books and was contemplating re-reading *Shadow Ranch*. No, I told myself sternly. You'll bend a page, you'll crack the spine. Quit while you're ahead.

My extreme enthusiasm as I unwrapped each book on Christmas morning might have been a tip-off to less trusting parents. Their faces flushed with my reflected delight. Cradling my treasures in my arms, I curled myself up in a corner of the couch and in the flickering tree lights settled down to indulge myself in a full Christmas morning of re-reading.

My criminal activity continued during the next three Christmas seasons. It might have gone on much longer had I not made a major faux pas in my eagerness to defend the work of my then-favourite author, L. M. Montgomery. I'd read all of the Anne books and had been longing for one of the author's more mature stories entitled *The Blue Castle*. Not an easy book to find, it was proving as elusive as *The Secret of Shadow Ranch*.

But joy of joys! A week before Christmas it appeared in the cedar chest. Reading it by the light of my torch, I thrilled to the courage of heroine Valancy Stirling and identified with her need for freedom and self-expression. It was so romantic, the ending absolutely wonderful. When I finished reading two days before Christmas, I hugged it in the darkness beside the cedar chest.

On Christmas morning a bevy of relatives descended on our home. It was my parents' turn to host the Yuletide dinner. One of my maternal aunts wandered into the living room as she waited for the meal to be served and found me in my usual reading corner of the couch, absorbed in *The Blue Castle*.

"Well, Gail, I see you got another book," she sighed in mild exasperation. Not book-addicted, she couldn't understand my fascination.

"Yes, a perfectly lovely book." I put my finger between the pages of the first chapter to mark my place and beamed up at her.

"Another novel, no doubt," she scoffed sitting down opposite me. "I never read anything but the newspaper myself. Those things are nothing but nonsense."

"Oh no they aren't!" I couldn't bear to hear my beloved books defamed. "This one is about a girl who leaves home to nurse a sick friend and falls in love with the town outcast. Later she discovers he's really a millionaire, they get married and live happily ever after."

"Do they now?" I turned to see my mother standing in the living room doorway. My finger slipped from its place at page six.

Her lips curled up into a smile, she winked and turned back into the kitchen.

My mother died three Christmases later, a victim of cancer. Her legacy to my love of literature, however, lives on in my heart and home. Thornton Burgess's *The Adventures of Reddy Fox* and *The Secret of Shadow Ranch* remain beloved parts of my library. *The Blue Castle* occupies a place of honour beside the family Bible.

As for the cedar chest, filled with family photos, it sits in my living room, symbolic of those happy Christmases when a book could make my dreams come true and a mother who understood.

~Gail MacMillan

Chicken Soup for the Soul: O Canada

Gifts

The meaning of life is to find your gift.
The purpose of life is to give it away.
~Pablo Picasso

I was in fifth grade when my father broke his hip and femur in several places. He had slipped on the morning dew while splitting wood in the back yard. The freak accident was devastating and it would take a considerable amount of time and many surgeries for my father to recover.

At the time, my father had just switched employers and our family didn't have any medical or disability benefits. So Mom became the single breadwinner supporting our family of five. She had significant health issues herself and was in and out of the hospital.

Further complicating our situation was the fact that the fixer-upper, old farmhouse we were living in was not insulated. I often found myself staring at pretty patterns of ice etched on the inside of the windows. I would use my fingernail to write my name and draw hearts in the ice. We stuffed old socks in every hole to block the cold, and we huddled in the kitchen next to the stove when Mom was cooking, as it was the only source of heat in that part of the house.

My dad stayed in a hospital bed in our living room, so we put blankets across the entranceway and heated only that room to conserve money. In the cold of an upstate New York winter of blustery winds and subzero temperatures, we could see our breaths in the other rooms of the house.

We sold everything we could to keep food on our plates, the house partly heated, and the lights on. We lived in the country and were isolated from neighbors. To my surprise, the people who did know of our difficulties didn't seem to want to get involved.

We were thankful when my mom would get the farmers' surplus food once a month from a local church — large containers of cheese, peanut butter, and powdered milk. Meat was scarce and my teenage brothers took to hunting for rabbits and deer. We couldn't afford a butcher so Mom and every one of us kids helped to butcher the deer. We were so thankful for the food and didn't let anything go to waste. My mom canned and froze whatever she could to help sustain us.

Sometimes I wondered if Dad would ever walk again. His surgery had not been successful so far, and as his pain increased, his screaming was unbearable to hear. With Mom sick too, I worried about what would become of us.

The Christmas season came along, and we knew that my parents had been whispering about how they couldn't buy us many presents. My mother had knit some items for us, and we were wise enough to know that we would be grateful for those things when we received them.

On Christmas Eve we sat in our cold dining room eating venison and peaches that Mom had canned. She had made the canned venison into a warm gravy over toast. We were enjoying our meal when we heard an unexpected knock at the door. Mom pushed her hair to the side and smoothed her shirt before taking a deep breath and answering the door.

Two men who worked with my dad walked in carrying a box wrapped in Christmas paper. They said, "Ho, Ho, Ho," with deep voices. They placed the box in front of my dad, who we had maneuvered to the table for Christmas Eve dinner. Dad looked sad and Mom had tears welling up in her eyes. Mom slowly pulled each piece of wrapping paper away. It was as if her hands were apprehensive and couldn't imagine touching something joyful.

The two men said, "Open it. All the guys miss you at work. We wanted to do something to let you know we care." Mom and Dad opened the box. It was stuffed with wadded up newspaper and money. Mom held her hands like she was praying. She then touched her praying hands to her heart then lips, and tears streamed down her cheeks. My father bowed his head and shielded his eyes with his hand. I saw a single tear hit the table.

They gave us $1,300. We were so thankful. That money would help us survive a few more months, until the harsh, dark winter eased into spring. The men didn't even know the true Christmas present they gave us was much bigger than money. It was the gift of feeling cared about. We were not being forgotten after all, and this gave us hope.

By the time summer arrived, each of us kids had found a job. My parents took the situation they had been handed and recreated themselves, each of them pursuing work that accommodated their medical issues. Little did our parents know that through their tragedies they blessed their children with an abundance of gifts, including resilience and compassion.

To this day, if I know of anyone struggling with medical and financial burdens I try to help them, whether it's letting them know I care or bringing them dinner. I always remember what was done for our family and how very much it meant to us.

~Kelly Hennigan

Chicken Soup for the Soul: The Power of Gratitude

Meet Our Contributors

We are pleased to introduce you to the writers whose stories were compiled from our past books to create this new Christmas collection. These bios were the ones that ran in the original books and were current as of their publication dates.

Angela N. Abbott is a fifth grade teacher who earned her Master's degree from Pittsburg State University; she speaks professionally for Abbott Learning (abbottlearning.org), and was named Wal-Mart Teacher of the Year. More than anything, she enjoys spending time with her family. Angela can be contacted at abbottlearning@yahoo.com.

Adrienne A. Aguirre is a graduate of CSU San Marcos, and has a Master of Arts in Theology from Bethel Seminary San Diego. Adrienne is a hospice chaplain and freelance journalist. She's also working on her first book. Adrienne enjoys roller skating and walking her neighbors' dogs. E-mail her at 2240521@gmail.com.

Martha Ajango taught first grade for thirty-one years in Fort Atkinson, WI. She has written *Messages Everywhere*, a collection of short, inspirational vignettes about how she discovers God in commonplace experiences. E-mail her at majango@charter.net.

Mary M. Alward lives in southern Ontario. Her work has been published in both print and online venues. When Mary isn't writing, she enjoys spending time with her family, reading and blogging. E-mail her at malward2002@yahoo.ca.

Peggy Archer is the author of picture books for children, including *Turkey Surprise*, a *New York Times* bestseller. Besides writing, she enjoys walking, line dancing, and time with her grandchildren. She and her husband have six children and eleven grandchildren. They live in O'Fallon, MO. Visit her at peggyarcher.com.

Bryan Aubrey is a former professor of English and is the author of two books, as well as numerous articles and reviews.

Karena Delite Bailey received her BS degree in Journalism, with honors, from Illinois State University. She is a published writer and speaker, with a background in technology. A believer in miracles, Karena meditates to create inner peace and a closer connection to the divine within us. E-mail her at karenadbailey@gmail.com.

Dan Bain is an award-winning features and humor writer from Raleigh, NC. He's been writing for others' entertainment since the "Kick Me" incident of second grade, and hopes one day to prove to his beleaguered ex-teachers that yes, he amounted to something. Please see www.danbain.net for more damaging information.

Jean Ballard retired from teaching sociology at the University of the Fraser Valley, and enjoys writing and photography on Vancouver Island. She is a regular contributor to the *Chemainus Valley Courier* and volunteers with several animal rescue groups. She can be contacted via her blog at mylifewiththecritters.blogspot.com.

Celeste Barnard received her Practical Theology degree from Christ for the Nations with a third-year advanced study in Youth Ministry. She is currently a contributing author for *Destiny in Bloom*, an online magazine. She plans on doing more writing and speaking in the future. Learn more at celestebarnard.wordpress.com.

Christine Barnes is a human resources/organization development professional who has worked in Canada and the United States. Currently she works in San Francisco for a large technology company and is seeking others to network with about spirituality in business and leadership.

Patricia Barrett is an English teacher at Foothill High School in Sacramento, CA. She has an M.Ed. and has worked as a freelance newspaper correspondent covering issues in education. Her published poetry spans over thirty years of creative endeavors. Passionate about teaching, today she inspires her students to write and publish.

Barbara Bartlein, RN, MSW, is a professional speaker, author and consultant. A motivational humorist, she presents across the country and has appeared at the Comedy Club. Her column, "Success Matters," appears in numerous publications. Her latest book *Why Did I Marry You Anyway?* is scheduled for release in 2002. E-mail her at balance4u@ aol.com. Or visit her website at successmatters.org.

Beverly M. Bartlett, a native of San Francisco, now resides in Cleveland with her husband, after living in Germany for several years. Though she had traveled to and even studied in Europe before living in its hub, her time in Germany was an eye-opening experience. Meeting others, including refugees, and learning their languages and cultures will long be treasured. She owns a customized trading card business.

Richard Bauman has been a freelance writer for over twenty-five years. His articles about spirituality, history, travel, and self help have appeared in numerous national publications. Richard and Donna, his wife of thirty-eight years, reside in West Covina, CA. They have two adult children and three grandsons.

Gail Neff Bell is retired and a grandmother. She was formerly a teacher and a lawyer. She lives with her husband in Tsawwassen, BC, where she enjoys swimming, walking with stride poles, trying new recipes, and organizing community groups.

Lisa Beringer is a piano teacher who writes inspirational stories, humorous plays, and daily e-mails to her four children who have spread their wings and left the nest. She lives with her husband, Dale, in Ontario, Canada, where they enjoy fishing aboard "Audacious" and acting together in their church family drama troupe.

Pegge Bernecker is a spiritual director, retreat leader, and author of *Your Spiritual Garden: Tending to the Presence of God*, and *God: Any Time, Any Place*. The death of her son magnifies her desire for deep meaning and service. She lives in Kasilof, AK, with her husband and dogs. Pegge can be reached through her website at www.PeggeBernecker.com.

Georgia A. Brackett and her husband are retired. They owned and operated an HVAC/R company and general construction company for thirty years. She has a passion for helping her community through the local police department Community Watch Program. Penny Childers suggested she write and submit her story.

Ellie Braun-Haley started her writing career as a newspaper correspondent. Later she wrote books for adults who work with young children. Eventually her research took her to investigating miracles, a topic she thoroughly enjoyed! She has also written children's stories, true short stories and rhymes! She presents talks on miracles.

John Briley is an "in the trenches" pediatrician who is also a writer and Irish-style storyteller. His proudest accomplishment, other than his children, is helping to establish an infant development (child enrichment) program on Maui where he lives with his wife, who somehow puts up with him!

Valaree Brough received her Bachelor of Arts degree in Elementary Education, with a dual minor in English and French, from Utah State University in 1971. She has four children and twelve grandchildren. Valaree enjoys writing, reading, playing the piano, teaching, and family history.

Jane Brzozowski comes from a family of writers, including her husband Steve and her daughters Kat and Sally. This is her first published work. Her sister, Lava Mueller, got her hooked on the *Chicken Soup for the Soul* series.

Pastor Wanda Christy-Shaner runs a Facebook page called "Good News Only," a site developed for prayer and praise. She has been previously published in the *Chicken Soup for the Soul* series, as well as *War Cry*. She is an award-winning speaker, actress and adrenaline junkie. E-mail her at seekingtruth65@yahoo.com.

Helen Colella is a writer of educational books/materials, magazine articles/stories for adults/children. Her stories have appeared in several *Chicken Soup for the Soul* books and parenting magazines. She works for Blue13Creative, a professional writing, editing, and creative services company in Denver, CO. Learn more at www.underthecuckooclock.org.

Bonnie Walsh Davidson, M.Ed., of Marion, MA, is the author of *Breast Friends*. Davidson has turned her breast cancer experience into an avocation, publishing numerous pieces on breast cancer in several national magazines, as well as *Chicken Soup for Every Mom's Soul*. Her husband, Paul, encouraged her to spread her wings with a website, PinkRibbon.com, in the hopes of assisting other women diagnosed with breast cancer. Davidson is a mother of three and a full-time real estate associate for Jack Conway & Company, Inc., in Mattapoisett, MA, and chairperson of the Relay for Life in her community.

Inga Dore is a retired teacher and freelance writer who enjoys growing organic vegetables, walking, and visiting shut-ins.

Neither blindness at thirty-one, unthinkable tragedy nor painful injustice defeated **Janet Perez Eckles**. Rather, in spite of adversity, she has become an international keynote speaker for Spanish and English-speaking audiences. She is a #1 best-selling author, radio host, life coach, master interpreter, columnist, and ministry leader.

Barbara Jeanne Fisher resides in Fremont, OH. A prolific writer, she has published articles in numerous national magazines. Although fictional, her first novel, *Stolen Moments*, is based on her dealing with lupus in her own life. Her goal in writing is to use the feelings of her heart to touch the hearts of others. Contact her at mentorsfriend@cros.net.

Carol Chiodo Fleischman's writing has appeared in books, newspapers, and a textbook. Her topics cover a wide range of everyday events. A recurring theme is life as a blind person, especially the joys and challenges of using a seeing-eye dog. Pelican Publishing has scheduled a release for a children's book about her guide dog, Nadine.

Sally Friedman is a graduate of the University of Pennsylvania. Her personal essays have appeared in *The New York Times*, *Family Circle*, *Ladies' Home Journal* and *The Huffington Post*. Her family provides ample material for musings about how we live our lives. E-mail her at pinegander@aol.com.

Johnnie Ann Gaskill writes a weekly inspirational column for two newspapers. A former teacher and education director, Johnnie enjoys having extended time to write. She and her husband live in Thomaston, GA, where their two daughters often bring grandchildren for them to spoil. E-mail her at jjgask@charter.net.

Lenore Gavigan has been a teacher for thirty-two years. She currently teaches English, as well as English as a Second Language for the North Rockland School District in New York State. As an adjunct instructor for the Regional Training Center, she conducts courses for teachers on how to convey the art of writing to their students. She and her husband of thirty-two years, Jack, have three children, Tara (married to Sinclair), Sean and Mary Beth, and two grandchildren, Meghan and Justin, who bring great joy to their lives.

Michael Gingerich lives in Hershey, PA, with his wife Kathy and his son Matthew. He is also the father of two other sons—Adam and David. He is an author, counselor and pastor. E-mail Michael at michael.gingerich@hotmail.com.

Gwen Hart teaches writing at Buena Vista University in Storm Lake, IA. She is the author of the poetry collections *The Empress of Kisses* (Texas Review Press) and *Lost and Found* (David Robert Books). Her short stories have appeared in magazines and anthologies such as *Calliope 2013*, *Litro*, and *Eclectically Vegas, Baby!*.

Kristi Hemingway loves her life in Denver, CO, where she works as a teacher, writer and actress. Her perfect day includes gardening, biking, French food, dancing and snuggling with her husband and two children. She has recently completed a snarky spiritual memoir and her first novel. E-mail her at klhemingway@comcast.net.

Kelly Hennigan loves spending time with her family in upstate New York. She credits her high school English teachers Mr. Moriarty and Mr. Haynes for encouraging her writing. Kelly would like to thank Chicken Soup for the Soul for this opportunity. You can read more of her writing by following her blog at frommygut.weebly.com.

Mary Hickey is a backgammon champion and teacher, and has co-authored a book on middle game strategy for that game. She is the author of *Arise and Call Her Blessed*, about Mary the mother of Jesus as we know her from the Bible, and is currently writing a book about the experience of moving from the city to the country.

Morgan Hill is a former TV/radio account executive, broadcaster and actress. She has a Master of Science in Special Education. Teaching in Los Angeles, she hopes insights from her own background will inspire her inner-city high school students towards getting their first job and making positive plans after graduation. E-mail her at mhwriter5@gmail.com.

Michael Hogan wanted to travel the world but, because of his excessive weight, was having trouble walking three blocks. If you'd like to know how he learned to manage obstructive sleep apnea, lose eighty-five pounds and have some fun getting fit, contact him at michael.hogan@shaw.ca.

Mariane Holbrook earned her degree from Nyack (NY) College and from High Point (NC) University. She and her husband John are retired teachers living in Kure Beach, NC. Mariane is the author of two books, *Prisms of the Heart* and *Humor Me*. She has two sons and six grandchildren.

Don Jackson is the former host of Canada's #1 evening FM radio program, *Lovers and Other Strangers*. He now produces a unique webcast about life, love and relationships on his website heartbeatoftheinternet.com, where he can also be reached. He plans to write inspirational books and novels. He is married and a father of two.

Crystal Johnson finds great joy in writing — it feeds her soul and acts as her creative outlet. She has worked as a Speech Language Pathologist in hospitals since 2008 and feels privileged to work with clients and learn with and from them. She has a supportive family who stand by her in her many and varied endeavours.

Tom Kaden is counselor at Someone To Tell It To which can be found at www.someonetotellitto.org. He is a graduate of Messiah College and Asbury Theological Seminary. Tom and his wife Sarah and their four children live in Carlisle, PA.

L.A. Kennedy is a writer and an artist. She began journaling when she was twelve. Her unusual and humorous experiences are the source for many of her short stories. Her works in progress include two novels. She also sculpts and creates folk art. E-mail her at elkaynca@aol.com.

Mimi Greenwood Knight is a mother of four and freelance writer with over four hundred articles and essays in print. She lives in South Louisiana with her husband, David, and enjoys Bible study, butterfly gardening, artisan bread making and the lost art of letter writing. Visit her blog at blog.nola.com/faith/mimi_greenwood_knight.

Kathleen Kohler is a writer and speaker from the Pacific Northwest. Her articles, rooted in personal experience, appear in books and magazines. She and her husband have three children and seven grandchildren. Kathleen enjoys gardening, travel, and watercolor painting. Visit www. kathleenkohler.com to read more of her published work.

Patricia Lorenz is a frequent contributor to the *Chicken Soup for the Soul* series with stories in nearly sixty of them. She's also the author of fourteen books, her latest being *57 STEPS TO PARADISE: Finding Love in Midlife and Beyond.* E-mail her at patricialorenz4@gmail.com to contact her as a speaker for your group.

Linda Lowen is a radio producer/co-host, writing instructor, parenting magazine columnist and freelance writer. She's won regional and national awards for her online, broadcast and print work covering women's issues, politics, health, wellness and motherhood. Her two daughters keep her young — her husband keeps her solvent.

Gail MacMillan is an award-winning author of dog books. A graduate of Queen's University, Gail has had her work published in Canada, the United States and the UK. She lives with her husband and three wonderful dogs. Contact Gail through her website at www.gailmacmillan.com.

Teddi Eberly Martin received her BS from BYU, and her Master of Education from CSU, San Bernardino. After many years working in the field of education, she currently is raising her family in Texas. Teddi enjoys traveling, writing, reading, and long car rides. E-mail her at teddiebs@gmail.com.

Nada Mazzei has a Bachelor of Arts in French and Italian and a Master of Theology from the University of Toronto. She received her Master of Arts in Theology from the University of St. Michael's College. Nada is currently a freelance writer in Toronto. She enjoys reading, music, and art.

Annette McDermott is a freelance writer and children's author whose work has been published in both adult and children's magazines and online. She enjoys writing about a wide variety of subjects but specializes in holistic living topics. When she's not busy writing and raising her family, Annette enjoys singing, gardening, and reading. E-mail her at annette@annettemcdermott.net.

Though her career is in music, **Cynthia McGarity** has an international following for her blog, *God's Daily Message… for the terminally dense*. She's a Master Teaching Artist for The Young Americans and The Walt Disney Company. Her latest project, the "Branching Out in Faith" app, is available through iTunes. God is the greatest!

Nancy McIntosh works as a Food Bank Community & Development Coordinator. She's been a radio announcer, newspaper columnist, clothing and art designer and won numerous awards for corporate window displays, merchandising and advertising campaigns. She intends to focus on traveling, painting and illustrating children's books. E-mail her at nancymcintosh4@hotmail.com.

Sharon Melnicer is a writer, artist and teacher in Winnipeg, Manitoba. She has frequently aired her "Slice of Life" pieces on CBC radio. A retired high school English teacher and university instructor, she continues to teach life-story writing to adults and is a recognized artist who shows and sells throughout North America.

Cathy Miller is a Canadian teacher and freelance writer. "Delayed Delivery" first won a short story contest in her hometown of Sudbury, Ontario, in 1992. The following year it was published in *Christmas in My Heart 2*, edited by Joe Wheeler, Review & Herald Publishing, Hagerstown, MD. It has since been reprinted in several anthologies and magazines.

Martha Moore, a retired Texas English teacher, spends her time tutoring at a community college and writing. She is the author of three novels, including *Under the Mermaid Angel* which won the Delacorte Press Prize for a First Young Adult Novel. She enjoys inspiring others to tell their own stories.

Courtney Lynn Mroch is the Ambassador of Dark and Paranormal Tourism for Haunt Jaunts, a travel site and radio show for restless spirits. When she's not exploring haunted places or writing, it's a safe bet you'll find her on a tennis court or yoga mat somewhere. She lives in Nashville, TN with her husband.

A visual artist by training, **Susan Mulder** left a career teaching and speaking in her field to pursue new directions. A chronic maker of handcrafted goods, book nerd and doting Mim (as her "grands" call her), she also loves to cook and writes a little here and there. Susan resides in Michigan with her husband and an ornery cat named Bo.

Eric Myers currently resides in Austin, TX, with his wife, Jennifer, and daughter, Lydia. They are currently approved for another adoption. Eric received his BS from Harding University and a BS in physical therapy from the University of Oklahoma.

Linda O'Connell is an accomplished writer and teacher from St. Louis, MO. A positive thinker, she writes from the heart, bares her soul, and finds humor in everyday situations. Linda enjoys a hearty laugh, the beach, and will write for dark chocolate. Read more at lindaoconnell. blogspot.com

Ivy Olson created the Angel Network Charities in 1989 to help the homeless. Ivy passed away in 2002, but her legacy is an organization that has a successful rate of 95 percent in supporting individuals in becoming self-sufficient again. The Angel Network Charities can be reached at (808) 377-1841.

Vincent Olson served four years in the U.S. Air Force and later received his bachelor's in English Education from Southern Illinois University. He and his wife have one son. He teaches high school English in Illinois. In addition to short stories, Vincent also writes screenplays, poetry and novels, and is a freelance animator.

LaVerne Otis lives in Southern California where she loves writing, photography, bird watching, gardening and spending time with family. LaVerne is recently retired and is taking classes at a local community college. She has been published in *Chicken Soup for the Soul* books and various magazines. E-mail her at lotiswrites@msn.com.

Jeanne Pallos has several stories in the *Chicken Soup for the Soul* series and is the author of stories for adults and children. She is passionate about writing family stories and preserving the memories of loved ones for future generations. She lives in Laguna Niguel, CA. E-mail her at jlpallos@cox.net.

Leslie A. Paradise learned about Horses Help, a therapeutic riding program for people with special needs, when her husband, John, suddenly passed away. Leslie joined as a volunteer and went on to become a therapeutic riding and driving instructor through NARHA (North American Riding for the Handicapped Association). She has been teaching for six years and owns two horses. Visit Horses Help at www.horseshelp.org.

J. C. Pinkerton graduated from Stonewall Jackson Nursing School and attended Southern Sem College in Virginia. After a career in nursing, she now enjoys freelance writing. She is constantly researching ancient history, America in the 1800s and children's stories. For more information on J. C. Pinkerton, e-mail her at pinkerton@rockbridge.net.

Susan R. Ray writes a weekly newspaper column entitled "Where We Are" available at susanrray.com. A retired teacher, she volunteers in a second grade classroom, and she writes, reads, and takes field trips with her eight grandchildren. Susan likes to travel, bake bread, and quilt.

Jennifer Reed received her MFA in Writing from Vermont College of Fine Arts in 2013. She has published over thirty books for children, with a focus on educational nonfiction books. Jennifer enjoys traveling, gardening and paper quilling. She lives in Maryland with her husband and two dogs.

Cara Rifkin is a born and raised Chicagoan who received her Bachelor of Science in Mathematics from DePaul University. She volunteers her free time promoting social justice and human welfare causes. A self-proclaimed "news junkie," she also researches and writes about a variety of business topics.

C. L. Robinson has written for the online *Inside Out Travel Magazine*, the magazines *France Today* and *Destinations Abroad*, and recently placed eleventh in the 74th Annual Writer's Digest Writing Competition, for which there were almost 18,000 entries.

Nancy Rue is the bestselling author of over sixty books for children and young people, including the current top-selling *Lily* series. She is a former high school teacher and theater director, and she now teaches workshops for young writers nationwide. Nancy lives in Lebanon, TN.

Victoria Schlintz, RN, MA, is a registered nurse and has a Master's degree in education. She has an emergency nursing background, and currently directs education services at a Northern California hospital. She is also a student at the Graduate Theological Union, Berkeley, CA, and an ordination candidate in the United Methodist Church.

Kim Seeley is a former teacher and librarian. She loves to travel, read, and write. She is a frequent contributor to *Sasee* magazine and has written several articles for the *Chicken Soup for the Soul* series.

Janet Seever and her family have lived in Alberta, Canada since 1993, where she writes for a mission organization. She also enjoys doing freelance work. She and her husband have two adult children, one of whom is married, and a grandchild.

Gail Sellers enjoys writing poetry and short stories. Her hobbies include swimming, reading, attending concerts, travelling and relaxing at the cottage. She loves animals, especially cats. She plans on writing inspirational children's stories, animal stories and poetry. E-mail her at gailsellers2011@gmail.com.

Jodi Iachini Severson earned her Bachelor's degree from the University of Pittsburgh and she now lives in central Wisconsin where she works for the State Public Defender. As a freelance writer, she has been a frequent contributor to the *Chicken Soup for the Soul* series since 2002. E-mail her at seversonjl@gmail.com.

Diane M. Smith is an award-winning freelance writer and a certified veterinary technician whose particular interests lie in the fields of feline health and nutrition. Her work has appeared in a number of publications, including *Cats* magazine, *Cat Fancy* and *CATsumer Report*. She is a member of the Cat Writers' Association. Diane lives with her husband, David, and four cats.

Judith Smith lives in Peterborough, ON, where she received her PSW, and social services worker diploma. She is working with intellectually disabled adults, assisting them to live independently in their own home. She also has her own women's clothing consignment boutique called Back of the Closet Consignment Boutique.

Mary Z. Smith is a regular contributor to *Angels on Earth* and *Guideposts* magazines. She resides in Richmond, VA with her husband Barry. They have four grown children, two biological and two adopted. Mary loves writing for the Lord, walking, and gardening. E-mail her at stillbrook@comcast.net.

Michael T. Smith lives in Caldwell, ID with his lovely wife Ginny. He works as a project manager and writes inspiration in his spare time. Sign up for a weekly story at visitor.constantcontact.com/d.jsp?m=1101828445578&p=oi or read more stories at ourecho.com/biography-353-Michael-Timothy-Smith.shtml#stories.

Lizanne Southgate is an Oregon screenwriter and ghostwriter. She can be reached at lizannesghost@msn.com.

Ruth Spiro lives in Illinois with her husband and two daughters. Her articles and essays have appeared in *Child, Woman's World,* and *Family Fun,* as well as several anthologies. She is also the author of a children's book, *The Bubble Gum Artist.* She can be reached at ruthspiro.com.

Alan Struthers, Jr. is a business and financial writer. Alan has written for major corporations and for government officials. Articles based on his speeches have appeared in the *Washington Post, The New York Times* and other newspapers. He has a successful Christian financial planning practice in northern New Jersey. He is also a musician who has recorded two CDs playing the bluegrass banjo.

Denise Taylor is the busy mom of eleven children, eight of whom are still living at home. Thankfully she has her husband Todd to help out around the house. She also keeps company with one cat named Flower P. Cat. Denise loves to write, camp, hunt and fish in the quiet forests of Michigan's Upper Peninsula where she resides.

Jodi Renee Thomas has published stories on many subjects, from relationships to women's rights. She is a featured speaker for the women's movement and award-winning author of *aMused.* She lives happily in Florida with her teenage daughter, husband and three dogs that like to bother her while she types.

Ted A. Thompson is a former copywriter and freelance author. He presently works as a chimney sweep in Harrison, AR.

Paula Maugiri Tindall, RN, writes her stories and finds her inspiration from personal life experiences and through nature while overlooking the lake where she resides in Florida, completing her first book. Her work has been previously published in *Chicken Soup for the Grandma's Soul*. E-mail her at lucylu54@aol.com.

Todd W. Van Beck is the school director of the New England Institute of Funeral Service education at Mount Ida College in Newton Center, Massachusetts. Mr. Van Beck is in demand as a motivational speaker and seminar leader on a wide range of human service topics. Mr. Van Beck can be reached at ToddVanBeck@aol.com.

Mary Vaughn earned her education from raising five kids and a husband. She was driven by strong faith and love for family and friends. For her, every day was a chance to do the Lord's work. Sally O'Brien's stories have appeared in several publications. Contact Sally at sobrien95@ msn.com.

Carrie O'Maley Voliva is a public librarian, writer, and mother in Indianapolis, IN. She received her BA degree in Journalism from Butler University and her MLS degree from Indiana University. Carrie misses her mother every day, but feels grateful for the time they shared and all the lessons her mother passed on.

Nicole Webster has been interested in writing since the age of eight. Her other interests include reading, scrapbooking, cooking, cross stitching, and being outdoors. She is a stay-at-home mom and currently resides in Utah with her husband and four children.

Bob White resides in Willis, TX, with his wife of twenty-five years. He is employed by a major international airline. He enjoys traveling, sailing, flyfishing and indulging his two wonderful grandchildren. "A Christmas Gift" is his first published work. Bob can be contacted at bwsail@msn.com.

John White graduated from Harding College in 1968, is a Vietnam veteran and has worked as a long-term care administrator since 1976. John continues to serve seniors today, has been married for forty-five years, is a high school umpire in Alabama, plays baseball in national tournaments and enjoys his four grandchildren.

Following a career in Nuclear Medicine, **Melissa Wootan** is joyfully exploring her creative side. She enjoys writing and is a regular guest on *San Antonio Living*, an hour-long lifestyle show on San Antonio's NBC affiliate, where she shares all of her best DIY/decorating tips. Contact her through facebook.com/chicvintique.

Amy Catlin Wozniak shares her life with her soul mate, four children, two grandsons, and a Great Pyrenees named Scarlett O'Hara, who has absolutely no problem living up to her namesake. She resides in Northeast Ohio, where she writes inspirational fiction and nonfiction that reflects God's hope.

Sandra Wright loves to write to inspire others. If she's not writing she enjoys the outdoors, spending time with her family, and travelling. E-mail her at sandrawright@a1.net.

Lynn Yates is a writer, editor, and public speaker in the southeastern United States. She has been proudly married to her husband, Dan, for thirty-three years. Honoring his wishes, she is using a pseudonym for "The Least We Can Do."

Meet Amy Newmark

Amy Newmark is the bestselling author, editor-in-chief, and publisher of the *Chicken Soup for the Soul* book series. Since 2008, she has published 140 new books, most of them national bestsellers in the U.S. and Canada, more than doubling the number of Chicken Soup for the Soul titles in print today. She is also the author of *Simply Happy*, a crash course in Chicken Soup for the Soul advice and wisdom that is filled with easy-to-implement, practical tips for having a better life.

Amy is credited with revitalizing the Chicken Soup for the Soul brand, which has been a publishing industry phenomenon since the first book came out in 1993. By compiling inspirational and aspirational true stories curated from ordinary people who have had extraordinary experiences, Amy has kept the twenty-four-year-old Chicken Soup for the Soul brand fresh and relevant.

Amy graduated *magna cum laude* from Harvard University where she majored in Portuguese and minored in French. She then embarked on a three-decade career as a Wall Street analyst, a hedge fund manager, and a corporate executive in the technology field. She is a Chartered Financial Analyst.

Her return to literary pursuits was inevitable, as her honors thesis in college involved traveling throughout Brazil's impoverished northeast region, collecting stories from regular people. She is delighted to have come full circle in her writing career — from collecting stories "from the people" in Brazil as a twenty-year-old to, three decades later, collecting stories "from the people" for Chicken Soup for the Soul.

When Amy and her husband Bill, the CEO of Chicken Soup for the Soul, are not working, they are visiting their four grown children and their first grandchild.

Follow Amy on Twitter @amynewmark. Listen to her free podcast, The Chicken Soup for the Soul Podcast, at www.chickensoup.podbean. com, or find it on iTunes, the Podcasts app on iPhone, or on your favorite podcast app on other devices.

About Toys for Tots

Your purchase of this *Chicken Soup for the Soul* book supports Toys for Tots and helps create Christmas miracles for children who might not receive gifts otherwise! The mission of the U.S. Marine Corps Reserve Toys for Tots Program is to collect new, unwrapped toys during October, November and December each year, and distribute those toys as Christmas gifts to less fortunate children in the community in which the campaign is conducted.

You can contribute to your local Toys for Tots campaign in several ways. You can donate a toy at one of the area toy drop locations, host a Toys for Tots event at your home, office or other venue and collect toys for Toys for Tots, or volunteer at the local warehouse.

Local campaigns are conducted annually in over 800 communities covering all 50 U.S. states, the District of Columbia and Puerto Rico. Local toy collection campaigns begin in October and last until mid to late December. Toy distribution also takes place mid to late December.

Members of the community drop new, unwrapped toys in collection boxes positioned in local businesses. Coordinators pick up these toys and store them in central warehouses where the toys are sorted by age and gender. At Christmas, Coordinators, with the assistance of local social welfare agencies, church groups, and other local community agencies, distribute the toys to the less fortunate children of the community.

Over the years, Marines have established close working relationships with social welfare agencies, churches and other local community agencies which are well qualified to identify the needy children in the community and play important roles in the distribution of the toys. While Toys for Tots Coordinators organize, coordinate and manage the campaign, the ultimate success depends on the support of the local community and the generosity of the people who donate toys.

You can learn more about Toys for Tots by visiting their website at https://www.toysfortots.org.

Sharing Happiness, Inspiration, and Hope

Real people sharing real stories, every day, all over the world. In 2007, *USA Today* named *Chicken Soup for the Soul* one of the five most memorable books in the last quarter-century. With over 100 million books sold to date in the U.S. and Canada alone, more than 250 titles in print, and translations into nearly fifty languages, "chicken soup for the soul®" is one of the world's best-known phrases.

Today, twenty-four years after we first began sharing happiness, inspiration and hope through our books, we continue to delight our readers with new titles, but have also evolved beyond the bookstore with super premium pet food, television shows, podcasts, positive journalism from aplus.com, and licensed products, all revolving around true stories, as we continue "changing the world one story at a time®." Thanks for reading!

Share with Us

We all have had Chicken Soup for the Soul moments in our lives. If you would like to share your story or poem with millions of people around the world, go to chickensoup.com and click on "Submit Your Story." You may be able to help another reader and become a published author at the same time. Some of our past contributors have launched writing and speaking careers from the publication of their stories in our books!

We only accept story submissions via our website. They are no longer accepted via mail or fax.

To contact us regarding other matters, please send us an e-mail through webmaster@chickensoupforthesoul.com, or fax or write us at:

Chicken Soup for the Soul
P.O. Box 700
Cos Cob, CT 06807-0700
Fax: 203-861-7194

One more note from your friends at Chicken Soup for the Soul: Occasionally, we receive an unsolicited book manuscript from one of our readers, and we would like to respectfully inform you that we do not accept unsolicited manuscripts and we must discard the ones that appear.

Chicken Soup for the Soul.

A Book of Miracles

101 True Stories of Healing, Faith, Divine Intervention, and Answered Prayers

Jack Canfield,
Mark Victor Hansen
& LeAnn Thieman

Paperback: 978-1-935096-51-1
eBook: 978-1-61159-133-0

More hope and inspiration

Chicken Soup for the Soul®

Answered Prayers

101 Stories of Hope,
Miracles, Faith,
Divine Intervention,
and the Power of Prayer

Jack Canfield,
Mark Victor Hansen,
and LeAnn Thieman

Paperback: 978-1-935096-76-4
eBook: 978-1-61159-195-8

every day of the year

Changing lives one story at a time®
www.chickensoup.com